Thinking for a Living

Thinking for a Living

*Education and the
Wealth of Nations*

RAY MARSHALL
and MARC TUCKER

BasicBooks
A Division of HarperCollins*Publishers*

Table on page 18 reprinted by permission of the publishers from David Tyack, *The One Best System* (Cambridge: Harvard University Press). Copyright © 1974 by the President and Fellows of Harvard College.

Library of Congress Cataloging-in-Publication Data

Marshall, Ray, 1928–
    Thinking for a living: education and the wealth of nations
/ Ray Marshall and Marc Tucker.
      p. cm.
    Includes bibliographical references and index.
    ISBN 0–465–08555–5
    1. Education—Economic aspects—United States. 2.
Economic development—Effect of education on. 3. Labor
supply—United States—Effect of education on. 4. Industry and
education—United States. 5. Educational change—United
States. I. Tucker, Marc, 1939–   . II. Title.
LC66.M37 1992
370.19′361′0973—dc20   91–58596
                                            CIP

Designed by Ellen Levine

92 93 94 95 CC/RRD 9 8 7 6 5 4

No nation can achieve greatness unless it believes in something—and unless that something has the moral dimensions to sustain a great civilization. The release of human potential, the enhancement of individual dignity, the liberation of the human spirit—those are the deepest and truest goals to be conceived by the hearts and minds of the American people. And those are ideas that can sustain and strengthen a great civilization—if we believe in them, if we are honest about them, if we have the courage and stamina to live for them.

—John Gardner

Contents

Part III
The Challenge

Part IV
The New American System: Strategies for High Performance

Part V
Two Futures: Which Will We Choose?

Acknowledgments

Sometime in the fall of 1984, Governor Jim Hunt of North Carolina approached David Hamburg, the newly appointed president of Carnegie Corporation of New York, and suggested that Carnegie invite fifty leading Americans to a one-day gathering in New York City to discuss whether Carnegie should launch a major effort on the theme of education and economic growth. The answer was a resounding yes, and, a few months later, Carnegie asked Marc Tucker to help design and serve as executive director of the new Carnegie Forum on Education and the Economy. Dr. Hamburg asked Ray Marshall, a trustee of Carnegie, to serve on the forum's advisory council. Thus was born a partnership that has endured and prospered to the present.

This book emerges from the work of the Carnegie Forum and of the National Center on Education and the Economy, created as an independent not-for-profit organization in 1987 to carry on the forum's work activities. Our purpose in writing *Thinking for a Living* has been to present the ideas growing out of that work as an integrated whole, in the hope that by doing so, we can make available to a wider public those ideas on which so many have worked.

The authors are deeply indebted to the people whose contributions to the work of both organizations—as trustees, advisory council, and commission members, as well as staff—constitute the intellectual capital on which we have drawn: Robert Atkinson, Donald Baker, William Baker, David Barram, Harvey Berson, Owen Bieber, Lewis Branscomb, William Brock, Allan Campbell, R. Carlos Carballada, Edward Carlough, Pete Carlson, Anthony Carnevale, Edward Caron,

Paul Choquette, Jr., Henry Cisneros, Sarah Cleveland, Hillary Rodham Clinton, Michael Cohen, Richard Cohon, Thomas Cole, Mario Cuomo, Norman Deets, Henrik Dullea, John Foley, Badi Foster, Gloria Frazier, Mary Futrell, John Gardner, Thomas Gonzales, Fred Hechinger, David Hamburg, Van Buren Hansford, Jr., Louis Harris, Barbara Hatton, Guilbert Hentschke, Sonia Hernandez, Rear Admiral W. J. Holland, Jr., Bill Honig, David Hornbeck, James Houghton, James Hunt, John Hurley, John Jacob, Cynthia Jorgensen, Vera Katz, Thomas Kean, Donald Kennedy, Dan Kinley, William Kohlberg, William Lucy, Judith Lanier, Arturo Madrid, Ira Magaziner, Lynn Margherio, William Maroni, Shirley McBay, Peter McWalters, Margaret McVicar, Shirley Malcom, David Mandel, Richard Mills, Eleanor Holmes Norton, Karen Nussbaum, Michael O'Keefe, Mary Louise Peterson, Peter Pestillo, Edward Porter, Philip Power, Ruth Randall, Lauren Resnick, David Rockefeller, Jr., Betsy Brown Ruzzi, Kjell-Jon Rye, Howard Samuel, Robert Schwartz, John Sculley, Albert Shanker, Peter Smith, Catherine Spangenburg, William Spring, Susan Sullivan, John Taylor III, Anthony Trujillo, Laura D'Andrea Tyson, Adam Urbanski, James Van Erden, Robert Wagner, Jr., Robert White, Kay Whitmore, Joan Wills, William Woodside, and Alan Wurtzel.

We are deeply grateful to Dr. David Hamburg, to the Board of Trustees of Carnegie Corporation, and to Alden Dunham, Vivien Stewart, and Barbara Finberg of the Carnegie staff for their steadfast support of our work. Governor Mario Cuomo's support of the National Center's work has been indispensable. Peter Gerber of the John D. and Catherine T. MacArthur Foundation made possible the work of the New Standards Project. Robert Schwartz, director of the education program of the Pew Charitable Trusts, has provided wise counsel from the beginning. His support of the National Alliance for Restructuring Education, along with that of Stanley Goldstein of the Melville Corporation, and of the New Standards Project, made the work of those programs possible.

There would have been no Carnegie report without Lewis Branscomb, the chair of the Carnegie Task Force on Teaching as a Profession. Branscomb's commanding intelligence and deft hand enabled a very diverse group of American leaders to come to a consensus that has held ever since, to provide the foundation upon which everything else we have done has been built. James Hunt played the same role as chair of the planning group for the National Board for Professional Teaching Standards. We owe a considerable intellectual debt to Ira Magaziner, the chair of the Commission on the Skills of the American Workforce and the guiding spirit behind the Commission's report, *America's Choice: high skills or low wages!*, for, among other things, his penetrating conception of the role that the organization of work plays in the fate of nations.

Many people were kind enough to read parts or the whole of various drafts of this book and to comment on them. Among them were Andrea Camp, Sarah Cleveland, Hillary Clinton, Norman Deets, Edward Finein, John Foley, Robert Glover, David Hornbeck, Cynthia Jorgensen, Cheryl McVay, Hillary Pennington, Lauren Resnick, and Jon Wainwright. These people contributed much to whatever strengths can be found in the text; they are hardly responsible for its shortcomings.

Our thanks, too, to Martin Kessler, our indefatigable editor and publisher, for cajoling, pushing, and enticing this book into existence.

And, finally, a deep note of thanks to our families, most especially Kathleen Bonk and Pat Marshall, for putting up with all the lost weekends and holidays, for their steadfast encouragement and unflagging faith.

The American Economy: Point of Decision

For much of this century, and indeed, right up to the present, American enterprise has been organized on the principle that most of us do not need to know
much to do the work that has to be done. This system may have worked
brilliantly for us until recently, but it will do so no longer.

The future now belongs to societies that organize themselves for learning.
What we know and can do holds the key to economic progress, just as command
of natural resources once did. Everything depends on what firms can learn from
and teach to their customers and suppliers, on what countries can learn from one
another, on what workers can learn from each other and the work they do, on the
learning environment that families provide, and, of course, on what we learn in
school. More than ever before, nations that want high incomes and full employment must develop policies that emphasize the acquisition of knowledge and
skills by everyone, not just a select few. The prize will go to those countries that
are organized as national learning systems, and where all institutions are organized to learn and to act on what they learn.

Our most formidable competitors know this. Many newly industrialized countries know it and are vaulting forward as a result. But the United States does not.
Because this country continues to operate on the premise that, for the country to
be successful, only a few need to know or be able to do very much, we are poised
on the precipice of a steep decline in national income, with all that this implies
for our material well-being and the stability of our society.

Perhaps we are blinded by our seeming good fortune. Through the 1980s,
America appeared to have every reason to rest on its laurels. We have the highest

per capita income of any major industrial country. The last decade generated a larger increase in employment for us than for any of our competitors, and the close of the decade witnessed the triumph of our basic economic and political philosophy on the world stage.

But there is every reason to believe that if we continue on our current path, our national prosperity will evaporate. A rising proportion of our people will sink into poverty and the well-being of our middle class will slowly decline, thereby rending the political fabric of America, perhaps beyond repair.

As it is, our prosperity is costing us dear. We are actually consuming more each year than we are producing. Between 1980 and 1986 real consumption per worker increased by $3,100 per year and real output per worker by only $950.[1] Like any family that consumes more than it earns, the country is making up the difference by borrowing and depreciating our capital. Our economy is propped up by unparalleled levels of public and private debt.

Borrowing is not, of course, necessarily bad. When borrowed money is invested in something productive, it can provide handsome returns. But the money we borrowed during the 1980s was used to sustain our consumption. To borrow it, we had to offer high interest rates, which raised the cost of capital here at home, discouraging business investment. As individuals saved less in order to consume more, the sources of investment funds dried up even further. In 1988, the United States saved and invested 2.9 percent of its gross national product, compared to an average of 7.7 percent for the seven economic-summit nations (Canada, France, Germany, Italy, Japan, the United Kingdom, and the United States).[2]

We are in every way eating into the future to pay for the present. When the borrowed money is gone, there will be little to show for it except mountains of debt stretching far into the future. The interest payments to foreign holders of our debt will act like a tax on income for years to come, reducing our standard of living just as surely as a cut in pay.

In the business world, much of the borrowing that went on in the 1980s was related to takeover threats. As firms were threatened by takeovers, they went deep into debt, using the proceeds to buy back their stock, and thereby driving stock prices up to levels that made the companies unattractive to the raiders. Some managers used the same techniques in the form of leveraged buyouts, borrowing enough money to buy back all the stock of the company. Still others bought back their stock to keep share prices and per-share earnings up, because their own tenure and income depended on these indicators. Thus enormous debt was accumulated without many new assets being added to America's productive capacity.

One of the side effects is that large amounts of stock were removed from the pool of stock available for purchase on the country's securities markets. People in other countries who, unlike us, saved their money rather than spending it, used this money to purchase financial assets like stocks and real property in the

United States as the value of the dollar declined relative to their currencies, making our assets a real bargain for them. Because stocks were dwindling in supply as demand from abroad increased, stock prices went up relentlessly, thereby adding to the illusion of a healthy American economy.

The main reason our economy has continued to grow in recent years is that more people have been working than ever before, especially women. In 1973, 42 percent of our people were employed. Today, that figure has risen to 50 percent.[3] But productivity growth has been stagnant. We produced more because there were more workers to produce it, not because we were more efficient producers.

The catch is that today far fewer people are entering the work force. During the 1970s, our labor force grew at an average annual rate of 2.7 percent. During the 1980s, it grew at a rate of 1.6 percent per year.[4] Because of the baby bust that started in the late 1960s and lasted for twenty years, there were 15 percent fewer teenagers in 1985 than in 1975.[5] And it will not end there. The labor-market share of sixteen- to twenty-four-year-olds will decline from about 21 percent of the work force in 1985 to about 16 percent by 2000.[6]

At the same time that fewer people are entering the labor market, the country as a whole is growing older. Birth rates are falling and people are living longer. As these demographic trends converge, the net result is that each worker must support a growing number of those who do not work. In 1990 there were about sixty-two dependents for every hundred potential workers; fifty years hence there will be seventy-four.[7] By that time, other things being equal, each worker will have to produce on average almost 20 percent more for the population at large than one of today's workers to sustain the same standard of living we enjoy now. If productivity growth rates do not improve, our current standard of living will fall substantially.

Yet productivity is not growing. It is virtually stagnant. The result is that real incomes are declining. Consider what happens to the "typical man" as he ages from forty to fifty.[8] Between 1953 and 1963, he experienced real growth in income of 36 percent; between 1963 and 1973, that figure was 25 percent. But between 1973 and 1983, his income declined by 14 percent. Little wonder that millions of women entered the labor force in those years. It began to take two incomes to support a family where one had been enough before. Little wonder, too, that the number of people working at more than one job hit a record high in 1989.[9] Overall, average real wages in the United States have fallen 13 percent since 1969. The average American working person is getting poorer—and so, therefore, is the country.[10]

What these figures conceal, however, is what has been happening to the middle class and the working poor. Between 1979 and 1988, real family income for the poorest fifth of our people declined by 4.5 percent while that of the richest fifth increased by 14 percent.[11] For single mothers, a rising proportion of the bottom fifth, life is very bleak. But it is not just the poorest who are in trouble. The middle class, the key to social stability in the United States, is also in difficulty. Overall, the top 30 percent of our people in terms of income distribution have been getting richer while the bottom 70 percent have been getting poorer.[12]

In the simplest terms, our people have been trying to maintain their standard of living by borrowing money, putting more family members to work, and working at more jobs. But with fewer people entering the work force, the string will run out on these strategies. We will run out of additional family members who can enter the work force, there will not be enough hours in the day to work more jobs, and our creditors will not increase the amount they are willing to lend us at rates we can afford. We know that a real slide in our standard of living is coming; the only question is how quickly.

The only way to avoid this chilling scenario is to find a way to improve our productivity dramatically. A major improvement in productivity would enable us to reduce our debt, lower interest rates, invest in the future, and provide rising incomes for everyone.

Virtually all the major nations suffered lowered productivity growth rates after the oil shock in the 1970s. The United States was hit harder than most, however, and whereas many other countries have since recovered to make strong progress, we have not. Why? Many factors have contributed to our own weak performance, but none is as important as our relative inattention to the quality of our human resources and our failure to make the most productive use of our people in the workplace.

Other nations have pursued creative human-resource policies in part to improve their competitiveness in a rapidly integrating world economy. But becoming more competitive is in itself no challenge at all. There are only two ways to compete—reducing incomes or improving productivity and quality. We can, in other words, become more competitive simply by lowering the price of our goods and services in world markets, either directly or by lowering the value of the dollar in relation to other currencies. That, however, is simply the path to lower income and a diminished standard of living for all Americans—and it is the path we now tread. The challenge is to be competitive while maintaining high incomes and full employment. This is now impossible without high productivity growth rates, and these, in turn, cannot be achieved without very high-quality human resources.

The thesis of this book is simple. The key to both productivity and competitiveness is the skills of our people and our capacity to use highly educated and trained people to maximum advantage in the workplace. In fact, however, the guiding principle on which our educational and industrial systems have been built is profoundly different; this guiding principle, for long highly successful, is now outmoded and harmful, and the time has come to change it.

In the first part of this century, we adopted the principle of mass-producing low-quality education to create a low-skilled work force for mass-production industry. Building on this principle, our education and business systems became very tightly linked, evolving into a single system that brilliantly capitalized on our advantages and enabled us to create the most powerful economy and the largest middle class the world had ever seen. The education system, modeled on industrial organization, was crafted to supply the work force that the industrial economy needed. America's systems of school organization and industrial organization were beautifully matched, each highly dependent on the other for its success, each the envy of the world.

But most of the competitive advantages enjoyed at the beginning of the century had faded away by midcentury, and advances in technology during and after the war slowly altered the structure of the domestic and world economy in ways that turned these principles of American business and school organization into liabilities rather than assets.

Economic theory should have predicted these problems and provided clues to their solution. But modern economic theory evolved in the face of the problems presented by the Great Depression. It is virtually silent on the problems of the quality of goods and services, of improving productivity, and of capital formation in nations that must compete in the global economy. Furthermore, modern economic theory has almost nothing to say about the causes or consequences of failures in the supply of human skills.

That is why American business has suffered increasingly from the competitive assault, government has responded with economic policies based in part on theories that were blind to the most serious problems posed by the changing shape of the international economy, and business executives have pursued strategies that had worked in the past, but were counterproductive in the present. Educational institutions, for their part, proud of past successes and largely unaware of the changes in the world's economic structure, and therefore in domestic skill requirements, have continued to pursue policies that are wholly inadequate for the present and future.

But the countries that have had the most economic success in recent years have pursued a different course. Committed to the broad goals of full employment and high wages, these nations have built policies firmly grounded on the assumption that they would be able to provide high incomes for everyone only if the quality of their human resources was very high and employers were organized to use those highly educated people effectively in the workplace. What is striking is how similar these policies are in countries as dissimilar in other ways as Japan and Germany, Singapore and Sweden. It is vital for us as a nation to understand how our competitors link economic, labor-market, and education policy into one integrated strategy, how the practices of firms and education and training institutions are affected by this strategy, and what the outcomes are for their people.

In the United States, individual firms and public programs can be found that are among the best in the world, but because we lack a consensus on strategy, we also lack the powerful systems of policy and practice that our competitors have developed. Our country is locked in a time warp, wedded to a worldview and to strategies long since outmoded by events. U.S. industry does not depend on an abundant supply of highly skilled labor, and this has a debilitating effect on our education and training system. Though the top executives of our best firms are among the most ardent advocates of school reform, the vast majority of American employers do not want more than eighth-grade-level skills in the people that they hire for their front-line work force. Because what our schools are producing is in rough balance with what employers actually want, the schools have little incentive to perform at world-class levels. Conversely, if our employers organized work in the way that the most successful firms around the world do, there would be an instant skills crisis. Our front-line workers—those in non-managerial and nontechnical positions, working directly on the plant floor or in direct contact with customers, on whom we will depend to produce the turn-around in productivity on which our future depends—may be the least skilled among those of all the major industrial nations.

The picture that emerges is one that most Americans will find startling. The United States appears to be home to the most elitist work organization and education system in the industrial world. Here more than anywhere else, those who do not have and are not on their way to getting a baccalaureate degree— more than 70 percent of the population—are held in low regard, have little claim on the nation's goods and services, and are in no position to make the contribution at work of which they are capable. They are our single most valuable—and most wasted—resource. In comparing our human-resources system for our front-line workers point for point with that of our competitors, we find a staggering cumulative deficit.

In a way, America is the victim of its success. Although in fact our economic system was outdated by the late 1930s, our achievements in the war and our economic dominance afterwards persuaded us that we still had the best system in the world. There was no incentive to change it. For those who have since become our most formidable competitors, however, the situation was very different. Their social institutions, not just their physical plants, had been destroyed by war and largely discredited. Looking at the future with a clearer eye than we could, they were able to build new social and economic systems far better adapted to post-war realities, while our systems, vigorously defended by a host of vested interests, continued to be rooted in the past.

But the picture is hardly bleak. Everywhere one looks, among firms, schools, government programs and agencies, and unions, there are good examples of the policies and practices on which a world-class system can be built. Throughout the country, the elements of the new system are fighting to emerge from the shadow of the old. In this book, we lay out a comprehensive program for America, a plan not for equaling the performance of our best competitors, but for improving on it. Proposals are made for national economic and family policy, for changes in employer and union practices, for the schools, and for our training programs. Taken together, these proposals are intended to constitute a seamless web, an institutional fabric that will enable the society and its members to learn constantly and to put that learning to work, to enable us once again to lead the world in productivity growth.

As this is written, the former members of the Communist bloc in Eastern Europe and the Soviet Union are setting out to fashion new societies. It is a rare, perhaps unparalleled, event in human history when so many peoples in so many countries have an opportunity to sit down and write a new set of rules for themselves. Many of those countries have done a better job than we of building effective human-resource development programs, and, for that reason, may yet surprise the world in economic prowess, if they can solve their political problems.

But we in the United States face a similar challenge of rebuilding our social institutions. Our main purpose in writing this book lies in our hope and belief that our people and our political leaders will rise to the challenge now, before it is too late.

PART I

America Preeminent: Riding the Second Industrial Revolution to Success

CHAPTER 1

The Mass-Production Economy: The American Way

It must have seemed to others that America came out of nowhere to capture the flag as the world's leading economy. In the 1870s, Germany and Britain were the undisputed economic and technological leaders of the world. Then, suddenly, we appeared in the vanguard. In 1926, we produced about 45 percent of the world's industrial output, including 80 percent of the world's automobiles and 50 percent of its steel, electricity, and crude oil.[1] We were the world's leading exporter. We had already become, thirteen years earlier, the world's largest and wealthiest market for manufactured products. It had all happened very quickly. Wages of American workers in 1920 were five times as high as they were in 1900, the value of goods and services was six times as high, and the number of wage earners had doubled.[2]

The methods we had used to accomplish that meteoric rise were destined to mold our national character, to frame our thinking to this day. They shaped our institutions, our laws, our politics, our values, and our attitudes. They had a decisive effect on the way we view the role of human resources in our economy and society.

A brief look at the rise of two companies, United States Steel and the Ford Motor Company, will set the context.

Andrew Carnegie, whose nineteenth-century steel empire eventually became United States Steel, epitomized the turn-of-the-century entrepreneur.[3] His basic approach was to acquire the latest technology, usually from abroad, establish efficient operating procedures, and engage in active price competition, the very strategy that would be used with equal success a century later by the Japanese against the United States. A very shrewd businessman, Carnegie would maintain and even build capacity during recessions, and then profit handsomely during the next upswing, when his competitors were caught short of capacity, another technique recently employed with great effectiveness against American business by the Japanese.

Carnegie, like the other captains of industry in his era, thought it essential to crush the craft unions of his time. His enormous investments in machinery could only be recovered by continuous operation of the mills, which meant, as he saw it, the least possible interference from labor.

That same machinery provided the means. The technology made it possible to redesign the work so that it could be broken down into repetitive tasks, none of which required much in the way of skill or training. There was no shortage of immigrants and former farm workers who were happy to get these unskilled jobs. Mass-production methods worked as well in the steel mills as they were later to do in the automobile assembly plant.

The Amalgamated Association of Iron and Steel Workers was indeed crushed, most notably in the famous Homestead Strike of 1892. After the union's power was broken, working conditions deteriorated. These workers would not be effectively organized again until the 1930s, in the midst of the Great Depression.

The economies of scale that Carnegie could achieve with these methods worked the same wonders for him that they did for Henry Ford. The cost of a ton of steel declined from $36.52 in 1878 to $12.00 in 1898. The profits were enormous. Carnegie earned $40 million in 1900 alone, on an initial capitalization of only $25 million.[4]

J. P. Morgan bought out Carnegie in 1901 to form United States Steel from his holdings. Morgan and his associates were financiers whose main interest was in making money, not steel. Led by United States Steel, all the steel company managements quickly learned that the way to maximize profit was to get the industry down to a few big firms that would keep their prices up and reduce their output when the inevitable recessions came. This was the opposite, of course, of what Carnegie had done.

As successful as the steel industry became with the use of advanced technology and the de-skilling of labor, the greatest triumphs in this area were achieved by the auto industry, exemplified by the pioneer of the mass-produced automobile, Henry Ford. Ford made his first car in 1896, but it was not until 1908 that he introduced the Model T, one of the greatest commercial and technological successes of all time.[5] Ford's sales went from 10,607 in 1908–9 to 730,041 in 1916–17. At the same time the price of a touring car fell from $850 to $360, and Ford's share of the auto market rose from 9.4 percent in 1908 to 48 percent in 1914. Productivity in the industry more than quadrupled between 1889 and 1919.[6]

The assembly line and mass production were largely responsible for the great reduction in Ford's prices. Ford's approach to the use of these twin pillars of modern production methods was heavily influenced by the teachings of Frederick Winslow Taylor. Taylor did not invent mass-production methods, but he perfected them, provided a rationale for them, and served as their most effective champion.

Under Taylor's approach to scientific management, all the ordinary work of the organization was to be studied by engineers on "time and motion" principles, so as to break it down into very simple tasks that could be quickly and easily learned by someone with little education. On the basis of his analysis, the engineer would determine the one best—or most efficient—way to perform that task, and that was the way in which everyone was henceforth to do it. Each worker would be assigned one task, to be repeated with "machine-like efficiency" countless times during the day.

> The worker's equal division of work was to do what he was told to do by management and his share of the responsibility was that responsibility to do what he was told. In his system the judgment of the individual workman was replaced by the laws, rules, principles, etc., of the science of the job which was developed by management.... The whole attitude of Taylor in this respect was described by a mechanic who worked with him.... Taylor would tell him that he was "not supposed to think, there are other people paid for thinking around here."[7]

Taylor, like his colleagues elsewhere in business, was interested in reducing the control that skilled workers had over production and transferring that control to management. But he was also taking into account what he perceived as the low quality of labor available to staff enterprises.

The issue of labor quality was very real. In the late nineteenth century the country had begun to experience the greatest wave of immigration that the world had ever seen. Fourteen million immigrants arrived between 1865 and 1900. After 1900, they continued to pour in at the rate of one million a year. Most of these immigrants were desperately poor; most could not speak English; and few could claim to be more than semiliterate in any language. Thus the industrial system was designed around workers who were presumed to have very few intellectual skills. Ordinary workers were expected to do as they were told. In order to do so, they needed to be able to follow simple written and oral instructions—Taylor's system involved the development of countless manuals describing in great detail how each job was to be done—and to do simple arithmetic. Mainly, though, the system required obedience and discipline.

Taylor knew that his system required an array of people above and around the ordinary workers to direct and support their activities. But he believed that whatever bureaucracy evolved to design the work and monitor and supervise and support the front-line worker, it would more than pay for itself in the efficiencies that could be achieved by his method.

Unenlightened and unfair as this system may seem to us now, it was part and parcel of the mass-production system that was to produce astonishing economic progress for everyone concerned. Very large investments in complex and expensive machinery, designed to be operated by people with minimal skills, could turn out standardized products in profusion at very low unit costs. Rates of productivity increase from this method were, as we have seen, very high. Great gains in industrial output and a rapid improvement in our standard of living were made possible in this way.

Another important consequence was that the ability to lay off as many workers as needed became a key to profitability. Since technology and Taylorism had deskilled the work and there was a seemingly inexhaustible pool of immigrants and rural migrants ready to take the jobs of those who had been let go in a recession, there was not much of a problem in implementing this strategy, so long as the unions were weak. The replacements could be trained easily in a day or two for the work they had to do. Keeping prices steady even in a downturn was no problem either, as long as the few firms that dominated the market had no competition from abroad, which was indeed the case.

The steady improvements in technology and its application that fueled the enormous productivity improvements in manufacturing were paralleled in agriculture. Here, the productivity growth was spurred by labor shortages caused by people leaving the farm for the higher wages offered in the cities. The mechanization of the farm between 1910 and 1919 was nothing short of phenomenal. In 1910, there were only 1,000 tractors on American farms, no trucks, and 50,000 automobiles; only nine years later there were 158,000 tractors, 100,000 trucks, and 1.8 million automobiles.[8] In turn, the productivity growth in agriculture spurred the growth in manufacturing, by making it cheaper to live in the cities. The system fed on itself.

It actually did so in many ways. Among the most important was the steady lowering of prices for a steadily widening range of products, made possible by the mass-production method combined with the steady advance of technology. Lowered prices brought these products into the buying range of many more people. This increased demand, which increased the size of the market, and in turn made it possible to produce even more at even lower prices.

But these low prices depended heavily on the ability to produce very long runs of identical or nearly identical items. America's enormous and rapidly growing domestic market made this high-volume production profitable, but only, as Morgan and his colleagues learned, if the large firms that controlled production also controlled prices and the pace at which new products were introduced. One had to recoup the enormous capital costs of the plant and machinery required to produce one product before going on to the next. That, of course, is why Henry Ford declared that the public could have the Model T in any color it wanted, as long as it was black.

For all these reasons, oligopoly—the control of a given market by a small number of firms willing to cooperate with one another—was a key element of the system. Real price competition or the unbridled introduction of new products would have killed the system by making it impossible to recover the enormous capital investments involved. So, the managers thought, would caving in to demands for worker job security, because layoffs in time of weak demand were essential to lowering variable costs when sales were off. Oligopoly made it possible to control both markets and workers.

But real trouble developed in the system in the 1920s. Productivity was increasing faster than the real wages of the workers, which had been kept down by the financiers who controlled business. That meant that, over time, the workers had less and less money available to purchase the rising volume of products and services available. The scale was tipped by the farmers. Farm production had greatly expanded to meet the needs of the Western allies in the First World War. As the Allies got back on their feet, the foreign market dwindled. Since the needs of the domestic market were already being met, farm prices plunged. To make up for their losses, the farmers planted even more, driving prices down further. As their incomes plummeted, so did their purchasing power. Manufacturers did what they always did in a recession; they laid off the workers they did not need, while trying to keep prices up. With so many people out of work on farms and in the cities, demand collapsed. The stock-market crash only worsened the Depression that was already well underway, pulling down a vastly overextended financial structure made weak at every point by rampant speculation.

The policies of the Roosevelt administration and the war put the system back on its feet. Keynesian economics correctly interpreted the economic problem as insufficient demand for the available production capacity. It legitimized the role of government in putting money in people's hands in downturns so they could purchase more, creating more demand, which then enabled employers to hire people to meet the demand, thereby pulling the economy out of its rut. Before the Great Depression, most economists had said flatly that such an event was impossible. After it, most were persuaded that they had finally learned how to fine-tune the economy with good demand management, and they held this view long after the Keynesian mass-production synthesis was invalidated by economic and technological change. As we shall see later, they were no better prepared for the future than their predecessors who had denied the possibility of a depression ever happening.

The Depression years also brought the passage of strong labor legislation. American labor leaders had argued that the only way to protect workers' interests was to take laborers out of competition with one another within companies through collective bargaining and the common rule (equal pay for equal work); between companies by "pattern bargaining" (threatening to strike first one company and then another) and multi-employer bargaining; and between industries through government regulations and pattern bargaining.

Virtually all of this package of ideas was enacted into law in the 1930s and

1940s. It fit nicely with the Keynesian analysis that the problem was insufficient purchasing power in the hands of consumers (read "labor") and was put forward as a way for labor to gain enough "countervailing power" in the system to get its fair share of the productivity dividend, thereby making another depression less likely.

But we should note carefully that labor, in taking this approach, had fully embraced the basic premises of the system as we have described it. No challenge was laid down to the Taylorist work organization, the prerogatives of management, or the assembly line's definition of tasks and roles. The Taylorist dividing line between management and labor was encased in law, their relations defined as adversarial. Labor eschewed any role in management, agreeing with Taylor that it was management's role to tell laborers what to do and how to do it (assuming of course that the laborer's pay was fair and the working conditions were safe and "fair"). The divisions Taylor made among jobs were cast in stone in the union contract, and management was not allowed to assign a worker to a different job. Unions used this tactic to protect jobs, and it also served to reinforce the Taylorist method of work organization.

Furthermore, in the Roosevelt era labor borrowed from management the use of oligopolistic practices. Its value proved itself in the pattern bargaining that took place in the automobile industry, among others. The United Automobile Workers would threaten to strike one of the Big Three auto makers, making it clear that the workers at the unstruck firms would subsidize those at the struck firm as long as necessary, thereby paralyzing the struck firm indefinitely. The threatened firm would grant a substantial wage increase. The other two would quickly fall into line, knowing that one of them would be next if they did not. But there was no big penalty for submitting to these wage demands. The Big Three controlled between them the price of cars. As long as they did not compete on price, a practice that they all believed would be ruinous to everyone, they could simply pass the wage increases on to the consumers, who had no one else to buy cars from, and so paid the price demanded. Much the same thing happened, with variations, in all the basic industries. In this way, workers with no more than an eighth-grade education and little in the way of technical skills could end up drawing paychecks that enabled them to have two cars, a vacation cottage as well as a principal residence, and maybe a boat for fishing and water skiing. The system worked for everyone.

At least it worked for those in the big industrial unions. In the 1930s and 1940s, the American industrial labor movement concentrated its organizing efforts on a few key industries, primarily those controlled by monopolies and oligopolies of the sort we have just described. The result now is that in this country, unlike the countries that are our most formidable competitors, the majority of workers are not union members. This difference in strategy would years later have fateful consequences.

Then there were the craft unions, very different from the unions organized around industries like steel and automobiles. The craft workers are the elite of the American work force. Confined largely to the building trades, the machinists, and a handful of other occupations, they represent the small number of jobs that could not be deskilled by advancing technology, the assembly line, and the Taylorist methods of mass production. Many, of course, are individual entrepreneurs, and therefore managers, themselves. Typically far more skilled than their industrial union counterparts, they constitute a small fraction of the American labor force.

Though many owners and managers of firms were very bitter about the changes that took place in the Roosevelt years, it is clear in retrospect that far from destroying the system, his administration actually saved it. Management remained firmly in control, and the proceeds of productivity increases were distributed equally enough between owners and workers to ensure that sufficient funds were available both for investment and for demand. Workers were still expected, however, to "leave their heads at the factory gate." Neither their bosses nor their shop stewards expected them to think for a living. In fact, the legal structure that the New Deal put in place simply reinforced a system in which the workers were prevented from doing so.

During this period, leadership passed from the financiers of the Morgan era into the hands of professional managers. In 1900, only 12.5 percent of corporate managers were engineers; 19.5 percent were salaried managers. By 1925, these proportions had grown to 15.6 percent and 37.7 percent and by 1950 to 19.5 percent and 41.4 percent.[9] By midcentury the large mass-production company was controlled by a bureaucracy consisting of many layers of management. Work at the front-line level was done by people whose jobs were very narrowly defined and controlled by managerial elites through detailed regulations that more or less followed Taylor's scientific management method. The burgeoning bureaucracy scheduled production, dealt with suppliers, checked for quality, reworked broken parts and subassemblies, maintained the machines, and re-paired them when necessary, among countless other tasks. It got so large that a whole corps of middle managers arose that did nothing but manage the flow of information up and down the system.

In the days of the entrepreneurs, before the financiers ran the system, it had been possible to start out at the bottom of the pyramid and work one's way to the top. Gradually, as the professional managers came into ascendancy, this was less and less possible. Just as in the armies of earlier centuries it was common to see grizzled sergeants officered by boys from the upper classes commissioned in their teens, so it became common in business to see plant-floor workers with years of seniority supervised by young men right out of college or graduate schools of management. America was on its way to building the most elitist form of work organization in the world. Just as in the army officers and enlisted men

were not allowed to socialize, so in twentieth-century factories there were separate parking lots, dining areas, rest rooms, and even entrances, that served to
maintain the rigid segregation between the front-line workers and their social,
intellectual, and occupational superiors. In the end the boundary between blue
collar workers and managers became virtually hermetically sealed.

It is a sad irony that this closing of the bridge between exempt and nonexempt
workers was ultimately made possible by the great expansion of higher education in America following World War II. The granting of opportunity to some
effectively closed it off for many more. As soon as there were enough college
graduates to fill the jobs above the front line, those on the front line were faced
with a need-not-apply sign, no matter how experienced, knowledgeable, or capable they might be.

Through it all, the front-line worker was there, still, to do as he or she was told.
Product innovation, the main form of intellectual activity in the firm, was not
only a function to be organized and carried out exclusively by the managerial and
technical elite, it was to be driven by scientists and engineers with advanced
degrees who did the laboratory research. They passed on their findings to
engineers, who designed new products and processes based on the research, tried
them out as prototypes, then designed production models, and passed their
blueprints to the managers of production departments. These in turn organized
the work and told the workers what to do and how to do it. Because this whole
cycle took years and often cost many millions of dollars for a major product,
significant changes in the design rarely occurred except when new models came
out, which was generally every few years. Those changes were the result of new
basic and applied research and the resulting new technologies, combined with the
results of market research done by the marketing department. The front-line
workers were at the end of a long, linear process, on the bottom of a very large
and complex bureaucracy. It rarely occurred to anyone to ask these workers—
often three-quarters or more of the whole work force—how they thought the
product or the process might be improved, let alone actually to involve them in
the design process.

Nevertheless, this system made the front-line workers part of the largest and
richest middle class the world had ever seen. Through the 1950s and 1960s, they
were to enjoy an unprecedented prosperity. The system had worked not simply
well, but brilliantly, for sixty years.

But it was far more vulnerable than anyone imagined. There was one thread
that ran through almost all its weaknesses—its elitist character. We had built
a system of "coolie labor" surrounded by a managerial, technical, and support
elite.

Product changes could not be made quickly on the factory floor or at the point
of service delivery because innovation was a time-consuming linear process that
was driven by the research and development elite. What if competitors would

someday figure out how to create a partnership between the engineers who did the design work and a highly educated front-line work force that would contribute to a process of constant innovation? A partnership like that could short-circuit all the problems that arise when engineers, out of touch with the plant floor, design things that cannot be built or serviced. It could innovate continuously. It could get new marketing ideas into the product far faster than the system that only made changes in model-change years. But one does not ask coolies to innovate.

The system was wedded to long runs of standardized products because it was assumed that productivity improvement was a function of investment in very expensive machines, not in the ordinary worker on the floor. What if one assumed, instead, that large investments in workers would yield even greater returns? Then one might be able to invest less in the machines and be able to recover the capital investment more quickly, making it possible to compete by targeting narrower markets, or changing the product more frequently to match changing consumer tastes. But one does not make large investments in the training of coolie labor.

Ultimately, the American system resulted in a ratio of managers, support staff, and technical people on the one hand to front-line workers on the other that was the highest in the world. This was largely because of the Taylorist assumption that the front-line workers were incapable of thinking for themselves. What if it occurred to some firm, or even nation, that the front-line workers could bear the primary responsibility for quality control, for production scheduling, for their own supervision, or for countless other functions done by the elite? But one does not assign these functions to coolies.

The system depended on maintaining prices in downturns, which depended on being able to lay off workers whenever business was slow. But what if a competitor came along who viewed its highly trained front-line workers as its most important asset, had invested heavily in their training and therefore did not lay them off in downturns, but rather reduced prices and went for a bigger market share? But this tactic would not make much sense to employers who had invested little in their front-line workers, whose jobs had been deliberately designed to require little skill. Better to let the coolies go, and reduce the downside risk; one could always replace them later.

"Coolie" is, of course, a loaded word. We have used it deliberately, to help the reader gain a perspective on the system, a perspective that might be hard to get in another way because we are all so much a part of the system that it is hard to imagine how things might work differently. We do not mean to imply by the use of the word that management or anyone else now bears responsibility for the way things turned out. Labor, as we have noted, did little or nothing to change these features of the system, nor did government.

Whatever the system's origins, it now belonged not just to management, but to everyone. The Taylorist idea of how work is best organized had permeated the American workplace more completely than it had workplaces in any other country in the world. Three-quarters of a century after Taylorism became firmly entrenched, we would pay the price for so seriously underrating the contribution that 70 percent of our work force could make to the products and services their firms produced—and for building an education system that was perfectly matched to the needs of the Taylorist workplace.

CHAPTER 2

Mass-Producing Education

Americans have been curiously ambivalent about education at least since the founding of the republic. America was the first country to follow the Prussians in establishing a system of free public schools, and we have taken great and justifiable pride in our educational institutions ever since. Yet, since the Revolution, we have been suspicious of academics and intellectuals, associating them with the monarchies and class-based systems of the Europe against which we rebelled. For Americans, schooling has largely been a practical affair, its justification lying less in the path that it provides to the life of the mind than in its utility for maintaining our democracy, meeting our country's economic needs, and offsetting the advantages of social origins in the great race of life. We have a love affair with schooling but a deeply rooted distrust of truly educated people.

At no time in our history was this attitude more fateful than at the turn of the century. In the space of less than two decades, the American educational ideal shifted from schools whose purpose was to secure for some students real intellectual mastery of the core academic subjects to schools that would help almost all students adjust to the roles they would assume later in life, in particular their vocational roles in the developing industrial economy. In a remarkably short time, America performed a herculean task as it built a school system on the industrial mass-production model to fit the needs of a smokestack economy. In doing so, we will argue, it turned its back on an educational ideal that would be desperately needed years later when America's position in the world economy would be greatly changed. Even more serious, it built an institutional structure for education and legitimized public attitudes toward education that would leave it open to question whether the country could ever embrace an educational ideal based on real intellectual achievement by the masses of American students, the goal that is now required if the American economy is to prosper.

As the country moved from craft methods of production to factory methods and giant organizational structures were put together in vast and growing networks of business organization, skill requirements were changing radically. But skill requirements are not necessarily the same thing as intellectual requirements. William T. Harris, arguably the leading educator of his day, a preeminent Hegel scholar and founder of an important journal of philosophy, commented that "in modern industrial society, 'conformity to the time of the train, to the starting of work in the manufactory,' and to other characteristic activities of the city requires absolute precision and regularity. . . . The student must have his lessons ready at the appointed time, must rise at the tap of the bell, move to the line, return; in short, go through all the evolutions with equal precision."[1]

No one who reads that passage can doubt that the education policy of the day was striving to meet the needs of the burgeoning industrial economy. Management, investing its capital in plant and equipment, was learning how to prevent disruption by skilled craft workers and make the most of less-skilled workers who had a reasonable command of reading, writing, and arithmetic, but little more.

Still, the challenge to educators to reach even this ideal was immense. As we have seen, as industrial wages rose, employment in America's big cities became very attractive to people on the farms and in poverty-stricken areas overseas. The schools had to cope somehow with a vast influx of uneducated people and make them fit for life in the factories, mills, offices, and stores.

Universal primary education had largely been accomplished. Public secondary schooling had been growing slowly in the cities since 1870. This was partly because the growing complexity of industrial organization required basic literacy among more workers. But there were other reasons as well. Successful campaigns against child labor were providing strong political support for raising the compulsory schooling age. Organized labor added to that support out of a desire to keep young primary-school graduates out of the labor market, so as to keep wages up as the supply of immigrant labor grew.

Prior to the close of the nineteenth century, few primary students went on to secondary school. Those who did usually went to private schools, often as boarders. By no means all of these students went on to college, but the secondary schools were unmistakably elite institutions that followed a classical curriculum. The growing number of public high schools were modeled on the private schools. Admission to "Boys' Latin" and "Classical High" was typically competitive, by examination. These public high schools, like their private counterparts, where one read Greek and Latin and studied the ancients, mathematics, and the natural sciences, put their students on paths intended to lead to the most prominent professional, business and social roles in the community. Those who attended were, in the main, highly motivated.

The onset of compulsory mass secondary schooling brought about a profound transformation in the character of the schools. Great masses of students had to be brought into a school structure based on village models of governance and organization. Schools and school districts were approaching the size of major corporations. As they did so, they were subject to increasing attacks on the grounds that their managements were corrupt and inefficient and their curriculums outmoded and irrelevant.

The leadership of the transformation in the schools was largely in the hands of the progressive reformers of the era, who were busy recasting local government in the mold of modern industrial organization and arranging for business executives and other "successful citizens" in the community to gain control of the institutions of local government.

While the reformers were determined to curb the excesses of the business community, they, like the public at large, lionized the captains of industry. A great wave of enthusiasm for the methods of scientific management was sweeping the country, and with it, a conviction that large, tax-supported institutions—controlled, as they were, by ward-based political organizations, which used them as an inexhaustible source of patronage—were a hotbed of corruption and inefficiency that had to be rooted out. The public believed that if only modern business methods could be applied to governmental institutions, great efficiencies could be achieved there as they had been in business. Disgusted with the corruption and apparent chaos of ward politics, and believing that the illiterate and dirty immigrants would ruin America if democracy went too far, the reformers were determined to run their government institutions in the same orderly and efficient way in which they thought business was run.

All these sentiments were first directed at municipal reform, but it was only a matter of time before they were applied to the schools with a vengeance. The city school boards at the turn of the century were typically organized on the ward system, with the total membership of ward committees and city boards sometimes numbering in the hundreds, dispensing jobs and requiring political loyalty in return. These large city school boards were divided into subcommittees that ran the schools, while superintendents were often no more than figureheads.

The program of the reformers was straightforward. The ward system of citizen management of schools must be replaced by a corporate style of organization, emulating the small board of directors that made broad policy, and these new boards must get their direction from a strong chief executive officer, in this case the superintendent of schools, who would function as a professional manager, and would be responsible for the direct management of the schools. The direction of the organization immediately under the superintendent should be placed in the hands of a professional management staff composed of people who specialized in specific operations of the schools. These professional managers should give detailed direction to the workers, the teachers, whose job it was to follow those directions with the strictest obedience. This approach had worked brilliantly for American private enterprise and there was no reason, the reformers argued, why it should not work for the schools.

To those critics who suggested that the burgeoning bureaucracy would take scarce resources from the education of children, the reformers replied that the research by Taylor and others on scientific management showed conclusively that the increased planning and administrative staff would pay for itself and produce additional savings through a manifold increase in the efficiency with which teachers worked.

Those who defended the old style of school governance on the grounds that it provided for broad public participation and responsiveness to the diverse interests of an increasingly heterogeneous population were quickly defeated by the administrative progressives. In 1893, the twenty-eight largest cities had central school boards (not counting the ward boards) averaging 21.5 members per city. By 1913 that ratio had dropped to 10.2, and the ward boards had largely withered away.[2] Election by wards, favoring popular leaders of modest means, had been replaced by at-large elections, which favored election of those "successful men" who could raise the large sums of money required to mount a successful citywide campaign. The leading businessmen and their allies were now in charge and in a position to install the methods of organization and staffing that they had found most efficient in their own sphere. These business-dominated boards turned from superintendents who concerned themselves mainly with such matters as the aims and purposes of education to those who could be counted on to manage the schools for rational efficiency. Inevitably, these new superintendents tended increasingly to identify themselves with the successful business executive.

Whether the schools in fact became more efficient is open to question, just as it is at least arguable that mass production and economies of scale, not scientific management, improved industrial efficiency. But there can be little doubt about the growth of administrative and supervisory staff. The U.S. Office of Education reported that in 1889, there was an average of four such officers in the 484 cities in which it collected such data. Between 1890 and 1920, however, the numbers grew from 9 to 144 in Baltimore, 7 to 159 in Boston, 10 to 159 in Cleveland, and 235 to 1,310 in New York. David Tyack quotes sociologists Robert and Helen Lynds[3] to the effect that "in 1890 in Middletown the superintendent was the only person in the system who did not teach, but by the 1920s there was 'a whole galaxy of principals, assistant principals, supervisors of special subjects, directors of vocational education and home economics, deans, attendance officers, and clerks, who do no teaching but are concerned in one way or another with keeping the system going.' Problems were met 'not by changes in its foundations but by adding fresh stories to its superstructure.' "[4]

The dictates of scientific management not only produced this bureaucracy, but prescribed its function. Franklin Bobbitt, instructor in educational administration at the University of Chicago, had taken on the role of translating Frederick Taylor's principles of scientific management into a form in which they could be used by educators. Bobbitt "believed with Taylor that efficiency depended on 'centralization of authority and definite direction by the supervisors of all processes performed. . . . The worker [that is, the teacher] . . . must be kept supplied with the detailed instructions as to the work to be done, the standards to be reached, the methods to be employed, and the appliances to be used. . . . The results of the work of the planning department had to be 'transmitted to the teachers so that there can never be any misunderstanding as to what is expected of a teacher in the way of results or in the matter of method. This means that instruction must be given as to everything that is to be done.' "[5] Thus were the principles of scientific management used to elevate the authority of the supervisors and limit the freedom of the teacher.

As the organization of schools was modeled by the reform administrations on the organization of smokestack industry, the teachers became the blue-collar workers. It was therefore inevitable, especially during the 1930s, after the union battles in the private sector had led to government approval of collective bargaining, that teaching would be become a unionized occupation.

One might ask why teaching, almost alone among the occupations requiring a college degree, should have become a blue-collar occupation rather than a profession. The answer lies in the matter of gender; the teachers were overwhelmingly women, the administrators overwhelmingly men. Just as managers in the industrial workplace had worked to arrange things so that they could employ as workers people over whom they could exercise maximum control, so the managers in the school workplace had chosen as line workers women, who had little power in the society, who could be expected to do as they were told, and who could be paid a wage well below what their education could otherwise command in the marketplace.

As long ago as 1848, John Philbrick, the new principal of the Quincy School in Massachusetts, invented the modern form of school organization, which remains largely unchanged to the present day. Abandoning the form in which teachers taught many subjects to many students of different ages, Philbrick decided on a separate classroom for each teacher, who taught students in one grade. Students were separated by ability. "Let the Principal or Superintendent have the general supervision and control of the whole, and let him have one male assistant or sub-principal, and ten female assistants, one for each room." Thus, says David Tyack, "was stamped on mid-century America not only the graded school but also the pedagogical harem."[6]

It was actually well into the nineteenth century before women came to dominate teaching. Before that, communities tended to turn to educated young men who would teach for a while before going on to some more rewarding occupation; to men to whom no other such occupation was available; or to men such as ministers, who were willing to combine teaching with some other vocation.

Economics changed all that. The steady rise in student population brought about by immigration, combined at the turn of the century with the onset of compulsory education up to the age of sixteen, created the need for a great increase in the number of teachers. Unwilling to pay what men would have required and been able to demand in such a market, America turned to its women. In 1870, women had become 59 percent of the teaching force. By 1900, the figure had risen to 70 percent. By 1920, 86 percent of our teachers were women.[7] These young women had the virtues of being of high moral character, undemanding with respect to pay, and, not least important, docile.

The exigencies of an ever-increasing student population produced a ceaseless quest for inexpensive teachers. Even in the middle of the nineteenth century, inquiries showed that women schoolteachers could be hired for less than women factory workers, presumably because teaching was respectable work for aspiring young women. School boards took full advantage of the limited opportunities available to young women. This is nowhere more succinctly demonstrated than by David Tyack in a table that shows the average salaries of women and men in three positions in 467 city systems in 1905.[8]

	Women	Men
Elementary Teacher	$650	$1,161
Elementary Principal	$970	$1,542
High School Teacher	$903	$1,303

But these young women were not very well educated and did not stay around very long. Required by convention, law, or regulation to quit teaching when they got married or had children, they had little commitment to teaching and little of the skill that only experience could confer. As late as the 1919–20 school year, "half of America's schoolteachers were under twenty-five, half served in the schools for not more than four or five years, and half had no more than four years of education beyond the eighth grade."[9]

Nevertheless, these young women fit the needs of the evolving bureaucratic system very well. Everyone agreed that they were more likely to take direction from those in charge of the system than men. The growth in the feminization of teaching closely parallels the growth of the new system, as does the reservation of administrative posts for men. The scientific method of management required that the worker be told in detail what to do by those in authority. The system worked, or at least was tolerated, in the factory, where the worker had little education. But schoolteaching required somewhat more education than factory-floor work. How, then, to make the method work when the workers in the schools had more education than the average blue-collar worker, in fact enough education to qualify them for positions in management? The answer, clearly, was to hire young women, who, because they were both young and women, could be counted on to give no more trouble than the blue-collar workers in the factory.

A work force of this character would undoubtedly have had great difficulty in administering an intellectually demanding curriculum to the vast numbers of students descending on turn-of-the-century schools. But, as things turned out, they were not required to do so.

The same reformers who demanded scientific management of the schools were also bitter critics of the prevailing classical curriculum, which they denounced as academic and irrelevant to the needs of the students. Not content with sadly admitting that the realities of overwhelming numbers, inadequate budgets, and unwilling students might make it impossible to pursue a curriculum that demanded real intellectual effort of all students, the critics instead denounced such an objective as archaic and undemocratic. Surely there was more than a grain of truth in the critique of the traditional nineteenth-century curriculum, but instead of heeding John Dewey's plea to create a modern curriculum with real intellectual substance, the critics, in Richard Hofstadter's words, "entered upon a crusade to exalt the academically uninterested or ungifted child into a kind of culture hero."[10]

The dominant view through the end of the nineteenth century and into the beginning of the twentieth was that the purpose of education was to discipline the mind (what we mean today when we say "learn how to think" or "learn how to learn"). The way to achieve that end was through the mastery of core subjects in the curriculum. Each child, it was held, should be pushed down this road as far as his or her talents permitted. According to this view, these goals were appropriate whether or not the student was college bound, because the habits of mind that they produced were as useful in life as they were in college. The most authoritative statement of this view came from the NEA's famous Committee of Ten, which was chaired by President Charles Eliot of Harvard and included other leading college presidents and professors. The committee recommended that all students, wherever destined, should take a minimum high-school curriculum consisting of four years of English, four of foreign language, three of history, three of mathematics, and three of science. The purpose of this was to train "the powers of observation, memory, expression, and reasoning. . . . Every subject which is taught at all in a secondary school should be taught in the same way and to the same extent to every pupil . . ."[11]

In 1911, another NEA body, the Committee of Nine, issued a very different report. This time the chairman was a teacher at the Manual Training School of Brooklyn. There were no college presidents, distinguished professors, or heads of private academies among the group. The purpose of high school, this committee said, was "to lay the foundations of good citizenship and to help in the wise choice of vocation. . . . An organic conception of education demands the early introduction of training for individual usefulness, thereby blending the liberal and the vocational. . . . By means of excessively bookish curricula false ideals of culture are developed. A chasm is created between the producers of material wealth and the distributors and consumers thereof." The committee recommended abolishing any requirement for the study of any subject for four years as a prerequisite for college entrance. Finally, in 1918, an NEA Commission on the Reorganization of Secondary Education recommended that teachers should abandon methods of teaching based on the conception of a subject as a "logically organized science."

> This Commission . . . regards the following as the main objectives of education: 1. Health. 2. Command of fundamental processes [It became clear in context that this meant elementary skills in the three R's, in which the commission, no doubt quite rightly, felt that continued instruction was now needed at the secondary level.] 3. Worthy home-membership. 4. Vocation. 5. Citizenship. 6. Worthy use of leisure. 7. Ethical character.

The child, as Richard Hofstadter puts it, was now to be conceived "not as a mind to be developed but as a citizen to be trained by the schools."[12]

This profound shift in goals and values for American schools came about in part at the urging of American business and industry. Indignant at what they perceived to be the irrelevance and waste of the classical style of education, business leaders were quick to embrace goals that would supply their firms with a steady stream of workers who had mastered the three R's, had some vocational skills, and were well disciplined.

But professional educators had their own reasons for adopting, even championing, the new order. They were pressed by circumstance to take in vast numbers of students whose parents had little education and who themselves did not want to be in school and had little appetite for intellectual activity. They strove mightily to create an institution that could rise to the challenge (1918, the year in which the last of this trio of NEA reports was issued, was also the year in which the last state—Mississippi—passed a compulsory education law). Pressed by the business community to turn out students with practical skills, and perceiving the traditional intellectual goals to be undemocratic, they sought to create an ethos for schooling with which they could be personally comfortable and which, not incidentally, would provide them with a rationale for offering something that could appeal to each segment of their now immensely diverse clientele. Thus did the schools eagerly embrace an anti-intellectual conception of their purpose when it was offered. In this way did mastery of the basic skills become the de facto American intellectual standard of schooling. Here, as in the other matters we have related, the evolving needs of American industry and those of the schools were joined in a symbiotic relationship that persisted for decades.

In many respects, this turn of events was the occasion of a decades-long estrangement between the schools and the nation's intellectual establishment in the great universities—except, perversely, in one important respect. The developing discipline of psychology provided powerful support for the turn away from an intellectually demanding curriculum. Researchers using the new intelligence tests maintained that their research showed conclusively that a large segment of the American population had a mental age not exceeding fourteen. A few used this "information" to argue for an elitist approach to schooling. But most did the opposite, arguing that in a democratic country, the only fair response to this information was to construct an intellectually undemanding curriculum for everyone.

In time, this sort of testing would come to haunt American education. While educators in other countries would continue to insist that all children could learn demanding material, those of America would accustom their fellow citizens to the view that their children vary widely in their inherited ability and intelligence, and not too much should be expected of those with low measured ability.

And indeed it was not. In 1910 more students were taking any one of the subjects of foreign languages, mathematics, science, or English than all the nonacademic subjects combined. During the following forty years, the academic subjects fell from three-quarters to about one-fifth of the high-school subjects offered.[13]

Sad to say, science was used, sometimes retrospectively, to justify this trajectory. In 1940, Lewis Terman, a respected psychologist, opined that an IQ of 110 was required for serious academic study.[14] He estimated that less than 40 percent of American youth had an IQ of 110 or above, showing, he said, that 60 percent were not fit for intellectual activity. It appeared to matter little that other psychologists did not believe that IQ was unalterable from birth, and actually showed that increases in measured IQ on the order of fifteen to twenty points could be produced by education.

In part, what replaced the academic subjects was vocational education. As the industrial system grew in strength in the latter part of the nineteenth century, the need of firms for mechanics and other skilled and semiskilled laborers increased accordingly. But even as the need was growing, the supply of qualified people was dropping. The factory system made a long period of apprenticeship unattractive to boys who could get immediate employment in the factory. More important, under the factory system, the old independent masters were no longer independent and it no longer paid them to teach aspirants to the trade. As workers themselves became interchangeable parts, it no longer paid an employer to invest heavily in the skills of the worker, who could get up and take his skills with him whenever he wished.

As the apprenticeship system shrank, youth employment became youth exploitation, and the reform forces sought to remove these young people from the labor market altogether. This tendency was supported by the growing labor unions, as we noted earlier, because that enabled them to keep the wages of their members up.

Employers, "locked in mortal combat with Germany and England yet hamstrung by hidebound high schools, monopolistic union regulation of apprenticeship, and the 'outrageous opposition of organized labor' to trade education,"[15] made the establishment of trade schools a top priority, thus locking horns in combat with the unions. However, leading educators made it their business to reach out to both management and labor to bridge the political gap. The unions, fearing that industrial education would be wholly controlled by the employers if they stood aside, endorsed the idea of public trade schools, provided that those schools be advised by representatives of both management and labor.

In 1910, several independent forces converged. The American Federation of Labor joined the National Association of Manufacturers in lobbying for vocational education in the schools. The farmers' associations stepped up their demand for agricultural education in rural schools. The National Education Association lauded vocational training as "the central and dominant factor" in the education of students who would work in industry."[16] By 1917, this loose coalition of forces had ironed out their differences sufficiently to win passage of the Smith-Hughes Act, which provided direct federal aid to the states for vocational education.

This victory no doubt strengthened the American economy of the time, but it sowed the seeds of problems to come.

As Paul Douglas pointed out in perceptive criticism written shortly after World War I, the very sort of craft-oriented instruction to which the Smith-Hughes Act had committed the nation had already been left behind by the onrush of technological advances. The craftsmen who left industry to become teachers of vocational subjects too easily isolated themselves from the mainstream of industrial innovation; while the machinery purchased for school use was itself soon outmoded by technological improvement. It took less than forty years for American industry, facing a new apprenticeship crisis after World War II, to reclaim for itself educational responsibilities it had so easily abandoned in the early decades of the century.[17]

The system of secondary vocational education established at the turn of the century, however, like all the other features of the larger system of education we have described, continued on to the present, long after its usefulness had been greatly diminished by swiftly changing events in the society at large—a living relic of the past.

Without question, it was a striking achievement to turn out, in the early decades of this century, an entire nation of workers, including millions of immigrants, who could read and write English with reasonable proficiency, do their sums, exhibit the necessary qualities of personal health, industriousness, obedience, and punctuality that would be indispensable to their employers, and bring with them the initial vocational skills that those employers required. By the standards of the time, we had one of the most highly educated work forces in the world. State by state, and community by community, America's "successful men" had, with broad public support, taken the controls of education policy to fashion a school system and a work force ideally suited to their needs.

Successful as the schools were, however, highly educated people were still in short supply. Little wonder that the managers and engineers of the time created approaches to the organization of work that assumed that most workers would have to be told what to do in detail by a small cadre of well-educated and highly trained technical specialists. The relationship between enterprise and the schools was in fact highly symbiotic. Schools organized to meet industry's needs. But the practical limitations on what the schools could accomplish produced constraints on industry that determined how work would be organized, human resources used, and capital employed.

At the core of our productive capacity were the basic industries, organized into giant oligopolies, run by the methods of rationalized scientific management. Enormous investment in very expensive machinery could be made to pay high dividends in these industries, because the very high production runs made possible by oligopolistic organization could result in very low unit prices to the final customer. Scientific management, used in the context of mass-production techniques, made it possible to turn out low-cost products of reliable quality with workers who had what we now regard as only rudimentary skills.

Of course, it worked. The labor force in these basic industries became fabulously wealthy in a few short decades, by historical standards. But a great price was paid for this success. Workers learned that they did not have to know very much to make high wages, and management learned that the key to higher profits and increased productivity was investment in physical, not human capital. The costs of these lessons would not be apparent for decades to come. Nor would the equally high prices paid for the public-policy choices made for the schools.

The school system worked in part for the same reason that sweated labor worked. Those who labored had few choices. Costs were kept low by recruiting line workers—teachers—from among college-educated women and minorities who, because they had few occupational choices other than teaching, were willing to work for wages and under conditions far below the market for most occupations requiring a college degree. The Japanese, and most European countries, made quite a different choice, opting for salaries closer to those of other professionals. The Japanese, for instance, set teachers' pay by law at the top of the pay ranks for career civil servants. Beginning teacher pay in Japan is now about the same as it is for beginning engineers. In the U.S., in the late 1970s and 1980s, when opportunities in the professions opened up for college-educated women and minorities, custom and resistance to increased taxes would make it very difficult to produce pay levels for teachers comparable with those of our competitors.

In time, the methods of business organization and management borrowed

from industry with good results at the beginning of the century would prove to
have corrosive effects on the schools as the second half of the century drew to
a close. The reader will recall that Taylor did not expect line workers to think.
When Bobbitt adapted Taylor's system to the schools, the same presumption
applied. Designing the system around line workers of whom little in the way of
intellectual accomplishment was expected was probably realistic and certainly
expedient. It made possible the rapid expansion of the system we have described.
But it was little wonder that teachers declined in the esteem of the public. What
was remarkable was that it took so long for that decline to occur. When America
came to demand teachers who could think for themselves and think well, a whole
system had been elaborated in the schools the purpose of which was to tell these
line workers what to do and how to do it, factory style. It would be little wonder
that intellectually able people who expected to think for themselves would flee
the schools at the first opportunity or, when they finally had the option, would
choose other careers in the first place.

Furthermore, the business model of governance imposed on the schools at the
turn of the century, combined with the idea that public education was to become
nonpolitical, would, in time, isolate the schools from their natural constituencies,
parents and other community members. When the politics of education shifted
in the urban trauma of the sixties, and school board positions became prizes for
politicians who aspired to rise higher, the "successful men" who turn-of-the-
century reformers had expected to run did so in far smaller numbers, often
leaving the field to people with narrow constituencies whose agendas had little
to do with sound educational goals or the broad needs of the community as a
whole. Because the reformers had succeeded in isolating the school from the
broader sweep of politics, those who held offices in general government found
they had little influence over a vital community function.

The professional administration model, and the bureaucracy it brought with
it, would create a maze of procedure and system that would discourage any but
the most persistent community members from involvement in their schools. The
reader will recall that the justification offered for this bureaucracy was that it
would more than pay for itself in the efficiencies it would introduce. But in the
competitive business environment the profit motive provides incentives for efficiency. No such incentives were put in place to influence the behavior of school
officials. If schools become demonstrably more efficient, their reward is to lose
funds and preside over smaller operations. No school district has ever gone out
of business because it was less efficiently run than another district. At the heart
of Taylor's system was exhaustive research, the purpose of which was to find out
how the job of the worker could be done at the highest level of quality for the
lowest cost. Because school officials had no incentives to run efficient operations,
they had no incentive to spend large sums—or, for that matter, anything at
all—on research that would show how teachers could teach most effectively. So

the schools got the bureaucracy, but not the efficient operation that was to be its justification.

Perhaps the most subtly corrosive influence of turn-of-the-century developments was the contribution of the psychologists and test makers. The idea that school achievement is a function of inherited intelligence not only provided a means of sorting children in the factory system of education, it legitimized that system in the minds of the public. The results were devastating. Children from low-income backgrounds, who had parents of little education and low educational aspiration for their children, were condemned to be assigned to educational tracks that virtually guaranteed their failure. Teachers had low expectations for such children, and those expectations were, of course, fulfilled, because these children were seldom challenged to produce their best. In the same way, the parents, told by their teachers that little could be expected of their children, demanded little of them. As we shall see, when society began to attend to the needs of these children in the 1960s, educators and society at large assumed that the fault lay in the children, not in the schools. One need only to look at the performance of children from Jewish and Asian families to see what happens when the contrary assumption is made, namely that educational achievement is a function not of inherited intelligence, but of supportive learning systems and the effort the student makes to learn.

Perhaps the most fateful of the decisions made at the turn of the century was the revolt of the reformers against an intellectual ideal for schooling. Declaring the classical curriculum archaic and aristocratic, they put forward the view that in a true democracy, there could be an aristocracy neither of students nor of curriculum. Intellectually gifted students, they declared, could take care of themselves, since their gifts would be nurtured by the larger society and could not be much affected by anything the school could do. And there could be no hierarchy of subjects; mathematics and science were no better or more important than homemaking and shop. Ideas and conceptual skills were banished in favor of the facts and operational skills that even the least able could be expected to master and which were taken to be the practical requirements of the industrial era. Once again, the psychologists of the day were brought in as expert witnesses to lend their weight to this fundamental shift in goals and values. They declared that the classical curriculum was irrelevant because science showed that learning does not transfer, the mind cannot be "trained." Hence the intellectually difficult core subjects in the classical curriculum had no bearing on the practical skills needed in the factory, office, and store. Best, then, to get on with the job of giving students the basic rote skills and then train them for the work at hand. Much good research since that time has shown these views to be nonsense, but the schools nevertheless continue to focus on transmitting the facts and providing low-level operational skills.

Perhaps the most noteworthy attempt to overcome the overwhelmingly anti-intellectual outlook of public educators was the work of John Dewey. Dewey was a leader of those who would make the schools an instrument of democratic society. He strongly rejected an elitist view of public education. But Dewey believed that the curriculum could be both democratic and intellectually demanding. Believing, with the reformers, that the classical ideal was dull and arid, he thought that the curriculum could combine both the head and the hand, that intellectual activity could be meshed with the application of ideas to real problems, making conceptual development inherently more interesting for the student and at the same time more useful. In this way, thought Dewey, a student could become fully engaged in the educational process, not just the recipient of what was taught, but an active participant in his or her own education.[18]

But the educational establishment, by that time finely tuned to the factory method of schooling, chose to hear only those parts of Dewey's message that reinforced their own views and policies. To the extent that Dewey's urgings toward a "democratic" view of their responsibilities reinforced their desire to demand little in the way of intellectual effort on the part of any student, they were eager to follow them. The same held true of Dewey's focus on gearing the curriculum to the child's needs and to activities that responded to the desire of children to work with their hands. But the other part of Dewey's message, that schools had an obligation to attend to the life of the mind, to serious intellectual development, was studiously ignored, not least by those who chose to describe themselves as Dewey's disciples. The reformers had recruited a corps of teachers on the criteria of cheapness and obedience, not of intellectual ability. They had fired the school leaders who had believed that an essential part of their job was to think about educational goals and replaced them with managers who were to be, first and foremost, efficiency experts. They were more concerned with efficiency of administration than with what was learned. It was little wonder that the schools were hostile territory for the essence of John Dewey's views. The die had already been cast.

Perhaps the greatest failure of the reformers was their blindness to the problems of black Americans. As the flood of Europeans streaming to our shores was interrupted by the First World War, black Americans from poor rural counties headed north to the cities. Under the ward system, the political organization of the day would have seen to it that the needs of these internal immigrants were paid attention to, much as those of the earlier foreign immigrants had been. But as the reformers destroyed the ward system and replaced it with government by "successful men," the blacks were doomed to be unrepresented in city government and in the governance of schools. The paraphernalia of science that the new managers brought into the schools made matters worse. Appallingly biased psychological testing confirmed prevailing views that blacks were psychological and intellectual cripples, virtually uneducable. The sociologists of the day found that even educated blacks could not get jobs commensurate with their education, and used this evidence to argue that it was not worth educating blacks. Though the educators were aware of the troubling conditions under which blacks were forced to live in the northern cities, and of the racism that prevented them from getting jobs other than dead-end work, they often used that knowledge to justify setting low goals for black students, rather than as the basis for attacks on a racist society.

Blacks were typically assigned to separate schools. Though many blacks trained as teachers, few were hired in these city systems, and when they were, they were almost exclusively assigned to these segregated schools. In 1930, Pittsburgh, with a black population of 54,938, had three black instructors or administrators; Newark, with 38,880 blacks, had eleven working as instructors or administrators; Springfield, Illinois, with 20,000 blacks living in the city, did not have a single black on its school staff.[19]

Blacks were themselves ambivalent about segregation. They knew that their children were in schools that were inferior to those to which whites were assigned. But black teachers knew they would be fired if the schools were integrated. Black parents, for their part, feared that their children would suffer even more if they went to predominantly white schools, because their parents had been disenfranchised at the polls and had no countervailing political power with which to offset the racism to which their children would be exposed in such schools. With the great expansion of the black ghettos in the years following 1940, tensions would mount dramatically, leading to violent explosion in the 1960s. By that time, generations of black children had been deprived of a decent education.

And yet, looking back, one can understand the pride that educators took in their accomplishments. They felt that there was little they could do about the racism of the larger society, and that on balance they had succeeded in fitting the great majority of American children for productive work and in preparing them to exercise their rights and obligations as citizens. They had cured the schools of waste and inefficiency and installed modern management methods that enabled them to manage a great mass of students at a cost the country could afford. The most admired men in society, the leading business executives, approved of their work and hired their products. Those who led the country's economic institutions and those who led its schools were operating in harmony. In time, however, the needs of the economy would change radically, while the character of the schools would not. Only then would the country realize how high a price had been paid for the turn-of-the-century reforms.

PART II

The Forces Changing the World Economy: Our Competitors Respond

CHAPTER 3

Technology, Competitiveness, and the New International Economy

The years following World War II were good to the United States. Between 1946 and 1969, the gross national product grew at an average annual rate of 3.7 percent, nowhere near the rates of the burgeoning twenties, but very good indeed. In 1922, total national wealth stood at $334 billion. By 1946, twenty-four years later, it had grown to $700 billion, about double. But by 1958, an interval of only twelve years, it had grown to $1.7 trillion. Between 1947 and 1969, family income rose in constant dollars from $4,531 to $8,473. Productivity growth was equally explosive: using an index set at 100 for 1958, output per man-hour had grown from 48.6 in 1929 to 68.7 in 1946, but by 1969 it was 135.6. America was booming.[1]

In part, the war itself accounted for this growth. The United States not only served as the "arsenal of democracy" during the war, but, because we alone among the major combatants survived the war with a productive capacity greater than when the war started, we also served as the major supplier of those combatants after the war, reaching out to a worldwide market hungry for whatever we could produce.

But these markets did not alone account for the remarkable growth in the nation's economy. The driving force was advancing technology. Here, too, the war had played its part. The war had been won as decisively in the laboratory as on the battlefield, as much by scientists and engineers as by foot soldiers. The United States profited at the close of the war by possessing the world's most advanced technology and many of its most capable scientists and engineers.

Having learned that public and private spending on technological development could pay handsome dividends, we made the most of the lesson. Between 1953 and 1969, total expenditure on research and development in the United States climbed from $5.2 billion to $26.2 billion, a fivefold increase.[2]

Even as advancing technology was providing the engine for our growth, however, it was steadily undermining the foundations of the American system, though we were not to see the results until the 1970s, thirty years or more after the war had come to an end. We shall discuss three ways in which technology would so change the economic context as to challenge the fundamental premises of our system: the growth of a truly integrated international economy; the decline in the importance of raw materials as a source of wealth; and the changing nature of work in the advanced economies. These three sweeping changes combined in a way that was to alter profoundly the basis of national wealth all over the world and have profound consequences for the importance of trained and educated labor as a determinant of economic well-being.

Technological advances in two critical areas, transportation and communications, were to have momentous effects on the shape of the international economy. In the years following the war, and partly as the result of wartime developments, advances in the technology of air transport and ocean shipping steadily reduced the cost per ton of international transportation to the point that, for a wide range of products, the cost of sending raw and finished materials from one nation to another became a small or even negligible portion of the final delivered price of the product. Through this whole period, the United States championed free trade because we, like Britain in earlier times, were the world's premier manufacturing nation and stood to gain the most from free trade. Though we benefited greatly in the short run, we were to find eventually that the reduction in shipping costs was to make it possible for faraway countries with lower commodity and labor costs to undercut us in many markets—including and especially our own—as they never could have before.

The revolution in communications was to have an equally profound impact. Advancing radio, telephone, and, eventually, computer communications made it possible for corporations to control operations on the other side of the globe with almost the same ease as they had earlier controlled them on the other side of town. At the same time, these developments facilitated the growth of international banking and finance networks that could transfer capital across national boundaries in seconds or less.

These developments in shipping, managerial control, and finance made possible the growth of a truly integrated international economy and of a new economic entity ideally matched to the opportunities it presented: the multinational corporation. A single corporation or combination of corporations could now purchase raw materials at the most advantageous price anywhere in the world, convert them into components, subassemblies, and finished products wherever labor was least expensive, and ship them to the country in which they could get the best price for them.

Until midcentury, America's oceanic isolation from the rest of the world's major manufacturing centers had made this country a captive market for its own domestic manufacturers. With the decline in the cost of shipping and the growth of multinational corporations, the world's largest market became the most important target for producers all over the world. The immediate consequence was a leap in the proportion of our gross national product entering international trade, from 5.9 percent in 1950 to 16.3 percent by 1979. That measure is deceptive, however, for the impact on our economy was far larger than even that figure would suggest. Most international trade is in goods, and our goods producers discovered in a few short years that 70 percent of all the goods produced in the United States were for the first time in competition with goods produced overseas.[3]

America's public and private policies were very badly matched to this new reality. The oligopolies of capital and labor we described earlier were predicated on isolation from foreign competition. The prices of goods could not be maintained when they were competing with lower-priced foreign goods of higher quality. Neither could the price of uneducated labor be maintained when multinational firms could get better-educated and better-trained labor at one-tenth the price abroad. As the seventies drew to a close, American business and labor found themselves under siege.

Business leaders responded mainly by finding ways to cut costs and shut foreign producers out of our domestic market. Cost reduction was achieved by automating to eliminate jobs and thus reduce labor costs, transferring production to other countries with lower labor costs, getting out of production altogether and becoming U.S. marketing agents for foreign firms with lower production costs, negotiating wage reductions with unions that saw massive job loss as the only alternative, and increasing the proportion of their work force composed of contingent labor—people who could be released on a moment's notice and who did not have to be paid fringe benefits. At the same time, the employers, aided by badly frightened labor unions, lobbied the Congress and the executive branch hard for "voluntary" and involuntary restrictions on goods entering domestic markets. Employers have succeeded in getting a lot of legislation passed, including the Trade Act of 1963, that actually provides tax subsidies for American firms that export production to foreign countries. The net effect of all these moves was to raise the prices that American consumers would have to pay for goods of all kinds, to lower the real incomes of American workers, and to eliminate thousands of American middle-income jobs.

The increasing penetration of our markets by high-quality, competitively priced goods from abroad also made it imperative that we lower imports and raise exports, so that we could pay for whatever we imported. Eventually, we lowered the value of the dollar relative to other currencies, making our exports less expensive for foreigners and their exports more expensive for our own citizens.

Thus, without ever having consciously decided to do so, we were choosing to compete in the newly integrated world economy by lowering our standard of living. As the reader will see later, there were other alternatives, and our most aggressive competitors were pursuing them.

Our macroeconomic policies proved to be as badly adapted to the changing shape of the world economy as our business policies. The Keynesian policies pursued by Republican and Democratic administrations since the days of Roosevelt were based on the assumption that the United States economy was virtually sealed off from the rest of the world. If demand fell significantly below capacity and therefore threatened to drag the country into recession, the solution was to lower interest rates and take other measures to pump money into the hands of consumers, thereby stimulating demand. If the economy was approaching capacity and driving prices up so that inflation threatened, the answer was to raise interest rates and take other measures to reduce demand, which would slow economic growth and thereby halt inflation before it reached runaway proportions.

But the growth of a truly international economy changed this neat calculus forever. Policymakers were to find that releasing money into a sluggish economy could simply increase spending on products supplied by foreign producers without increasing the intended demand for domestic products, thereby exacerbating the balance-of-payments problem without making much of a dent in the demand problem. It would take the stimulus of the enormous deficit created by the Reagan tax cut to create the domestic demand that a much more modest deficit would have produced before. That deficit could and would have the long-term effects of drying up investment, producing a crushing long-term debt, and forcing a further reduction in the value of the dollar. Similarly, using tight money to slow and reverse inflation could produce far more unemployment than before, not only because restricting the growth of the money supply choked off domestic investments through higher interest rates, but because those higher interest rates increased foreign demand for dollars. The increased value of the dollar raised the price of American goods to foreigners, thereby reducing American exports. This same process reduced the cost of foreign goods to American buyers, increasing imports.

Thus, the development of an international economy changed all the ground rules, ending the era of national control over national economies and requiring the development of new economic theories to account for problems Keynes had never considered. These problems will be discussed later.

One of America's most important advantages in the nineteenth and early twentieth centuries was its extraordinary store of raw materials and cheap energy sources. But the steady advance of technology after the Second World War has greatly diminished our natural advantage in raw materials. As the war progressed and combatants were cut off from their sources of supply of raw materials, they devoted increasing research and development resources to the search for synthetic substitutes for strategic materials like oil and rubber. After the war, these developments accelerated, producing an ever-lengthening list of synthetic versions of these materials, often cheaper and more serviceable than the varieties occurring in nature. Optical fiber made it possible to send thousands of communications simultaneously over cables made of processed sand, where before only hundreds of such communications could be sent over cables requiring highly refined copper. Carbon fiber, which uses as its raw material another of the most abundant materials found in nature, is replacing aluminum and high-grade steel alloys in aircraft bodies. Semiconductors made from silicon wafers, also derived from sand, have replaced tubes made from the alloys of rare metals in electronic components. Even more important, advancing technology often made obsolete the need for both the original and the substitute. Satellite and microwave communications, for example, limited the need to have either copper or optical fibers for point-to-point communications. The extent to which ideas, skills, and knowledge are being substituted for natural resources is suggested by the fact that 50 to 100 pounds of fiberglass cable transmits as many telephone conversations as one ton of copper wire.

In each of these cases and many more like them, the key to the replacement of the original material lay in research and development and in highly complex process and production technologies. In short, success was determined not by the accident of possession, but by the capacity to generate new knowledge and the ability of the work force to apply that knowledge skillfully in the production process. Thus, human resources—ideas, skills, and knowledge—replaced natural resources as a major source of production and wealth.

Finally, and most important, advancing technology was to have a profound impact on the organization of work and the skills demanded by the work to be done.

The impact of technology on employment and skills has been a recurring issue for economists since the dawn of the First Industrial Revolution. As steam power gradually replaced physical labor in the nineteenth century, people were thrown out of work and the prospect of widespread unemployment became quite real. But those who lost their jobs gained employment in other trades and occupations, many of them opening up in new industries created by advancing technology. The process through which technology both destroys and creates jobs is central to the phenomenon of productivity improvement. In this way the whole economic system becomes more efficient, eliminating relatively unproductive labor and transferring human resources to occupations in which people can produce more of what they need and want with any given amount of labor. Without this process of continual destruction and creation of jobs there can be no productivity improvement and therefore no improvement in the overall standard of living.

But what kinds of jobs would be created by the new technologies? Over the last ten or fifteen years, analysts have claimed to document two quite contradictory answers to that question. Some believe it is inevitable that technology will produce better jobs and a higher standard of living for everyone and others believe virtually the opposite. The advocates for each point of view have a plausible argument and are prepared to back it up with supporting data that purport to show that things are in fact falling out along the lines of their argument.

Those who argue that advancing technology will produce better jobs point out that competition will lead employers to automate jobs that now require little skill, leaving for humans the jobs that require more skill, greater autonomy, and more individual judgment—jobs that provide more satisfaction and higher pay. As professionals increasingly do their own typing and document preparation, secretaries spend more time gathering and analyzing information, dealing with other people inside and outside the immediate work unit, combining information from many sources into complex documents—in short, using their heads. Production workers who used to perform the same rote task at a machine over and over again now monitor robots that perform those tasks. They must be able to maintain and even program these highly complex machines, interpret data from many sources when trouble occurs, and act independently and with good judgment when they do so, holding in their heads a conceptual map of the intricate production- and process-control operations of which their machine forms an integral part. Telecommunications networks make it possible for the customer at the gas pump to slip into the pump a debit card that automatically debits the customer's bank account for the price of the gas pumped, eliminating the jobs of the gas-station attendant, the person who used to take the credit slip and enter its data into the credit-card company's records, the people at the bank who had to process the check written to the credit-card company, and many others. All these low-pay, low-skill jobs are being eliminated and in their place new, much more highly skilled and highly paid jobs are being created for the people who design, build, and maintain the new automated systems.

Those who argue that technology is, on balance, creating better-paid and more highly skilled jobs point to steady growth in the proportion of all jobs that require more education and pay well, and to a steady decline in the proportion of jobs that require less skill and pay less. Furthermore, they show that careful analysis of current shifts among a wide range of job categories reveals steadily escalating skill requirements in the new jobs that are being added to the economy.

Other analysts, however, are coming to quite different conclusions. They point to the growing use of technology to de-skill jobs and control workers. Workers' keystrokes are being counted to make sure that they never take a break, their phone calls are being monitored to make sure they never make personal calls, and the operations they complete are automatically counted as the basis of pay, reducing a workplace that had merely been dull to a modern-day sweatshop. Rather than increasing skill levels, responsibility, and autonomy, technology is being used by employers to push Taylorism to its extreme limits, fulfilling the original agenda of deskilling work and making employers' control over the work force virtually complete. These analysts present data showing that these developments are slowly eliminating middle-class jobs and producing an ever-widening gap between an increasingly well-off management and professional class and a working class that is getting increasingly poor.

It turns out that both groups of analysts are right. Some firms in some industries are taking full advantage of the potential of the technology to put more skill, responsibility, and autonomy in the jobs of their front-line workers, while other firms in the same and different industries are taking advantage of the equally great potential of the technology to de-skill jobs and control the lives of workers in minute detail. It is true that the long-term trend is toward a higher proportion of jobs on the higher rungs of the skills ladder, but it is also true that the middle class is shrinking and the real incomes of those at the bottom of the ladder are declining. Technology, in fact, is neutral. It can be put to either purpose, thereby realizing either the vision of the optimists or the worst fears of the pessimists. The question is, how will technology be used in the United States, to make work more highly skilled and better-paid, or to lower skills and reduce pay? .

The answer lies in the way firms choose to organize work. The best firms in the United States and elsewhere in the world are now organizing work around highly skilled, well-paid workers, using high-performance work organizations. The key to the method is the distinction between "direct" work and "indirect" work. Consider the automobile assembly plant. We will call the people who actually assemble the car the "direct" workers. The "indirect" workers are everyone else, those who do production scheduling, order the parts, repair and maintain the equipment, do the quality control, rework defective parts and assemblies, supervise the direct workers, coordinate all these tasks, and perform countless other functions. Worldwide, the ratio between indirect and direct workers in automobile assembly plants is about three to one. In the best plants, however, it is two to one. The difference is in how the work gets done. In the high-performance, high-productivity plants, much of the work done elsewhere by indirect workers is done by the direct workers. In one plant in Sweden, the direct workers are organized into teams of a dozen or so who are responsible for assembling large portions of a car. They get their orders at the beginning of the week. They decide how to schedule production, order the parts they need from internal and external suppliers, allocate tasks among themselves, fix their own machines when they break down and maintain them on a regular basis, do their own quality control, and perform many other tasks that used to be performed by the indirect staff. They solve a host of problems as they arise, rather than waiting for their supervisors to solve them.

The advantages of this form of work organization are enormous. The ranks of middle management and many support functions are thinned out, creating a very large productivity gain through cost reduction. Quality improves dramatically. There is better coordination of the myriad functions involved in building a car and many fewer mistakes are committed. Improvements in the design and construction of the cars are made constantly, instead of waiting for new model introductions, creating a strong market advantage. It becomes possible to go after small market segments, because success no longer depends on producing thousands or millions of identical products. Worker motivation and morale are greatly enhanced, because the workers take real pride in their work—they are no longer expected to leave their heads at the factory gate. Taken together, these changes give firms organizing this way a decisive advantage over their low-wage, low-skill competitors. Low-wage countries are in no position to compete using these methods of work organization because their workers lack the skills that are essential to its success.

This description does not apply only to automobile assembly plants. It works equally well in machine tools, insurance, banking and retail sales—in fact, across the whole spectrum of manufacturing and services.

There is a subtle point to be made here about the interaction between the choice of work organization and technology, on the one hand, and the choice of markets, on the other. Prior to the Second World War, most people were happy to get products and services that worked well enough to meet their needs at a price they could afford. Following the war, however, average incomes in the developed countries were so high as to create a new form of customer, the customer who became very discriminating with respect to quality and fit. These customers began to demand, and could afford, products of consistently high quality that appealed to their individual tastes. Price was less of a factor than it had been before. These demands had characterized the very rich for millennia; what was new was their appearance among a customer base much larger, vastly more sophisticated, and wealthier than ever before.

At the same time that customers were becoming more demanding, technology was evolving in ways that made it possible for farsighted firms to meet their needs. The advent of computer-based systems of all kinds created a world in which it became practical to manufacture very short runs of products for niche markets, to produce those products at consistently high quality levels, and to provide very high quality services customized to the needs of relatively small markets. In the world that was emerging, customers would gladly pay a premium for new products that were of higher quality and better adapted to their rapidly changing needs.

The firms and nations that could meet the needs of this sophisticated market could charge higher prices for their products and services, and therefore for their labor, and would become rich as a result. Success would depend on very large investments in research and development (to assure a competitive edge in new-product development and new process technology), conversion to the new forms of work organization (to assure high product quality, continuous product improvement, flexible response to shifting consumer demands, and competitive production costs), and very high-quality labor (without which the new forms of work organization cannot be successfully implemented).

The United States, however, was very poorly positioned to meet these requirements. Our overwhelming handicap was not lack of capital, nor lack of technological prowess, nor lack of natural resources—it was our own success. From the 1920s through the early 1970s our experience as the world's leading economic power had taught us that the lessons we had learned were winning lessons. Indeed, they formed a unified system of beliefs and practices that constitute what we have called the American System. We were not about to turn our backs on that system.

Employers had learned that price, not quality, was the key to profits. The source of productivity improvement was physical plant and equipment, not highly motivated and trained labor. Authoritarian methods of management produced the best results—labor was there to do as it was told. Job security was inconsistent with the ability to keep prices up in bad times; it was very important, in fact, to be able to keep labor costs down and to lay off workers when times got tough. Product improvement was the function of research, development, and marketing specialists, not the people on the front line. The greatest efficiency was gained when front-line work was de-skilled, leaving the skilled work to the professional, managerial, and senior technical staff. Strong unions would make their products uncompetitive, and the threat of unemployment, of course, kept wages down and therefore inflation and costs under control. Business functioned best when government was least involved.

Labor unions had learned that they stood to make the greatest gains in the basic industries that were controlled by the big oligopolies, and so concentrated their organizing efforts there, leaving many other industries largely unorganized. They had learned that they could make wage gains year in and year out in those industries, gains which were largely unrelated to productivity either there or in the economy as a whole. Just like the major employers, the big industrial unions were happy to trade high prices—in their case wages—for some unemployment, because their attractiveness lay in their capacity to offer higher wages than nonunionized workers with the same education levels could command elsewhere, and nonmembers do not vote. Thus the major players had learned that they could tolerate levels of unemployment much higher than in many other countries. Most important, the unions had learned that the steady improvements in the standard of living they made for their members were the result of organizing power and had little or nothing to do with the skills those members brought to the workplace.

Educators had learned that they could get steady real increases in funding year after year and broad public support if they met the nation's needs for adequately trained and educated management, professional, and senior technical personnel, and for skilled tradespeople. The economy would function quite well, and the education system would continue to get public support, if most of the rest—fully half the students—left school with no more than the equivalent of an eighth-grade education, including a substantial fraction who were functionally illiterate; in fact, it would function quite well if nearly a quarter of the students did not graduate at all.

The people responsible for running our publicly funded employment and training programs had learned that their responsibility was to the most disadvantaged members of our society—to provide a short-term safety net that would give them the very minimum of skills and labor-market connections. They had never been expected to offer a comprehensive system of services for a large fraction of the society for the purpose of providing high-level skills and efficient labor-market connections as part of a broad national labor-market policy, and they did not have the resources to do so.

Our economists had learned that demand management was the central problem of an advanced industrial economy. Spending, not saving, was necessary to sustain a high level of production and economic welfare. Inflation was to be controlled by slowing down demand; rising unemployment was an unfortunate but inescapable part of the formula.

Like the employers, the economists had learned that physical, not human, capital was the key to productivity growth. Few economists considered human-capital policy to be part of economic policy, nor did they concern themselves with the ways that skills, technology, and work organization combine to influence productivity, though virtually all economists were in agreement that productivity was the primary determinant of improvement in the national standard of living. Economists, like mass-production companies, were mainly concerned with prices and quantities and paid very little attention to quality. Like Frederick Taylor, they assumed there was "one best way" to compete and all successful companies would use it. They had learned that the United States could become and remain the world's leading economic power without taking such things into account, that the economy could be successfully managed through macroeconomic policy alone.

But the factors that had made all these views valid were disappearing. In their place were the new realities provided by advancing technology, an increasingly tightly knit international economy, and the need to be competitive in a game that had new rules.

Quality, flexibility, and responsiveness to changing consumer tastes would rule now in the world's richest markets, not price and the economies of mass production. Countries that chose to compete on the mass-production model would have to match the wages and hours of the less-developed countries. Productivity growth would still determine the rate of advance of a nation's standard of living, but it would be a function of human-resources policy and the organization of work even more than investment in plant and equipment. National governments that succeeded in providing a high standard of living for their citizens would be looking for ways to sustain high wages, not to keep them down. They would be searching for ways to reduce unemployment to virtually nothing, because they could not be internationally competitive if they had to pay large sums in transfer payments to unproductive adults.

Employers would find that authoritarian management methods and approaches to work organization would leave them at a severe disadvantage in the race for quality, flexibility, and productivity. Unions would find that they could no longer get high wages for unskilled labor, because, while the world had always been full of unskilled laborers willing to work for less, those unskilled foreign laborers could now sell the products of their labor in our domestic markets. They would also learn the need to work with employers to improve quality and productivity, not merely to leave these matters to managers.

Educators would find themselves in the midst of a storm of criticism, not because they were producing less well-educated workers than before, but because unskilled front-line workers could not sustain their wage levels in a newly international and highly competitive world economy.

Economists and political leaders would find that the theories that had shaped public policy for decades would not work anymore. It would be possible to have stagnation and inflation at the same time. Modest stimulation of demand in down times would not give domestic industry the boost it needed, and modest slowing down of the economy would not prove very effective against rising inflation. They would find that they had no theory at all to deal with the toughest problems the economy now faced: how to boost productivity, savings, and the quality of human resources. Still, our economists and policymakers failed to understand that economic decisions on these points could not be passively left to market forces. While this country operated on the old plan, the most successful countries were building a consensus for new national goals and policies as well as new strategies to achieve those goals.

In 1973, the oil crisis rocked the economies of the developed nations of the world. The United States was no exception. Somehow, it seemed, our competitors got back on their feet quickly, while we did not. They were getting richer while we were getting poorer.

The oil crisis itself did not account for our poor recovery. What it did was reveal a basic weakness in the American economy. That basic weakness was the American System itself. A source of enormous strength for more than six decades, it had become an unseen, unaccounted-for, pervasive liability in a greatly changed world.

In 1982, Richard Nelson and Sidney Winter advanced a theory of economic competition based on the ideas of Charles Darwin.[4] They speculated that economic success, like evolutionary success, may not be so much a matter of being smarter or more farsighted than one's competitor, but simply a matter of being lucky enough to have a strategy and a set of resources better adapted to new circumstances. Take two forms of plant life. One is well adapted to hot, dry climates and the other to cool, moist climates. As the environment turns cooler and moister over the course of a few thousand years, the latter plant flourishes and multiplies and the former dies out. So, said Nelson and Winter, firms and even national economies might rise and fall because their economic strategies and product offerings might be better or worse adapted to changing economic conditions.

In our case, that begs the question. What set of business practices, union strategies, and public policies might be better adapted to the changes in economic conditions we have painted than those embodied in the American System? In the next chapter, we show that many of our most successful competitors have chosen a different course, a course that enabled them to recover more effectively from the oil crisis and to forge ahead since. What is fascinating is that these countries, as different from one another as any advanced nations on earth, have practices and policies far more similar to those of each other than any are to those of the United States. We are the odd country out. Above all, what most distinguishes these countries from the United States is the importance they assign to the role of human resources in determining their standard of living.

CHAPTER 4

Our Competitors
Take the Lead:
The Path to Human-Resource
Capitalism

Forty-five years ago, Japan and West Germany were in ruins, devastated by war. Today, they are the twin colossi of the world economy. By 1985, West Germany, about the size of Oregon, with a population one-fifth of ours, rivaled us for the title of world's leading exporter and in 1990 had hourly compensation in manufacturing 40 percent higher than ours.[1] Japan, about the size of Montana, with half the population of the United States, had by then risen to the status of the world's economic juggernaut, with long-term rates of growth in gross national product, productivity, and real wages far exceeding our own.

For many years, observers in this country were able to dismiss the resurgence of these economies by saying that they were simply catching up, regaining their former—subordinate—position in the world economy. As they now outdistance us on one important indicator after another, that excuse is no longer valid.

Neither country has much in the way of natural resources. All that they have is their people and the means they have chosen to develop and organize their people for economic effort. In many ways, these two nations are as different from each other as any two major nations in the world. Yet we will argue that they have far more in common on the dimensions of greatest interest to us than either has with the United States. Our purpose here is not to recapitulate the enormous literature that has tried to identify and catalog all the sources of their success, but rather to draw together the essential threads that tie their approaches together and then to weave those threads into a general specification for a fabric of policies—both public and private—that the United States would do well to consider carefully.[2]

The devastation in Germany following the war verged on the unimaginable.

Twenty-four percent of the people born in 1924 were either dead or missing. Ten million homes had been demolished. Major cities were almost totally destroyed. Ninety percent of the factories in southern Germany were out of action; industrial output was running at five percent of former capacity.[3]

The crisis knit the society together. It was the decisive factor in the development of a bond among what came to be called the "social partners"—employers, labor, and government—drawing them into an unprecedented partnership that would guide the country out of its crippled economy into world economic leadership. These partners would act together in every important sphere of public policy and private economic activity, sharing power and responsibility in a way that has no parallel in the United States. What is most striking about the arrangement to an American was the implicit faith of the Germans that government had an important role to play in many matters that we regard as off limits. It was this belief that made it possible for government to guide and shape the rebuilding of the country as a full partner of business and labor.

In the years immediately following the war, the German unions agreed to keep wages low, persuaded that Germany needed low wages to be competitive. This led many economists to give the labor unions much of the credit for the "German miracle." Later, however, a system of "rigid" national wage determination was developed by the unions and employer associations to keep wages high and variations in wages low. The effect on employers is to force them into markets in which success depends less on price competition than on competition based on the quality of the product or service offered.

A policy of employment security was evolved that effectively makes it very difficult for employers to lay off employees, compelling them to keep workers in situations in which American employers would let them go. Large German employers are thereby forced to rely mainly on their existing work force. But the prospect of long-term employment makes German workers much more agreeable than American workers to the changes in work rules, assignments, and work organization occasioned by changing technology because they know they will not lose their jobs.

At the same time, German employers are much more likely than Americans to invest in the worker retraining required by such changes—because the employers know those workers will be around long enough for them to recoup their investment. But the legal provisions undergirding the German training system extend far beyond the employment security apparatus. The German skills development system begins early in school with *Arbeitslehre,* a formal learning program about industry that is compulsory for all students in all grades except those in the gymnasiums, secondary schools that prepare college-bound students. Then comes the system for vocational training. Built on regulations first issued in the 1930s and on an existing system that had been partly in place since the mid-nineteenth century, the Vocational Training Act of 1969 created the legal framework for the famed German apprenticeship approach to job training.

In 1869, a national industrial code provided that employers could be compelled to send their apprentices to a "continuation school" for further education and training. This was the first stirring of the system of dual education, under which employers and government assume joint responsibility for the training of the German work force, through a combination of formal schooling and on-the-job training. In 1938, part-time attendance for apprentices became mandatory, making the dual education system a reality for all apprentices. Now, under the 1969 act, most school graduates not going on to college become apprentices in one of 480 trades and occupations at the age of fifteen or sixteen.

The graduate seeks out an employer willing to enter into an apprenticeship contract lasting between two and three years. Getting a contract with a desirable employer depends on the applicant having a strong academic record and good recommendations from his or her teachers. At the end of this contract period, the apprentice faces a written examination and a careful review of selected work samples. Apprentices who pass are awarded a certificate honored by employers all over Germany, which attests to their having the skills required to assume journeyman status in their trade or occupation.

Apprentices typically spend a day a week at a *Berufsschule* (state vocational school) specializing in the student's trade, and four days in a structured program of training at the employer's work site, guided by a master of the trade. While in training, the apprentices receive a training wage, which increases through the course of the apprenticeship.

The terms of apprenticeship are set by the Vocational Training Act. The standards for the certificates are set through an elaborate consensus-building process involving employers, union members, government officials, and training experts—the social partners. The training curriculum is set by the federal government on the advice of the partners. Practical implementation of the apprenticeship system at the local level is in the hands of the Chambers of Industry and Commerce, to which all German firms must pay dues by law. The chambers are responsible for certifying companies providing training, registering contracts, administering examinations, and training and certifying trainers. Even the system for administering the examinations operates through social partners; the local examination boards consist of one representative each from the unions, teachers, and employers.

Companies are not compelled to offer apprenticeships, but half of all craft firms and virtually all the major firms do so. Those that do are not compensated for their costs, which are substantial. Firms that provide training must abide by the detailed regulations issued by the government and administered by the chambers, so as to avoid the possibility that the firms will simply exploit the apprentices as cheap labor.

Given the costs that must be borne by the firms and the detailed regulations that they must follow, one wonders why they bother. Why not just let the competition train future workers and then hire them away, much as American

...ᵤₒ would? The companies view apprenticeship training as an essential investment in their competitiveness. Ninety percent of the apprentices are employed by the firm that trained them. There is enough flexibility in the system so that the firms can tailor the training to their particular needs. Many managers came up through the apprenticeship system and take great pride in continuing the tradition. Because all the large firms provide training, none of them are afraid that a nonparticipating firm will take unfair advantage of them. Furthermore, when the economy enters a downturn, firms tempted to cut back on training programs find themselves confronted with strong public pressure to keep their numbers up. Knowing that these pressures are likely to lead to training quotas set by law if the voluntary enrollments fall, the firms keep their programs running at full bore.

The apprenticeships constitute a national system of mentoring under the guidance of caring and demanding masters. The system combines a concern for practical skill building and craftsmanship with an environment that builds confidence and self-esteem. It encompasses trades and occupations over the whole range of manufacturing and services. The result is a work force among the most highly skilled on the face of the earth, a youth unemployment rate that is among the lowest in all of the advanced industrial nations, and a sense of self-worth and competence among those starting out at work that would be the envy of all Americans who care about their kids.

The foundation of the success of the German apprenticeship system is a first-rate system for the academic preparation of students before they become apprentices, combined with social supports that assure the healthy growth and development of young children. Health insurance is universal and the federal government provides child allowances (about $1,600 annually per child) to all parents in Germany with children under the age of sixteen.

The performance of German students on international examinations is quite high. Some 76 percent of German intermediate-school graduates take national examinations that set a stiff standard of accomplishment. Many foreign observers, particularly in the United States, criticize the German system as being rigidly organized, feeding students at the end of the primary grades into one of three forms of intermediate school, and thereby determining irrevocably the course of their whole lives. Though there is some truth to the charge, there is less than meets the eye. The choices made for these students are not irrevocable. Fully one-third of Germany's graduate engineers came up through the apprenticeship system and then went to university. Seventeen percent of Germany's gymnasium graduates, qualified under the German system to go to college, prefer instead to enroll first in the dual education system, and the proportion is rising. This is hardly surprising, since, especially in technical fields, German employers increasingly prefer candidates for jobs who have both the theoretical background provided in the university and the practical preparation afforded by the apprenticeship system.

The superb preparation of the German front-line worker is a key factor in

German economic success. It provides workers who are not only well trained for specific occupations, but, because of the quality of the basic school system, creates a pool of workers with the flexibility to learn new skills quickly, contributing heavily to the capacity of the German industrial system to respond quickly to changes in consumer taste. The same factor makes it possible to give German workers the skills they need to function effectively in high-performance work organizations, taking on tasks that in the United States would rarely be assigned to anyone below the management and professional ranks. The direct involvement of the social partners in the design of training and further schooling assures that graduates coming into the system have been trained to standards that reflect real employer requirements.

But the system for initial education and training does not stand alone. It is part of a much larger system of skill development. In 1952, the federal parliament put the social partners in charge of the Federal Institution for Placement and Unemployment Insurance. The institution, a quasi-governmental agency, run by the social partners, was given a key role in the further development of a highly skilled labor force that would prove the basis for a dynamic, growing economy. With the addition of the provisions of the Employment Promotion Act of 1969, German law had created a statutory right for all German nationals, as well as nationals from other Common Market countries, to unemployment benefits that would last up to fifty-two weeks at the rate of 69 percent of previous net earnings; family allowances for the unemployed of $24 a month for the first child, $38 for the second, and $70 for each additional child; unemployment assistance for those who had exhausted their unemployment benefits of 58 percent of prior earnings; and, critically important, fully reimbursed training, further retaining, or rehabilitation, over and above income support.

Under the German system, unemployment benefits and what we call welfare are a last resort. Counseling, training and retraining, active job placement, incentives to employers for the maintenance and creation of jobs, and wage subsidies and payments to employers to keep people on whom they would otherwise lay off—all these measures are used before the welfare and unemployment provisions are invoked. Germany does not regard itself as a welfare state, even though, in 1977, it spent 32 percent of its gross national product on social services. It regards the "dole" with horror, a measure to be used only when all of the active measures to develop people's capacity and promote their employment have failed.

Reliance on the social partners did not stop at the making and administration of policy governing the use of public revenues. A series of enactments that began with the Works Constitution Act of 1952 and included The Codetermination Act of 1976 changed fundamentally the way private enterprise was to be run.

First, the laws provided that all corporations and limited partnerships with more than two thousand employees were to be run by supervisory boards composed equally of representatives of management and labor. This act built on the Works Constitution Act of 1952, which created a more limited version of the new act, applying only to the coal and iron and steel industries. The new supervisory boards were to hire, fire, and supervise management, as well as approve the major financial transactions recommended by management. Thus the German government provided labor with a role equal to that of management in making the crucial decisions facing large firms.

Because workers under codetermination have a strong voice in the management of the firm, they are far more willing than American workers to take the long view, foregoing short-term benefits for the long range. That makes it possible for management, in turn, to concentrate on the long term too. Both management and labor are in this way significantly isolated from some of the short-term pressures that operate on American employers.

The key companion to codetermination at the firm level in the German workplace is the works council, an institution dating back to 1848. Works councils, made up exclusively of employees, are charged with working together with unions and management on such matters as working hours, the introduction of new technologies, abandonment of industrial plants, and the fixing of performance-related compensation. They have, in addition, the right by law to participate with management in the design and redesign of work, manpower planning, and training. The councils, as we noted earlier, can refuse to permit the dismissal of any employee until and unless they are overruled in court.

For our purposes, one of the crucial features of the German system has to do with the rules regarding the organization of work. Employers are required by government action and pressured by the works councils—the other social partners again—to design jobs more broadly than they would otherwise.

One result of this system is labor peace. But there are others, even more far reaching: de-Taylorization of the work place and a steady increase in the responsibilities of line workers, coming about in response to calls for job enrichment. Workers are able to meet these increased responsibilities in part because of the investments employers make in their skills, which are in turn made necessary, as we have seen, by the limitations on the employers' rights to fire their employees. The de-Taylorization of the work organization, combined with the high pay enforced on employers by the national wage determination system, induces employers to seek markets in which the new forms of work organization will give them the marketplace advantage they need to recover their high labor costs.

The whole German system, then, is self-reinforcing at all the vital points. Its irresistible tendency is to push the decisions of private employers constantly toward business strategies that emphasize competition on productivity and quality rather than price, that enable them to pay ever higher wages and improve their competitiveness. While pushing the employers in these ways with one hand, it provides support for those strategies with the other—especially a constant supply of broadly educated and well-trained employees, and a system of social supports for workers and their families that further augments the quality of human resources available and cushions the effects of economic downturns.

All these factors combine to produce an economy that is booming in good times, recovers quickly in bad times, and provides a high level of income to a society in which that income is far more evenly distributed than in the United States. The unmistakable foundation of success is careful attention to human resources, paralleled by measures that induce employers to make the most of those resources through worker participation in management and high-performance work organizations that both demand high worker skills and use them to good effect.

The very same factors are also responsible for the parallel "economic miracle" of Japan. The Japanese economy, like the German, was devastated by the war. Like the Germans, the Japanese redesigned and rebuilt not just their physical plant but their social institutions in the decades that followed defeat. Few cultures could be more different than the German and the Japanese, but, remarkably, the institutions these countries built, though very unlike, end up serving almost identical functions in the economy.

The term "social partners" is used in Japan just as it is in Germany. Prior to the war, the prevailing view among top business executives was very like that of the American rugged individualist. As in Germany, however, the crisis provoked by defeat shifted the balance toward those who believed that business must join with the other major economic actors in the task of rebuilding the society, tying its own goals in with the larger interests of the nation as a whole. We should note, however, that the Japanese system of labor-management cooperation was not established immediately after World War II. Initially, labor-management relations were based on class warfare, which was also compatible with Japanese history. In the 1950s, following a wave of very debilitating strikes, a consensus emerged among Japanese leaders in the unions, companies, and government that cooperation was necessary. The key actors in government, industry, and labor now view each other, and are viewed by others, as a team. These three sectors act as collaborators, rather than as adversaries. It is, in fact, often hard for outsiders to locate the power centers in Japan, so diffuse is the distribution of authority and so dependent is the Japanese system on the existence of consensus among the partners before action is taken on any important matter. Here again, government, though hardly regarded as perfect or infallible, is regarded with respect as a valued player.

Though Japan does not have the same system of national wage determination that Germany does, the nation has set high wages as a primary national goal and pursues that goal relentlessly. While the United States was the only major industrial country to experience declining real wages between 1979 and 1988,[4] those years saw real hourly compensation for Japanese production workers grow by 6.92 percent a year in the same period. Japanese manufacturing workers' compensation costs increased from 48 percent of the United States' to 92 percent in 1988, falling back to 86 percent in 1990.[5] The annual growth in productivity was 2.93 percent for Japan, but only 1.09 percent for the United States between 1979 and 1988.[6] The criticism is often made of the Japanese that the extraordinary growth of their economy has been purchased at the expense of the Japanese consumer, since policies heavily favor reinvestment of the national earnings in productive capacity rather than the return of those earnings to private individuals for consumption. But given the spectacular growth of real income in Japan and its parallel decline in the United States, it is hardly clear that the consumption-oriented policies that we inherited from the Keynesian demand management era have served us well at all. What is important here, however, is that the Japanese do not view low wages as the key to their competitive future. To the contrary, as with the Germans, their explicit goal is to raise wages, often at the expense of other policy objectives.

The effect, as in Germany, is to drive Japanese employers toward business strategies that enable them to make a profit with high-cost labor, strategies that concentrate on markets that value quality over price and responsiveness to changing consumer tastes over long production runs geared to stable mass markets. But in Japan, business strategy is almost inseparable from national economic strategy. The drive to world economic leadership has been an overriding Japanese goal for forty years or more. At each successive point on Japan's climb up the ladder, the consensus has, as a matter of both government policy and firm practice, supported the progressive abandonment of low-wage, low-value-added industries to suppliers in other countries and embraced those industries that represented the next step in the evolution toward high-wage, high-value-added industry.

The formal mechanism for this process of consensus building is indicative planning, a process in which government holds up a vision of what the future should hold for Japan, developed with much advice and counsel from business and labor, and then business and labor in turn act to implement the vision. While an early version of the agency at the center of the indicative planning process, the Ministry of International Trade and Industry (MITI), was created in 1927, it did not attain its now central role in the making of a strong national industrial policy until after the war. While Germany does not practice formal indicative planning, the political process in Germany, aided by the close collaboration among the social partners, operates to produce much the same result, a consensus on social goals and economic objectives very similar to those that prevail in Japan that then guides the actions of millions of people acting in public and private capacities.

Germany imposed a system of employment security on its large employers by law in the years following the war, as we have seen. The same result was brought about by quite different means in Japan. Japan was very late to industrialize. In the years following the turn of the century, private employers seeking to attract people from the small pool of trained workers found that one of the most effective means to do so was to follow the lead of the first manufacturers, those owned by the government—to offer lifetime employment and advancement based on seniority. This practice grew rapidly among the big employers after the First World War and acquired the status of a major national institution following the Second World War, strongly aided by government policies, particularly those of the Ministry of International Trade and Industry and the Ministry of Finance.

However different the origins, the effect was the same as in Germany. Front-line workers in these large Japanese firms eagerly embrace changes in work organization and job assignments that, in the judgment of management, are likely to result in higher productivity and increased competitiveness, and, as we will discuss later, firms are more likely to invest heavily in the continuing education and training of their employees.

The methods by which these two countries arrange for a high level of vocational competence among their front-line workers could not be more different, but, here again, the result is the same: both nations boast work forces among the most highly skilled anywhere in the world.

The difference has its origins in dissimilar relationships between the worker and his or her work. In Germany, work is built on a centuries-old craft tradition without parallel in Japan. German workers, as a consequence, tend to think of themselves in terms of the trade or occupation in which they apprenticed, became a journeyman, and achieve—or hope to achieve—master status. In Japan, the workers identify not with the kind of work they do, but with the firm. When asked what they do, the German is likely to respond by saying that he is a master mechanic, but the Japanese worker is more likely to say that she works for Mitsubishi. Workers in Japanese firms are expected to do whatever kind of work is required to make the firm successful, so the expectation is that they will do many different kinds of work over their career with the firm. That means, among other things, that whereas the German firm is primarily concerned that new workers be fully competent at the specific task they are hired to perform, the Japanese employer is primarily concerned that the new worker be able to learn how to do a long succession of new jobs easily and well.

The implications both for schooling and for vocational education are profound. Large Japanese employers expect to provide virtually all the vocational education that new recruits need after they are hired. By 1992, for example, Toyota plans to put every new high-school graduate it hires for the front line through a two-year full-time course in digital electronics and mechatronics before they ever see the assembly line. Its assembly-line workers will have, as a result, roughly the same qualifications as do junior engineers in the United States. As far as they are concerned, the most desirable vocational qualification is the highest possible level of "general intelligence" in a recruit. General intelligence does not mean in Japan what it means here. To our definition—native ability—

the Japanese would add something they regard as more important: the effort put into learning. Unused intelligence, they would say, is of little value. It is intelligence actually applied that makes a difference.

Thus, although Japan does have a vocational education system, it is in no way remarkable. The large employers rely mainly on the academic high schools for their recruits, not on the vocational education system. Because this is so, and because the Japanese set such a high premium on general intelligence, the basic education standard set by the Japanese school system is probably the highest in the world. Many observers believe that the average Japanese high-school graduate reaches a level of achievement in the native language, science, and mathematics equal to or higher than that of the average American baccalaureate degree holder. If that is so, then by American standards, the vast majority of those entering the Japanese work force have the equivalent of an American four-year college degree. That is why Toyota can expect the people it recruits from high school to master an engineering curriculum when they report for work on the assembly line.

Just as in Germany, how students perform in school makes all the difference when it comes time to look for a job. Japanese employers, just like the Germans, want to know how the applicant performed in school and listen hard to the recommendations they get from teachers and principals. In fact, there are very close relationships between employers and individual high schools, and employers count heavily on both the reputation of the school and the integrity of the recommending official. The schools, for their part, can hardly afford to recommend someone not up to the employer's expectations, for fear of souring a very important relationship.

Again, much as in Germany, the excellence of the school system rests in turn on the firm foundation of the society's commitment to children. Though Japan offers some of the same public benefits for children that Germany does, including a modest child-allowance program for the less well-to-do, Japan's approach to this issue rests on custom and private effort rather than public policy. Mothers in Japan are expected to devote themselves to their children. They sleep in their rooms at night, sit up with them when they study, take their seats in school when they are sick and take notes for them, and, in countless ways, signal their unqualified love and support for them, always communicating their high expectations for their children's success in school and later in life. There is virtually no public child care in Japan, because Japanese mothers are expected to be at home caring for their children. While Americans are hardly likely to adopt such a system, having deep reservations about the ways in which it curtails women's opportunities, it provides a kind and quality of support for children that serve the Japanese well.

In much the same way, the Japanese provide the same extensive program of continual training and retraining of adult workers that the Germans do, probably at an even higher level of investment in the large firms, but mainly as a matter of private practice rather than public policy. Here again, the system of lifetime employment in the large firms, combined with the Japanese practice of shifting workers from one job to another quite different one, makes the employers more than willing to invest, knowing that the investment will be recovered.

The Japanese worker's attitude toward continuing training is virtually unique. Joining a large Japanese firm is like joining a team or becoming a member of a family. Just as in the Japanese family, one can expect the warm support of one's colleagues, provided that one meets, or works at meeting, the expectations of these other "family members." One of the most important of these expectations, not only from management, but from one's fellow workers, is that one will learn what is necessary to do the job well and be able therefore to contribute fully to the team effort. The greatest source of shame is to let one's fellow workers down.

In Germany, as we have seen, the move toward new forms of work organization, de-Taylorization, and the professionalization of front-line work have come about as the result of a whole complex of public-policy initiatives. In Japan, the same result was produced through a close partnership between the public and private sectors. In the years following the war, the consensus view, as we have seen, was that Japan should strive to break out of the ranks of low-cost producers to the front rank of industrial powers. To do that, it was widely agreed, the country would have to shed its reputation for poor quality, adopting methods of quality improvement that originated in the United States, but which had been widely ignored in this country. These objectives became an important imperative for government planners and corporate managers. To achieve them required not only highly skilled workers, but also high-performance work organizations.

It was only after the Second World War that the now famed partnership emerged between government planners and the large firms practicing lifetime employment. Indicative planning supported the move toward high-performance work organizations from without. The structure of the large corporations and the evolving pattern of Japanese industrial relations supported it from within.

Unlike the situation in the United States, shareholders play a minor role in the life of large Japanese corporations. The directors of Japanese corporations are typically subordinates of the president. The major shareholders are typically banks and other corporations with which the firm has close ties, and they are not entitled to sit on the board. Japanese managers therefore identify closely with their employees, and, what is at least as important, the employees identify their interests with those of management and the corporation as a whole. Though the form is very different, then, the end result is very like the benefits that Germany gets from codetermination.

The close identification of top managers with the employees of the firm is partly a function of the absence of the sharp distinction between management and labor that characterizes the West. It is not at all unusual for top Japanese managers to have worked their way up the ranks from the front line. Blue-collar workers often make as much as graduate engineers. The distinctions so common in the West—from separate lunchrooms to dress codes—are largely absent from the Japanese firm.

Employees, once hired, are very rarely dismissed before the retirement age of fifty-five or sixty. As we pointed out earlier, this enables employers to recover fully the investments they make in the development of their employees, and, just as in Germany, this induces management to invest much more heavily in the skills of their front-line workers than American employers. The value of those investments would, of course, be lost if Japanese employers laid off their employees in slack times. So, even in the worst of times, large Japanese employers will price their products and services to sell at a loss so as to maintain employment levels. This loyalty to the workers is repaid handsomely by hard work, the virtual nonexistence of absenteeism, and a willingness to do whatever else must be done to help the firm succeed. As in Germany, the assurance of job security makes Japanese workers far more willing than their American counterparts to accommodate and even embrace the shifts in roles and assignments demanded by technological change.

The deep sense of affiliation with the interests of the firm in Japan is greatly reinforced by the system of seniority pay. In its purest form, this refers to the practice of setting pay not on the basis of performance, but rather on the basis of seniority. In the United States, where pay based on individual job requirements is the norm, the success of the firm does not necessarily translate into success for the individual. But, under the seniority pay system, corporate success and individual progress are closely tied.

This system has a very interesting effect on the development of human resources. In a system in which pay and advancement are tied to individual job requirements, as in the United States, managers have little incentive to share what they know with their subordinates, for fear that those subordinates will use what they learn to compete for their positions and the resulting pay. In Japan, where both pay and formal position are typically tied only to years of service, managers are far more willing to serve as tutors to their subordinates, thus greatly improving the function of the firm as a total learning system. In fact, just as in Germany, the teaching of subordinates is regarded as a key role and responsibility of front-line and middle managers throughout the firm.

The Japanese tendency to view the firm as a form of extended family is reinforced by the pattern of labor relations. In Japan, labor relations are more paternalistic than in Germany, where unions operate in the public arena, using the political process to get government to establish formal rules the employers must follow. Unions in Japan are organized by firm, not by industry or craft. A system of joint labor-management consultation (reminiscent of the German works council) is used to resolve a very wide range of problems, including rearrangement of production lines, new factory installations, moves into overseas markets, work environments, and welfare policies. Even issues like wage increases and working hours, until recently the exclusive province of formal collective bargaining, are increasingly resolved through this consultative process.

Everything we have discussed so far—the consensus on the need to compete on quality, lifetime employment, the identification of the worker with the interests of the firm, the high quality of the education system, the continuous investment in workers' skills, the system of labor-management relations, and much more—all comes together on the shop floor to shape the way work is organized.

Under the Taylor system of work organization common in the United States, the standards for the way each job is done are set forth in detailed manuals developed by college-trained industrial engineers. Supervisors are expected to make sure that the manuals are closely followed. Not so in Japan. There the workers themselves, operating in teams, perform the industrial engineering function, deciding among themselves what to do, how to do it and when. Engineers are largely confined to the research and development function.

In the United States, management sees its job as inducing labor to perform faster and unions are there to act as a brake. In Japan, management relies on the work teams to control the pace of the assembly line, knowing that they will speed it up as they work the kinks out of the production process. In the United States, working the kinks out of the production process is the job of management, of course. But in Japan, improvements in both product and process are as much the responsibility of the front-line work teams as of management. This leads to very different responses when new products and machinery are introduced in the two countries. In the United States, it is assumed that, after initial shakedown, neither product nor process will be changed until the next design cycle, perhaps years away. In Japan, the introduction of a new product or process is the beginning of a continuous process of improvement in the product or service and means used to produce it, led by the front-line workers.

In the United States, quality control is the responsibility of specialized departments. In Japan, quality control is in the hands of the work teams. So is most equipment maintenance, as well as many other functions that in the United States are reserved for the management, professional, and senior technical staff. Likewise, in the United States, foremen are supposed to pass instructions down from the management to the front-line worker and make sure those instructions are carried out. But in Japan, the foreman is leader and guide of a largely autonomous work group and is expected to pass the views of the workers up the line to management.

At bottom, it is the collective skill of the work team that forms the basis for the success of the Japanese firm. It is fundamental to the working of the team that skills are shared among its members. Senior and junior members are expected to teach and to learn from one another constantly. The primary mode of instruction in the firm is discussions run by the foreman. If any member of the team is not performing up to par, the others feel an obligation to teach him or her whatever is necessary to bring the performance of the whole group up to a high standard.

The work group, then, is a learning system, a form of social organization one of whose primary purposes is to foster a process of continual individual and group learning. It is in turn the core unit of a larger unit, the firm, which can also be viewed as an integrated learning system, as we have explained. The result, as in Germany, is a high rate of productivity growth, excellent product quality, and great flexibility. Thus the work group is the most important single factor in the success of the Japanese economy.

As we have seen, though the policies and institutions of Germany and Japan differ widely, these two countries have ended up pursuing strategies that are strikingly similar at key points. Wilhelm Streeck, a professor at the University of Wisconsin in Madison, has reviewed much of the literature on the German economic miracle in general, and in the region of Baden-Württemberg in particular. He suggests a conception of the requirements for national economic success that goes a long way toward explaining why the common elements of the strategies of these two countries work as well as they do, and why, conversely, the United States is having such trouble matching their growth records.[7]

Keynesian economic theory, he points out, pays very little attention to the problem of the supply of factors necessary to the production of goods and services in the economy, assuming that the market will provide them in the most efficient way at the lowest possible cost. Nor does it pay any more attention to the microeconomic functioning of firms, assuming that firms will address the market segments, produce the products and services, adopt the production technology, organize the work, develop the skills, and pay the wages necessary to create the greatest possible economic benefits for society. In this scheme of the self-regulated economy, the only proper function of government is to regulate consumer demand through fiscal and monetary policy.

But, during the 1980s, a growing body of scholars observed that key differences in the organization of the society as a whole, as well as within the firm, appear to account for substantial differences in the capacity of the economy to perform well, given the challenge presented by the newly integrated world economy we described in chapter 3. These patterns of organization do not automatically emerge as a result of the actions of market forces, but rather as a result of conscious choices made by governments, managers, and labor, choices that could spell the difference between national success and failure.

Streeck points out that, until recently, most analysts had drawn a sharp distinction between economies based on the production of standardized, mass-produced goods that competed on price and economies based instead on the production of customized quality-competitive goods.[8] The first prospered best using Taylorized work organizations and would lead to low wages. The second would require craft forms of organization and lead to high wages.

But, now, it appears to be a little more complicated than that. Researchers have identified a third alternative. Advanced forms of mass-production technology can now be used to make relatively short production runs efficient, and can also be employed by small craft producers to turn out high-quality products for mass markets at a competitive cost. This opens up the option of competing on the basis of high-volume production of customized quality-competitive goods. Craft producers could enter this market by increasing production volume. Mass marketers could enter it by upgrading product design and quality and increasing product variety. It is this approach that Streeck calls "diversified quality production."[9] And this is the approach that Germany and Japan are employing with such great success.

It turns out that a choice for diversified quality production is a choice for a companion set of social goals: high wages, a low wage spread, worker participation, and full employment. High wages require this form of production because competing on quality and productivity rather than price is the only way to command the high prices that alone can support high wages. A low wage spread results because diversified quality production requires a work organization in which the distinctions between management, professional, and nonprofessional are very blurred. Worker participation is needed because the active participation of workers in decision making is the key to the flexibility and quality of the production process. Full employment is also involved, because employment security is a precondition for the trust in management and motivation of the workers on which the system is based.

What is striking is that diversified quality production is not emerging as the dominant business strategy everywhere, but only in certain countries. This is because it requires not just individual firm decisions but rather the commitment of the entire society.

Firms cannot—and generally will not—get there alone. Left to pursue their own self-interest in the traditional laissez-faire (or, in our case, deregulated) economy, they will rationally choose to keep wages low, lay off workers in slack times, invest as little as possible in their workers for fear the competition will recruit them, keep as much prerogative in decision making for management as possible, and so on. Changing these choices means that, somehow, companies must face constraints that make decisions compatible with diversified quality production more rational.

After the war, as we have seen, both Germany and Japan responded to the crisis they faced by drawing government, employers, and labor into a social partnership that was able to come to consensus on the social goals we just listed. Germany then enacted legislation that changed the constraints on firms to produce a set of corporate decisions favoring the implementation of the whole range of changes in management style, organizational and social structure, allocation of decision-making power, human-resources policies, and so on that we have seen are required to make diversified quality production work. Japan used its consensus to create powerful social pressures, aided but not led by policy, that had the same effect.

But consensual decisions by government, management, and labor concerning quality production in the firm are not in themselves sufficient, because a firm's success is dependent in part on external forces, especially a highly educated labor force. Thus government must take the lead, with the participation of the other social partners, in greatly increasing the supply of this vital resource.

Streeck points out that the creation of these external resources, especially highly educated labor, requires substantial public investment—not just in a high-performance education system, but in all the systems, from child-support to public-health programs, that assure the healthy growth and development of children needed to produce a first-class work force.[10] The natural inclination of employers in a laissez-faire economy, on the other hand, is to keep taxes down. So, once again, the development of an economy based on diversified quality production depends on the existence of a national consensus among all the social partners—in this case a consensus strong enough to overcome the natural reluctance of employers to support the public investments on which the new system depends.

In this way, Germany and Japan have become societies whose members think for a living. The work units within their firms have become advanced learning systems. The skills of their workers are perceived by almost everyone to be their most vital national asset.

In Germany and Japan, we see not just a variation on capitalism, but, arguably, a vision of a new kind of capitalist society. Its distinguishing characteristics are a commitment to the twin goals of high wages and full employment, a policy preference for diversified quality production of goods and services, a joining together of government and private enterprise to achieve the consensus goals, and a deep belief that the quality of human resources and a de-Taylorized workplace hold the key to attainment of those goals.

Furthermore, the consensus on these goals runs from the cabinet secretary to the factory manager and the cab driver. With this consensus, it becomes possible for governments to formulate economic, social, educational, and labor-market policies that are coordinated and mutually reinforcing, whatever party is in power.

This is certainly not laissez-faire capitalism, for government involvement goes well beyond the management of macroeconomic policy. But it is not socialism either, if by socialism is meant the ownership and control of capital and industry by the community as a whole through government. Ownership of capital in both of the countries we have just looked at is decidedly private and competition in open markets is very intense.

We think of this new model as human-resource capitalism. The foundation of its power is a new conception of the role of human resources in the economy. It abandons the notion that the key resources are natural resources and that the key policy factors are adequate consumer demand and slow growth in the money supply. Instead, the crucial factors turn out to be an adequate supply of high-quality human resources, business strategies that emphasize quality and productivity, and a pattern of work organization that fosters both of these goals. Because the development of high-quality human resources requires very high levels of public expenditure over a long period of time, and because these highly trained people can be fully competitive only in an environment suffused with advanced technology, the required levels of continuous investment turn out to be unprecedented. Because this is so, national economic policies must favor investment over consumption, and because a strong consensus is required on the patterns of investment, close cooperation among government, employers, and labor is essential.

Some would say that the key features of the Japanese and German systems are so embedded in the cultures of those countries that the United States has little to learn from them. We disagree. The powerful Japanese combination of indicative planning coordinated by government and lifelong employment in the large firms is not ages old; it assumed its present shape only after the war. Many of the most effective Japanese institutions and strategies are actually a blend of old Japanese approaches with American forms and techniques imposed or borrowed during and after the occupation. Some became part of the fabric of Japanese economic life only after the bitter labor strife of the 1950s.[11] Similarly, in Germany, the institution of codetermination, the system for national wage setting, and much else that we described are postwar innovations in a system that had earlier in many ways followed a Taylorist pattern of work organization.

So far, however, the United States has largely ignored the German and Japanese lessons. As we will show in the next chapter, all we have to do to become a low-wage country with a low standard of living is to maintain our current course. While we could choose another, the one Japan and Germany have taken, doing so would require a sense of urgency that the American people apparently have yet to feel.

PART III

The Challenge

CHAPTER 5

America on the Precipice: Will We Boil the Frog?

We laid out the terms of America's coming crisis in the introduction. We are consuming, we said, more than we produce, making up for the difference by borrowing from abroad, selling off our national assets, and depreciating our capital. As the Germans shift their investments to the demands of eastern Germany and America's assets become less attractive to the Japanese with the declining value of the yen against the dollar, we will be forced to live within our means, which implies a declining standard of living. We did not go into deficit finance because of rising consumption—growth in consumption is actually slowing—but rather because real wages have been declining; we have borrowed and sold our assets in a losing bid to maintain our standard of living. That standard would have slipped a lot faster than it did but for the fact that, over the last two decades, we had a steadily growing supply of new workers—baby-boomers and women—to expand the supply of goods and services. But now, both sources of new workers have dried up, leaving us on the edge of an economic precipice. With stagnant productivity growth and a steep decline in the number of new entrants into the work force, national income will decline with accelerating speed, and our standard of living with it. When the baby-boomers retire after the year 2010, the precipice we now face could look like good times.

The only way to avoid this is through a radical improvement in productivity. In the past, we have improved productivity by giving our workers the most advanced equipment on the market. But the same equipment is now available to low-wage countries that can sell their products all over the world—including here in the United States—at prices way below ours. If we continue to compete with them on wages and hours—which is what we are now doing—then our wage rates will decline and our hours will increase until they match those of the low-wage competition.

There is an alternative. We can join the ranks of those countries that are engaged in diversified quality production, which, as we have seen, is the key to high productivity growth rates and high wages. But diversified quality production depends on high-performance work organization, which in turn depends on an unending supply of high-quality human resources.

American firms are not doing that, however. Fewer than 5 percent of American firms are embracing high-performance, high-productivity forms of work organization.[1] The rest appear to be stuck in the Taylorist mode that America pioneered after the turn of the century. They are choosing to compete with South Korea, Mexico, and the Philippines rather than Germany and Japan.

Because few of our firms see the need to move to new forms of work organization, they do not perceive a real skill shortage. Ninety-five percent of American employers report no shortage of skilled labor. The reason is simple: as we have seen, most of our employers have designed the jobs of their front-line workers so that they need little skilled labor. Thirty-four percent of jobs in the United States require less than an eighth-grade education. Another 36 percent of jobs require more than eighth-grade skills but less than a baccalaureate degree. Only the last 30 percent of our jobs—those of executives, managers, professionals, and senior technical workers—require a four-year college degree.[2]

The low level of skills required of most workers does not mean that employers have no complaints at all about skills. Eighty percent say they have trouble finding workers with a good work ethic and appropriate social skills. Many complain that the eighth-grade skills they need are lacking. But very few are concerned that their workers cannot do statistics or algebra, are unable to write a competent essay or letter, or cannot solve a real-life problem that demands a knowledge of basic science. Contrary to popular belief, there appears to be a rough balance between the skills American employers demand and the skills American educational institutions are supplying.

The reason American employers are not demanding higher skills is simple: they are maintaining outmoded, low-performance, low-productivity forms of work organization. The structure of employers' skills requirements in the United States looks more like the profile of skills requirements in Third World countries than in the leading industrial nations. As long as they do that, America will continue to pursue a path toward ever lower wages and a lower standard of living.

The essence of the new forms of work organization, as the German and Japanese experiences demonstrate, is simple: front-line workers are given many of the responsibilities of managers, technical staff, and professionals. The great increases in efficiency, effectiveness, and productivity made by these countries all result from this strategy. We elaborate on the nature of high-performance work organization in chapter 7. The point here is that those American corporations that are using or moving toward high-performance work organization report that the most serious obstacle they face is a shortage of well-educated and highly skilled labor. If the vast majority of employers were to embrace high-performance forms of work organization, there would be a shortage of skilled labor of epic proportions.

If the first part of the American crisis has to do with the economic prospects we face as a consequence of the inability of our business enterprises to raise productivity growth rates, then the second part has to do with the poor quality of our front-line labor force. As we have shown, the Japanese and the Europeans have realized for many years that the key to their economic success is high-quality front-line labor. We can take the measure of our skills crisis simply by comparing the American system for educating and training our front-line workers with those of our major competitors. The picture that emerges is of a cumulative deficit of very large proportions that begins at birth and continues to the end of one's working life.

More than one-quarter of all our future front-line workers are now growing up in poverty, a statistic unparalleled among the advanced industrialized nations. The rate of poverty among children in the United States is more than twice that in Japan or any leading industrial country in Europe. The consequences in terms of hunger, malnutrition, and impaired cognitive, social, and emotional development are incalculable.

Once in school, we fail to provide our front-line workers with an education that meets the standards even of some of the newly industrialized countries with which we compete. The newspapers have for years featured reports on the educational performance of our students compared with those of our principal competitors. The performance of our students in mathematics and science now falls well below that of South Korean students. In fact, the dropout rate in South Korea is now about 10 percent, and virtually all of the 90 percent of South Korean students who graduate have mastered basic skills, two targets to which this country has never even come close. That means that our future workers are less well educated than workers who earn less than one-tenth what our workers earn. We have priced ourselves out of the worldwide labor market. If—or perhaps the issue is when—there is equilibrium in the world market for front-line labor, tens of millions of American workers will be unemployed or employable only at wage rates that are below current South Korean wages.

What is quite extraordinary is how determined we are to resist the plain facts revealed by the steady stream of data that flows from the comparisons so often made between the academic performance of our students and the students of other countries. Most Americans dismiss such comparisons with the observation that they are unfair because we educate everyone, whereas our competitors educate only a small elite. That might have been true years ago, but it emphatically is not true now. In one country after another, greater proportions of high-school students are enrolled in courses in mathematics, science, and language, for example, than in the United States; and the scores of those students on international examinations are consistently higher than the scores of American students.[3]

Thirteen percent of our seniors, mainly those taking a college prep curriculum, took the algebra test administered by the Second International Mathematics Study. This compares to 12 percent of the Japanese, 19 percent of Canadian youth in Ontario, and 50 percent of the Hungarians in that age group. Our top students equaled the mean score of the much larger group of Hungarians and was well below that of the Canadians. Only 2 to 3 percent of the Americans could match the median score for the Japanese.[4] Likewise, according to the Second International Science Study, 25 percent of the Canadians know as much chemistry as the top 1 percent of American chemistry students. In biology the figures are 28 percent and 6 percent, respectively.[5]

These data make it clear that with respect to math and science, American students are way behind their counterparts in many other advanced industrial countries that do not have elite education systems. The First International Assessment of Educational Progress, released early in 1989, goes further. As we related earlier, it shows that the United States performs below some of the newly industrialized countries with which we compete, countries in which the wage rates are well below our own. "In Korea, 78 percent of the 13-year-olds can use intermediate mathematics skills to solve two-step problems compared to only 40 percent of their counterparts in the United States. Despite their poor overall performance, about two-thirds of the United States' 13-year-olds feel that 'they are good at mathematics.' Only 23 percent of their Korean counterparts, the best achievers, share the same attitude." The Koreans also scored at the top in science, when compared to the United States, the United Kingdom, Spain, Ireland, and four Canadian provinces. More than 70 percent of the 13-year-olds in Korea can use scientific procedures and analyze scientific data, compared to 35 percent to 40 percent of their peers in the United States.[6]

In a highly technological society, widespread mastery of the fundamentals of mathematics and science is an essential national asset. But it is hardly all that is required. We know far less, however, about how our students compare to those in other countries on measures of achievement in the other core subjects in the curriculum. It is much easier to compare students in the universal languages of mathematics and science than in communications, history, literature, and other subjects where differences in language, history, and culture make such comparisons very difficult. Yet the results in science give us little reason to suppose that American students would fare well in such comparisons.

Some dismiss the international comparisons because our curriculum is different, and our children cannot be expected to learn what they have not been taught. But that begs the question as to why we would tolerate such a curriculum. It is patently absurd to say that international comparisons of math achievement, for example, are irrelevant because few of our children have a curriculum that includes calculus, physics, statistics, or probability when all or most of these subjects are required for technological literacy in the modern world.

Half of our high-school students, and a much higher fraction of our future front-line workers—are in what is called the "general" curriculum. Most of them emerge from school—with or without a diploma—with eighth-grade academic skills or worse. In terms of its own goals, the system is not unsuccessful. Study after study shows that young Americans, in field after field, have the rudimentary skills to do the routine work required of most workers in the first half of this century.[7] They can decode a simple sentence and do their sums. They have a reasonable repertoire of facts and know some simple procedures. By the standards in place at the end of World War II, 95 percent are literate. But a great many cannot go much beyond that to do the work that is now required. Not only do they have great trouble going beyond basic rote skills to reasoning and problem solving, but their capacity for engaging in these more advanced mental activities has actually declined in recent years.

Fewer than 4 in 10 young adults can summarize in writing the main argument from a lengthy news column—1 in 4 whites, 1 in 4 blacks, and 2 in 10 Hispanics. Only 25 out of 100 young adults can use a bus schedule to select the appropriate bus for a given departure or arrival—3 in 100 blacks and 7 in 100 Hispanics. Only 10 percent of the total group can select the least costly product from a list of grocery items on the basis of unit-pricing information—12 in 100 whites, 1 in 100 blacks, and 4 in 100 Hispanics.[8]

These tasks are hardly complex, yet only small fractions of young people aged twenty-one through twenty-five can perform them. While those in college outperform those who are not, their performance, clearly, is not greatly better than the average (more than half of our high-school graduates go on to some form of postsecondary education).

These findings make it clear that only a tiny fraction of our workers can function effectively in an environment requiring strong communications skills and the application of sophisticated conceptual understanding to complex real-world problems.

What about noncognitive ability? Here the data are scanty, but employers widely report that students come out of school at all levels unprepared to work in teams and with few of the skills they need to resolve conflicts with one another.

If the majority of students fail to leave school with the skills they need, it is reasonable to ask whether those skills were taught. Here we find that the schools' curriculum and methods are matched to the needs of a half-century ago, rather than to today's requirements.

Fifty years ago, relatively few students needed sophisticated communications skills, so students were not required to write much and teachers were not asked to spend much time working with them to improve what they wrote. Students are still not required to write much and teachers are given very little time to help them improve their writing. Fifty years ago, it was assumed that only a small proportion of students were capable of demanding mental activity, which was fortunate because the labor market demanded only a small number who made their living with their heads. Today, the schools continue to provide general and vocational curricula that make relatively light demands on students with respect to analytical and conceptual thinking and provide relatively little opportunity to academic-track students to apply what they are learning in a real-world context. Despite the fact that the "vocations" increasingly require abstract thinking and the ability to do other kinds of sophisticated "head work," students who go through the academic track increasingly show themselves unable to apply what they know to real problems that have be solved in and out of school. Fifty years ago, most workers were expected to go to work and do what their boss told them to do. In the age of standardized mass production, only individual effort was rewarded in the workplace. School was—and continues to be—much the same, even though teamwork is what counts now in the workplace, and self-governing people are much more valuable than those who wait to be told what to do next. Fifty years ago, most workers did what they were told, whether it made sense to them or not, to get a paycheck. Today, in the schools, students are expected to study hard to get through the next hurdle, whether or not what they are studying appears to be of any value in the real world. Fifty years ago, most students left school to take on a highly defined, relatively simple job. They did not need to know how the various things they had studied related to one another in an interlaced scheme of knowledge. Now they do, but the organization of the curriculum into sealed compartments, unrelated to each other or to real phenomena outside the school, continues. And, as many have pointed out, fifty years ago, most people left school with all the book knowledge they needed for a lifetime of work. They did not need to know how to learn or how to get new information efficiently. Schools still try to cover the whole terrain of all the major subjects, as if students will never again have an opportunity to study these things, sacrificing the kind of real understanding of any of them that is required for continued learning.

With respect to strictly vocational skills, the position is no better. Twenty-five percent of the vocational courses in the United States are taken by these students; 50 percent of the vocational courses are taken by college-bound students. Only a portion of these courses are actually occupation-specific. It seems likely that fewer than one-eighth of our general curriculum students end up in jobs for which they had any training at all in school. The result is that more than half of our students—much more than half of our future front-line workers—leave school with academic and vocational skills that fall below those of virtually all the industrialized countries and many of the newly industrialized countries.[9]

More than one-quarter of American students—perhaps as much as half of our future front-line workers—drop out of school. We do virtually nothing to recover them. We spend about $4,300 a year on average on our high-school students, but, averaging out the cost of our second-chance programs across all the dropouts, we spend only $235 a year trying to give those who drop out the education and job skills they will need to survive in our economy.[10]

America has what may be the worst school-to-work transition program of any industrialized country in the world. The data show that most of our young people who leave school without going directly to college mill around in our labor market for years. They get a series of dead-end low-skill or unskilled jobs when they can and go on unemployment when they cannot, until about the age of twenty-five or twenty-six when, with precious few skills, they get their first "regular" job.[11] Millions of youngsters from impoverished backgrounds do not do even that well, so remote are they from knowing anyone who can help them get a job or acquire the skills they need to keep one.

Once our front-line workers actually get their first real job, they will not fare much better. American employers spend about $30 billion a year on the education and training of their workers. But two-thirds of this sum goes to their college-educated employees. Twenty-seven billion dollars of the $30 billion is paid out by only one-half of one percent of America's firms. The result is that the vast majority of American front-line workers get no further formal education and training at all after landing their first job.[12]

Our competitors, meanwhile, are taking much better care of their children than we do of ours. They have high educational standards for their future front-line workers, whereas we have virtually none. Many make intensive efforts to make sure that everyone—those who do not drop out and those who do—meets those standards in or out of school. The countries with which we compete either make it virtually impossible for students to drop out, bringing almost all their students up to a high educational standard (as is the case in Japan), or invest what is necessary in recovering almost all their dropouts (as do the leading industrial countries in Europe).

Our competitors also make extensive provision for the transition from school to work. Virtually all the nations of Central Europe have programs like Germany's, enrolling almost all students who do not go to college. These programs call for two to four years of combined work and education beyond the age of fifteen or sixteen, which results in everyone being highly trained for a wide range of occupations in manufacturing and services by the age of nineteen or twenty. The average twenty-five-year-old graduate in the United States has the eighth-grade academic skills and the virtually nonexistent vocational skills with which he or she emerged from high school, while the average nineteen-year-old in Europe or Japan has far higher academic skills, strong technical skills, good work habits, and an employer who knows what he or she can do.

Firms in these nations and some Far Eastern countries typically devote a far higher proportion of their education and training budgets to constantly improving the skills of their front-line work force. Their governments, without exception, require employers to commit an amount equal to at least 1 percent of their payroll to employee education and training.

In the chapters to come, we will explore some of these contrasts between American practices and those of other countries in more detail, as we seek ideas for the policies that might guide us in the years ahead. The point here, though, is to make it clear that our competitors have greatly outdistanced us in their provisions for their front-line workers at every point in the life cycle.

The problem, reduced to its simplest dimensions, is that we are trying to use Third World business strategies and a Third World education system to maintain a world-class standard of living.

The last chapter showed what our competitors are doing to choose another future, a high-wage, full-employment future. But there is no consensus in this country that the overriding goal of policy should be full employment and high wages. Policy at every level of our system is more supportive of firms whose business strategies are based on price competition and low-cost labor than it is of firms that compete based on quality and highly skilled labor. Americans' belief that the less government we have, the better off we are has, if anything, grown stronger in recent years, and there is little love lost between management and labor in this country. Our economic policy strongly favors consumption over investment. American firms are, as we have shown, more deeply in the grip of Taylorized methods of work organization than those of any other major country in the world.

There are those who will argue that there is little that can be done to change the situation. The United States is too big and too diverse ever to come to consensus on a narrow set of social goals. Our distrust of government runs too deep for us to rely on it to lead the way as it has in Germany and Japan. Firms would never submit to the kinds of constraints on their freedom of action to which enterprises in other countries have submitted. Because that is so, there are no effective ways in which policy will ever be able to create strong enough incentives to induce employers to abandon Taylorized methods of work organization. And our citizens will never agree to the level of taxes that would be required fully to develop our human resources.

But recall that the crucial measures taken by Germany and Japan to create this new form of capitalism were not the result of centuries of evolution. They were virtually all put in place following World War II, the result of a crisis in their societies that forced a reevaluation of much that they had held sacred for a long time. Winston Churchill once remarked that the United States always does the right thing—after it has exhausted all the alternatives. Will we do the right thing this time?

That depends in no small measure on whether we believe we face a crisis, a crisis of the same proportions that our defeated foes faced after the war. Clearly, we do, but we are not behaving as if we did. Why not?

The metaphor of the boiled frog is useful here. A frog dumped in boiling water will instantly jump out to save itself. But put the frog in cold water and slowly turn up the heat to boiling, and the frog will at first revel in the warmth and then, too groggy to do anything else, die as the water comes to a boil. The country as a whole is like the second frog. Unlike Germany and Japan after the war, the United States saw the war as validating its established ways of doing business—in both the public and private spheres. Our long and spectacular success following the war confirmed our belief in all the old ways of doing business. Save for a tiny fraction of American firms in recent years, no single shock has been strong enough to make the frog jump.

Part of the problem is our insularity. Until recently, when Ford, General Motors, and Chrysler judged their performance, they had only to compare it to their own performance at an earlier date and to that of the other two companies. When first Volkswagen, and then the Japanese auto makers, began to encroach on the low end of the market, they brushed this off, saying that the numbers were low, and, besides, the low end of the market was not very profitable anyway. Only when it was almost too late did they realize that the benchmarks they were using—their performance over time and relative to one another—were irrelevant. The only thing that mattered was their performance relative to the best performance in the world.

This insularity applies with even greater force to American education than to American business. When Americans look at their schools, they behave just like the Big Three automakers did earlier. We reported before that American educators measure their performance by comparing it to their performance at some earlier date. When average Americans are asked about the quality of America's schools, they raise serious questions about the quality of the system as a whole, are more approving of the schools in their state and locality, but report general satisfaction with the schools in their own school district. The citizens of upper-income communities, for example, will ask some very simple questions: How does our system compare to the other districts in our state with which we have historically compared ourselves? Are we getting the same proportion of our graduates into the Ivy League and the Big Ten as we used to? If the answers to these questions are positive, then home owners will feel that their real-estate values are secure and parents will be relieved. In working-class communities, parents see their sons and daughters taking courses very like the ones they used to take and getting jobs much like they got. What, they then ask, is the problem? Given all the attention by the press in recent years to the quality of education in the United States, especially in comparison to the achievements of students abroad, this seems inexplicable. But the fact is that there is no state board of education or local school board in the country that we know of that is asked to compare the performance of its graduates with that of graduates in other countries. It is not that we are ignorant, but rather that we, like the Big Three automakers earlier, choose to ignore the evidence because it seems irrelevant.

The entire system, then, is self-reinforcing. Only a handful of American firms do enough business outside of the United States not only to feel the hot breath of foreign competitors (many are in that position) but also to see that there is another way of organizing and managing that will enable them to succeed while still paying high wages. Most restaurants, laundries, banks, insurance companies, real-estate agencies, and electric companies go on as before, using Taylorist organization strategies, not worrying overmuch about quality or productivity improvement, and paying the lowest wages they can. Because that is so, American education and training institutions produce now what they have produced in the past, in the same ways they have always produced it. American parents are generally happy to find that the schools and colleges are doing now what they did before, because the same school results produce the same employment results they have always produced. Press elites begin to sound the alarm, but most Americans assume that alarm is about someone else because little in their own world seems unusual. There is nothing in their own experience that suggests that this comfortable circle is leading to a downward spiral in real wages and living standards for them. There is no sense of crisis.

This sense of a gulf between opinion leaders and the public on the issues with which this book is concerned is not speculation. Through 1989 and 1990, the Public Agenda Foundation conducted a wide-ranging series of focus groups across America on these issues. The result is a fascinating story.[13]

For our leaders, productivity and growth are the keys to a strong economy, but most Americans associate a strong economy with lots of jobs—any kind of jobs. They seem not to realize that everyone can be employed while the country is getting poorer or that everyone could be better off even if fewer people worked. "Virtually none of the respondents spontaneously grasped the . . . imperative to produce good products at good prices that sell well the world over." So they saw no need to improve productivity and did not connect the "country's economic health to the skills and motivation of the work force."[14]

The majority of Americans, albeit a slim one, believe they are better off than they were ten years ago, despite the fact that real wages have declined steadily over the last ten years for most Americans. Only 16 percent think they are worse off, though hundreds of thousands of families have had to put housewives into the labor force and take on an unprecedented debt burden to make ends meet.[15]

Americans know that there is a competitiveness problem, but they do not connect it to lagging productivity growth or skills deficiencies. Instead, they blame excessive foreign aid, the failure to "buy American," corporations that ship jobs offshore, cheap foreign labor (they seem unaware that many of our competitors pay higher wages than we do), labor-union greed, direct foreign investment in the United States, and thievery of our best ideas by others, especially the Japanese (few are aware that several foreign countries, including Japan, are world technology leaders in their own right).

When Americans think about problems in the work force and with the skills of the people in it, they think in moral terms: a failing work ethic, workers who do not care enough, permissiveness and lack of standards in the schools, lack of willingness on the part of parents to take responsibility for their children. "For the public, motivation, standards, values, and the work ethic are the most important elements to be addressed in rebuilding the American economy."[16] But because these are not things that can be much affected by public policy, Americans do not know what can be done to influence them. They believe the problem is will, not skills. For this reason, they think the country can bounce back any time it wants to—a quick fix is just around the corner. It will not take a great financial investment, great institutional change, or much time.

Americans certainly do not think that higher skills are necessary. To the contrary, the skills and values that were necessary when they were growing up will do the job nicely. Confronted with data showing that students in other countries do far better than that now, they simply refuse to believe it, asserting that foreigners' high scores are the result of the "fact" that they educate elites whereas we educate everyone. If there is an education problem, the public believes it is confined to the K–12 education system. They do not believe we face important problems with technical training, advanced skills training, adult literacy, or continuing education, in part because they do not see any important connection between skills and competitiveness. The purpose of the economy is to provide jobs; people with jobs do not need more education because they already have jobs. In fact, the public worries that we may be overeducating for the jobs that are available. They do not focus at all on the possibility that good jobs may go begging for lack of qualified people while there are too few bad jobs for those who only qualify for such jobs. Nor has it occurred to them that it is possible to have a full-employment economy in which virtually everyone is poor, though that was exactly the situation in the Soviet Union under the Communists.

While our analysis shows that the economic future of this country depends on having a front-line work force that is world-class, the public has not "grasped the idea that individuals in the bottom third are essential economic players."[17] They view grand plans to help such people attain strong skills as a form of social welfare, and they see such programs as perpetuating poverty rather than solving it.

Far from viewing technology as a handmaiden to economic progress and an essential element of economic growth, most of the public sees it as causing unemployment. Americans do not see the connection between good products and good technology. They think technology education will make students excessively narrow. Even those who take a positive view of the role of technology are unconvinced that we needed better education and training in technology because they believe we have outdistanced all the other nations in this area.[18]

The American frog is coming to a boil slowly. The American people seem not to notice the rising temperature and their leaders have done little, it seems, to engage them in a conversation that starts where they are. Fortunately, the Business–Higher Education Forum and the Public Agenda Foundation, the sponsors of the study we just reported on, have asked media outlets and universities all over the country to join them in just such an effort.

But the fact remains that the nation's failure to act as the Japanese and the Germans acted earlier is not so much the result of policy failure or even a lack of vision as it is of a broader, deeper problem—the failure of the American people to see there *is* a problem. That is why we have no consensus on the direction that policy should take. That is why our frog is coming to a slow boil. It is not that we lack a crisis; it is that we fail to see it.

But there is not much time. If we continue as we are, real wages will fall much faster in the next twenty years than they have in the last twenty. As that happens, and the proportion of our population in the work force continues to fall, tax revenue will fall even as tax rates continue to increase, and it will be harder and harder to reverse course, because the investment capital required to educate and train our front-line workers will be increasingly hard to come by, exactly the situation many states now face. If we do not change course before 2010, when the baby-boomers—77 million people—begin turning sixty-five and burdening our pension and health system resources, we could truly reach a point of no return.

If ever there was a time to make the choice for a high-skill, high-wage economy, it is now.

We have tried to show in this chapter the scope of the problem facing the United States and its leaders. The challenge is to move the country as a whole from a perception of reality that has remained essentially unchanged through most of this century to one quite different, and by doing so, to create the basis for a new consensus that will permit construction of an economy based on human-resource capitalism. This is not primarily a problem of policy or even of institutional design. It is a problem in politics—the setting of new priorities, the building of new coalitions, and the reallocation of resources that can only come from new priorities ordered by new coalitions. We see this as the central problem, and the greatest opportunity in domestic politics for the next decade. The next chapter shows how the political leadership has begun to redefine the skills problem for the American people. In doing so, it provides grounds for hope that the frog may yet wriggle out of the pot.

America does not lack powerful examples of good policy or effective programs. We have some of each that are as impressive as any in the world. What we lack are systems—systems that are pervasive, woven together into a universal fabric of public policy and institutional action that support human-resource capitalism. That is what we lack and our competitors have. Our object in the remainder of this book is to present a set of ideas that will make it possible to build the political foundation for such a system. These proposals are neither conservative nor liberal, neither Republican nor Democratic. They are pragmatic and humane. They provide hope for those left out, but none for those who will not help themselves. They call for high standards, but provide a means for all to achieve them. They call for less bureaucracy but more accountability. They would empower workers, but hold them to a higher standard of responsibility. They would make education much more interesting but demand far more of students. They would greatly reduce programs intended only for the poor, but greatly expand real opportunities for the disadvantaged. They call for more government spending on education, but they are not founded on the belief that more money alone will solve the problems in our schools. In all these ways and many more, they are intended to show how new coalitions can be formed to solve the central problems addressed in this book. Without a new politics, there will be no solution.

CHAPTER 6

Facing the Challenge— At Last

"If an unfriendly foreign power had attempted to impose on America the mediocre educational performance that exists today, we might well have viewed it as an act of war."[1] With these words, the National Commission on Excellence in Education issued in the spring of 1983 what was surely one of the most effective calls to arms the country has ever heard on the subject of education, inaugurating what may prove to be the most vigorous education reform era the United States has ever seen. Eight years old as this is written, it shows no signs of flagging. It seems, if anything, to be gathering strength.

While it succeeded brilliantly in focusing the attention of the nation on education, the commission's report, *A Nation at Risk: The Imperative for Educational Reform,* was flawed with respect to both its analysis of the problem and its prescription for solving it. As the commission saw it, the problem was decline from standards once met, brought about by a dismantling of "essential support systems" formerly in place and by a "rising tide of mediocrity" in the schools. Implicitly, the schools had once been excellent and the educators were at fault for permitting, even encouraging, the dismantling of the foundations of that excellence.

Overall, the report identified two key imperatives: first, standards had fallen a long way from what they had once been and must be restored; and second, those responsible for this "falling away" from the former standards, the school professionals, not least the teachers, had to be made to toe the line and shape up.

Many state and local policymakers responded in kind.[2] Graduation requirements and college entrance requirements were raised. Basic skills tests were administered to teachers and those who did not pass were threatened with dismissal. Efforts were made to identify those (presumably few) teachers who had the ability to teach well, and merit bonuses were offered to them as an inducement to others to improve their performance. States greatly expanded their student testing programs, mostly in the basic skills, and districts and schools showing the worst performance on these tests, almost invariably those enrolling high proportions of low-income and minority students, were told to shape up under the threat that their managements would be replaced. On the whole, policymakers responded to the crises by getting tough on the educators—and their unions—thought to be responsible for the mess.

The educators were hurt and angry at the criticism being leveled at the schools. *A Nation at Risk* and other reports, they said, had persuaded the public that student performance had suffered a catastrophic decline in recent years and their authors were holding educators accountable for that decline. But they pointed out that the data revealed a much more complicated picture. There were real declines in certain indicators of performance for high-school students, most notably in the scores on the Scholastic Aptitude Tests (SATs).[3] But a substantial part of that decline had occurred because many more students were taking the SATs, and other tests that purported to measure the same qualities, including other tests of aptitude for college, showed much more modest declines. More to the point, other measures revealed impressive improvements in the same period for poor and minority students (surely, the educators said, a major achievement for the beleaguered system), real improvements for elementary students, and modest gains for those in the middle grades.* On balance, the educators argued, the record evened out, with gains in some areas and losses in others. There was certainly no cause for the hue and cry getting underway.† To the extent that

*Gordon Berlin and Andrew Sum, in *Toward a More Perfect Union*, published by the Ford Foundation in 1988, reanalyzed several reports issued by the National Assessment of Educational Progress to show trends in achievement for several minority groups in our schools, compared with the white majority. The results support dramatically the earlier contention of many educators that the performance of some groups not only did not decline, but improved substantially. They examined changes in reading proficiency from 1971 to 1984 for nine-year-olds, thirteen-year-olds, and seventeen-year-olds. During that period, the reading proficiency of disadvantaged urban nine-year-olds improved 16.6 percent; for disadvantaged urban thirteen-year-olds, 7.2 percent; and for disadvantaged urban seventeen-year-olds, 6.5 percent. The change in the same period for all white thirteen-year-olds was 5.7 percent, for black thirteen-year-olds, 19.1 percent, and for Hispanic thirteen-year-olds, 10.1 percent. These are very large changes, larger than the far more frequently mentioned declines in SAT scores.
†These points were made by several leading educators in the months following release of *A Nation at Risk*, but it was not until three years later that the argument was confirmed in detail in Dan Koretz's study, *Trends in Educational Achievement*, released by the Congressional Budget Office (CBO) in April 1986. Koretz reported a decline in a whole range of test scores through the sixties and seventies in private as well as public schools in the United States and Canada. The decline, greater in the upper than the lower grades, was immediately followed in the mid-seventies (long before *A Nation at Risk* was released) by a rise that continued into the eighties. For young children, the rise more than wiped out the previous decline. The gains for minority and poor children were considerably greater than for children from more advantaged backgrounds, narrowing, though by no means closing the gap. None of this, of course, suggests that all is well. But it does confirm the view of the educators that the public view of steady decline toward mediocrity was simply wrong. In a subsequent study, *Educational Achievement: Explanations and Implications of Recent Trends*, released by

performance had actually declined, they said, it was due at least as much to parents' inattention to their children, the advance of poverty among the young, the phenomenal growth in the use of television as an automated babysitter, and the lack of support for teachers among parents, as it was to anything they had done or not done themselves.

To these educators, and to many people deeply concerned about the prospects for our minority and low-income children, the call for educational excellence looked like a thinly veiled argument for shifting educational priorities from the needs of the disadvantaged to a renewed focus on the needs of the elite. The reformers responded by saying that standards for all had fallen and all, not least the disadvantaged, would be well served by restoring the standards of the past.

Teachers saw the use of basic skills tests to decide who could teach as an insult to people who held master's degrees and regarded themselves as professionals. They viewed the pay-for-performance plans that had been put in place as thinly disguised methods for allowing school administrators once again to reward the loyal and punish the disloyal. Deeply angry, and increasingly alienated from a public they saw as interested only in scapegoating them, they dug in for the long haul.

Arthur Wise captured the spirit of the time in the title of his book, *Legislated Learning.*[4] According to the consensus of the 1980s, the educators had allowed the country to slip into mediocrity and they would be made to feel the country's sense of outrage. The school establishment was at fault and it was time for tough measures. If the educators could not or would not do the job themselves, then the public, acting through its elected representatives, would spell out in detail the new rules, whether they liked it or not.

The symbol and guiding spirit of this stage of the reform movement was William Bennett, the second secretary of education in the Reagan administration. In a major departure from the posture of every education commissioner and secretary before him, Bennett abandoned any pretense of identification with the professional education establishment and went on the attack with evident relish, making clear his belief that the deep educational problems of the nation were the fault of the establishment itself, an establishment in his view far more concerned with preserving its power and position and advancing the interests of its members than with the welfare of the students.

But while many could recognize the truth of many of the Secretary's observa-

---

the CBO in August 1987, Koretz examines the probable causes of the trends he described in the first study. Three points are of prime importance. First, much of the decline in SAT scores, the indicator whose decline most alarmed the public, was caused by increased numbers of people taking the test, and therefore cannot be correctly interpreted as signalling a catastrophic decline in the competence of American high-school students. Second, demographics played a significant role in the decline and subsequent rise: the baby boom produced crowded schools with unfavorable pupil-teacher ratios and the subsequent baby bust made possible a real improvement in those ratios. Third, none of the improvement in student performance can be attributed to the policy measures taken after release of *A Nation at Risk*, such as teacher competency tests or raised graduation standards, since the rise had actually begun several years before those measures were instituted.

tions on the problems of the present, he failed to present a compelling view of the future or of a way to reach a future worth striving for. In fact, Secretary Bennett's view of a desirable future looked suspiciously like a romantic return to an idealized past. The first stage of the reform movement led only to a cul de sac—a deepening antagonism between professional educators and the public, and a vision of the future that simply turned the clock back.

The reformers had badly misunderstood the problem, and, as a result, their program had little chance of success. If you believe that the problem is that performance has declined from a standard once met, then the challenge is to restore standards that were once in place. But if the problem is that circumstances require a much higher standard than has ever been met before, then reinstating former policies will certainly lead to failure.

The educators were partly right. On balance, the performance of the system had not deteriorated in anything like the measure that the reformers claimed; in fact, it had changed little over the decades. But that was in fact the problem. The requirements the world was placing on school graduates were dramatically higher, but performance had stayed the same.

Consider the real challenge facing our schools. We noted in chapter 5 that the South Koreans have achieved dropout rates of under 10 percent and virtually universal mastery of basic skills among their graduates, standards far beyond any that this country has ever achieved. But matching the South Korean achievement would simply qualify Americans for South Korean wages and hours when the world market for front-line labor reaches equilibrium—wages one-tenth of what American front-line labor makes now and nearly twice as many hours a year as we now work.

To maintain our current standard of living, we would have to do far better than that. As we have shown, the only way for the United States to maintain and improve its standard of living would be to embrace the new high-performance work organizations in every sector of the economy, and that would require us to make sure that the vast majority of our high-school graduates could take on tasks now assigned only to managers and professionals in our workplaces. That implies a standard way above the South Korean standard. It means that virtually all of our students will have to achieve at a level now met by no more than 15 percent of our high-school graduates. It means that educational performance in the United States will have to be at least as high as that of the Japanese and the leading European countries. We pointed out earlier that many experts believe that the performance of the average Japanese high-school graduate in his or her native language, mathematics, and science is equal to or exceeds the performance in those subjects of our average four-year college graduate, and that half of all Japanese high-school graduates perform as well or better in mathematics than the top 2 percent of graduates in the United States. The idea that all the United States need do is restore the status quo ante of the 1950s is simply wrong. Rather, most analysts now agree that the chang-

ing workplace demands not simply higher levels of mastery of the core subjects, but a different kind of education.[5]

We can sum up the emerging consensus on the skills needed to power a
modern economy as follows:

- a high capacity for abstract, conceptual thinking;
- the ability to apply that capacity for abstract thought to complex real-
  world problems—including problems that involve the use of scientific and
  technical knowledge—that are nonstandard, full of ambiguities, and have
  more than one right answer, as jobs change in response to a constantly
  changing market and the opportunities provided by advancing technology;
- the capacity to function effectively in an environment in which communication skills are vital—in work groups, through the use of computer-based
  systems that require real mastery of written English, and by reading
  technical manuals that necessarily presume a high degree of both reading
  ability and technical competence;
- the ability to work easily and well with others, and the skill required to
  resolve conflicts that arise with colleagues and assume responsibility for
  the work that needs to be done without requiring much supervision.

If these are the requirements that those now going into the work force must
meet, what can we say about how well the schools are preparing them for the
future? As we saw in chapter 5, whether one judges by comparison to the
performance of other countries or by comparison to the demands of the modern
workplace, school graduates fall far short of what is needed and what others have
achieved. With respect to mathematics and science, the top fifth of our students
are able to match only the median performance of our most able competitors, far
below the performance of their top fifth, and our bottom fifth clearly places in the
lowest ranks of all the countries tested, both the advanced countries and those
that are newly industrialized. Our curriculum reflects the needs of the economy
of fifty years ago as does the performance of the average student.

Yet our students, too, can learn the material they need to learn. The much
publicized success of Jaime Escalante in getting low-income Hispanic students to
take and pass the Advanced Placement Examination in calculus is but one of
many examples showing that students long thought to be capable of only minimal achievement can in fact achieve at the highest levels.[6]

It is worth dwelling on this example. Reasonable people may differ as to
whether it is important that all American students learn calculus. But everyone
agrees that calculus is a tough subject. What Escalante showed is that the
"worst" of our students can perform at levels equal to those of the best students
in the world. That means that virtually *all* students can perform at levels significantly above those at which they are now performing, and almost all can perform
as well as the best in the world.

Setting our sights on cutting our dropout rates in half and achieving universal mastery of basic skills—which is the de facto target in our urban districts and many other school systems—is to set a target of Third World wage levels. The fact is that if the American economy succeeds over the next ten or twenty years, most people who have—but have no more than—the basic skills will be unemployable.

There is another inescapable fact. By almost all indices, the poor and minority people who live in our inner cities and impoverished rural areas already live in Third World countries, in terms of health, nutrition, housing, and especially education and skills. They have long since been left behind by the seemingly flourishing economy around them. Even when general unemployment drops below the frictional unemployment rate, their unemployment rates are many times that. Good jobs go begging, because this large segment of the population is not qualified for any but the most marginal jobs. As the shortage of people with the qualifications for good jobs grows, the wage rates for those jobs go up. As the number of unskilled and semiskilled jobs dwindles in relation to the ever-increasing supply of people seeking them, the wage rates for those jobs decline. Thus the gap between rich and poor increases, the capacity of the unskilled to improve their lot declines, and the number of hopeless rises year by year. Big-city employers, apart from those who cannot leave for high-skill locations, have little incentive to hire applicants with Third World skills who cannot be employed at Third World wage rates. That is the harsh reality of the current labor market.

In our impoverished rural areas, the lack of skills among the general population makes it almost impossible to attract any but the lowest-paying industries and difficult to keep those that are already there. The old economic development formula so successfully employed by low-wage states in the past—low wages, no unions, tax rebates, free or low-cost developed land, and free vocational training—can now be employed to much greater advantage by much lower-cost countries beyond our borders. The only hope those states now have is to upgrade enormously the skills of their people. They will be either high-wage, high-skill states or economic basket cases. There is no other option.

The fact that all the evidence shows that poor and minority youngsters can achieve at world-class levels is therefore crucial. Whatever stands in the way of bringing our entire population up to world-class standards, it is not some inherent limitation of the youngsters themselves. It lies in the system we use to educate them.

So far, we have concentrated on the economic consequences of poor educational performance, for individuals and the society as a whole. To many educators, such an argument debases education, making it only an instrument for providing employers with the cogs in the wheel they need to make a profit. That view is outdated. For decades, as we have shown, employers in fact mainly needed workers who required only a modicum of skill, who would be content with the most boring and repetitious work, and who would carry out whatever instructions they were given. It is easy to be sympathetic with the serious educators who rejected the minimalist demands of such employers. But what employers need now are workers who bring the kinds of skills that such educators have always said they want to develop in their students. For the first time in this century, those skills are needed in the great majority of workers. This is a crucial departure from the past. The demand for a highly skilled work force is in fact a call for educators to realize what have always been their highest aspirations.

But there are other implications that are no less serious. It is becoming less possible with every passing year for the general population to assess accurately the meaning for them and for their country of the political, social, and technological changes that are taking place in a world in which faraway events can have consequences as far-reaching as any nearby. As Jefferson observed, the effectiveness of our form of government is absolutely dependent on an informed citizenry, able to comprehend, interpret, and act on the information they get. To the extent that they cannot do so, our democracy is in jeopardy. And it is also true that our failure to match world-class educational performance robs our people of the capacity to fully enjoy what this remarkable world has to offer, in particular their capacity to develop their intellectual and aesthetic abilities.

Only a dramatic improvement in the skills of our people can turn this situation around. Our task is to shift the whole curve of American educational performance radically upward, and at the same time to close substantially the gap between the bottom and the top of the curve. For the first time in American history, we have to have an education system that really educates everyone, our poor and our minorities as well as our most fortunate.

Given the standard we must meet, the use of dropout rates and scores on standardized tests of basic skills to measure the success of our schools is an insidious form of unintended fraud. Just getting kids in school will not be enough to match our competitors. Just mastering the basic skills, as these skills are measured by the tests, will condemn these students to Third World wages at best and unemployment at worst. Minimum competency is institutionalized mediocrity.

Saying that we must raise the whole curve of American students' performance and greatly reduce the gap between the best performance and worst is to indicate a direction but stops a long way short of setting explicit standards. In fact, the United States has never officially embraced a set of explicit educational standards, much less a strategy for achieving them. Our Constitution makes no mention of a federal role in education, and the states have jealously guarded their right to make policy in this area. There has never been any mechanism for setting and enforcing national goals in education. This was hardly an oversight. Unlike the citizens of other nations, we thought we would be far better off if the national government had little or nothing to say about this potent mechanism for shaping our citizens' thoughts and values.

It is this that makes the events of 1989 and 1990 quite remarkable. In the space of a few short months, the nation's political leaders agreed on the goals that would guide construction of a comprehensive national human-resources development system, and began to elaborate a set of strategies for achieving them.

Galvanized by the poor performance of our education system and the growing realization that dramatic measures might be required to prevent low educational achievement from crippling economic performance, in September 1989 the president asked the governors to join him in an extraordinary summit meeting on education at the University of Virginia in Charlottesville. This was only the third time in the history of the United States that a president has summoned the governors to a meeting, and the first time that the topic was education. In a joint declaration issued at the end of the meeting, the governors and the president agreed to work together on developing a set of educational goals for the nation.

In his state-of-the-union address on January 31, 1990, President Bush made the first public statement of those goals. That statement was further elaborated by the governors when they met at their annual midwinter meeting in Washington in February 1990. Recognizing that goals alone are not enough to drive the fundamental changes necessary to realize them, both the governors and the White House announced at that meeting that they would work together to agree on a set of strategies for implementing the goals and would establish a high-level panel that would monitor the nation's progress toward achieving them, report periodically to the public, and keep the issue high on the national agenda.

Many educators at the time viewed this entire process as motivated only by shallow political considerations, an attempt by the politicians to ride the wave of public attention to the education issue. But no one who was present at that February meeting could doubt the seriousness of purpose of those who were there. The Governors' Education Task Force met the day before the official opening of the meeting. Not only were all the task force members present, but they were outnumbered by governors who had not been assigned to it. At most such meetings, the governors come and go, relying on their staffers to keep track of the proceedings and tell them when an important vote is coming up. Other attendees typically crowd the back of the room, carrying on conversations and paying little attention to the proceedings. But in this case, the governors came early and kept their seats. There was hardly a whisper from the onlookers. The only side conversations occurred when Roger Porter, the president's chief domestic policy adviser, and Governors Campbell, Clinton, and Gardner left the table to negotiate a troublesome point before bringing it back to their colleagues.

There were deep divisions between the White House and the governors on many specific issues of substance and procedure. It must surely have been tempting to both sides to play these differences out in the press, which almost certainly would have happened if the parties had only been seeking short-term political advantage from the occasion. But it did not. They knew they were working on a task of great importance to the nation. Guided by a patient and determined Governor Bill

Clinton, the chair of the task force, they overcame what often seemed insuperable partisan and institutional differences to reach agreement.

The skeptics were certain that neither the White House nor the governors had any real intention of holding themselves accountable for actually doing anything to achieve the goals they had agreed on, that even if some among them were serious on this score, the differences between the White House and the governors would prevent the creation of any but the most emasculated form of public monitoring mechanism. But when the governors met for their annual summer meeting at Mobile, Alabama at the end of July, they emerged with an agreement with the White House on the structure of a monitoring panel that had the potential for becoming a powerful influence on the course of American education.

The panel was composed of six governors, four senior administration officials appointed by the president, and four members of Congress, serving ex officio. The president appointed John Sununu, White House chief of staff; Roger Porter, assistant to the president for economic and domestic policy; Richard Darman, director of the Office of Management and Budget; and Lauro Cavazos, secretary of education. Governor Booth Gardner, chairman of the National Governors' Association, appointed Governor Roy Romer of Colorado, Governor Carroll Campbell of South Carolina, Governor Evan Bayh of Indiana, Governor Terry Branstead of Iowa, Governor John Ashcroft of Missouri, and himself to the panel and named Governor Romer as chairman. The congressional members include Senate majority leader George Mitchell, Senate minority leader Robert Dole, House majority leader Richard Gephardt, and House minority leader Robert Michael. The members of Congress were deeply angered that they had been given only a nonvoting role in the work of this panel. Nevertheless, this was a formidable group indeed to deal with an issue that, up to then, had been left to the individual states.

Not long after he was appointed to chair the panel, Governor Romer remarked to the authors of this book that he was certain that this assignment could prove to be the most important of his career. He has since thrown himself into the task with extraordinary determination and ability.

The seriousness with which Governor Romer addressed his assignment has been matched by the reaction of the country to the goals statement. Despite the initial skepticism about the national goal-setting process, educators all over the country have held meetings, issued statements, written journal articles, and found a myriad of other ways to consider how they might elaborate on the goals and make a contribution to their achievement. The Mathematical Sciences Board and the National Council of Teachers of School Mathematics have produced detailed goals for school mathematics that reflect broad consensus among school-teachers, university mathematicians, teacher educators, employers, and others. The American Association for the Advancement of Science has organized the scientific societies to produce a comparable set of goals for school science. The Secretary of Labor has formed a commission under former labor secretary Bill

Brock to tell the country what skills students need to succeed at work. The Council of Great City Schools has designed an elaborate procedure for involving people nationwide in developing a consensus on goals for urban education that build on the goals structure laid down by the president and the governors.

School districts, state governments, associations of school officials, teachers' organizations, and others all over the country show every sign of taking these goals as the starting point for their long-range planning. The Business Round-table, arguably the nation's most prestigious business organization, has assembled a special task force on education, chaired by John Akers, the chief executive officer of IBM, and committed itself to a ten-year effort to work with the governors and the White House to help the country achieve the new goals. Many other organizations have made similar commitments. It is hardly the case that the battle has been won. It is not at all clear that its nature is widely understood. But there is every sign that it has at long last been joined.

These are the six goals adopted by the governors and the president:[7]

- By the year 2000, all children in America will start school ready to learn;
- By the year 2000, the high-school graduation rate will increase to at least 90 percent;
- By the year 2000, American students will leave grades four, eight, and twelve having demonstrated competency in challenging subject matter including English, mathematics, science, history, and geography, and every school in America will ensure that all students learn to use their minds well, so they may be prepared for responsible citizenship, further learning, and productive employment in our modern economy;
- By the year 2000, U.S. students will be first in the world in mathematics and science achievement;
- By the year 2000, every adult American will be literate and will possess the knowledge and skills necessary to compete in a global economy and exercise the rights and responsibilities of citizenship;
- By the year 2000, every school in America will be free of drugs and violence and will offer a disciplined environment conducive to learning;

When the governors met in Mobile at the end of July 1990, they issued a report laying out strategies for reaching those goals. They were very much aware of the enormity of the task they had set for themselves and the country. They had observed at their meeting the preceding February that "meeting [these goals] will require that the performance of our highest achievers be boosted to levels that equal or exceed the performance of the best students anywhere. What our best students can achieve now, our average students must be able to achieve by the end of the century." In July they declared that "to achieve the new national goals, we must invent a new education system," and then laid out the criteria that system would have to meet:

- The system must be lifelong, recognizing that lifelong learning begins at birth, not at school, and continues throughout life, and does not end at graduation;
- The system must focus on prevention, avoiding damage to young children and removing barriers to learning for all, rather than paying the higher price of compensating for preventable learning difficulties after they develop;
- The system must be performance-oriented, with an unwavering commitment to achieving results rather than to maintaining existing procedures, practices, or institutions;
- The system must be flexible. Professionals should decide how best to help each individual achieve at high levels, rather than being told what to do and how to do it by distant authorities;
- The system and those who work in it must be accountable for the results they achieve. There must be real rewards for high performance and significant consequences for failure;
- The system must attract and retain talented professionals and ensure that they receive continued support and professional development;
- The system must provide meaningful choices to students, parents, and adult learners by recognizing and accommodating their varying learning needs and styles.[8]

How far the nation had come in the seven years since *A Nation at Risk* had been released! The 1983 report had said the problem was decline and it could be solved by restoring lost standards; the 1990 report said the problem was a failure to reach targets to which the country had never before aspired. The 1983 report had suggested that the reform effort could succeed if confined to the schools; the 1990 report said that success would be ours only if we addressed problems reaching far beyond the schools, ranging from child nutrition to adult literacy. The 1983 report implied that school professionals were the problem and the answer was to get tough; the 1990 report said that they were a vital resource and needed to be accorded a degree of professional autonomy they have never had before in order to get the job done. The 1983 report implied that there was a trade-off between equity and excellence and the nation needed to resolve it in favor of excellence; the 1990 report plainly said that the nation can and must have both. The 1983 report accepted the structure of the system as given; the 1990 report said the system is the problem and must be restructured from the ground up to provide very different incentives to the professionals who work in it.

In seven years, the nature of the problem as well as the framework for solution had been almost wholly redefined. No less important, the nation's political leaders had taken responsibility for meeting the challenge in a way that is without precedent in the entire history of the United States. We will make it plain how truly daunting that challenge is. But the growing consensus around the new definition of the problem and the general shape of the solution is an asset that cannot be overstated.

The United States is still far behind Germany and Japan. There is still no consensus on the need to focus economic and social policy on securing a high-wage future. We still do not even see the need for a coherent labor-market policy. Reducing poverty among the young is still viewed here as an obligation that can be put off rather than as a vital investment essential to our future. We have yet to agree on the need to build a system that really meets the needs of those not headed for a baccalaureate. Employers have not even thought about taking on a substantial share of the responsibility for building the skills of young people. Few business leaders are committed to the introduction of high-performance work organization. Nor is there broad agreement yet that a coherent national strategy for human-resources development is the key to economic success. And the president has yet to display the kind of leadership on these issues that he displayed to a dazzled world in the Middle East crisis.

But one can see in the goals structure and strategy statement developed by the president and the governors the outlines of a program comprehensive enough to match the problems we face and ambitious enough to meet the challenge.

PART IV

The New American System: Strategies for High Performance

CHAPTER 7

The Demand for Excellence: Can—and Will—Employers and Labor Lead the Way?

For many people, David Kearns personifies business leaders' commitment to the reform of public education. Coauthor with Denis Doyle of an influential book on the subject[1]—the only one we know of to be written by a business executive—Kearns has stumped the nation from one end to the other. This is not surprising, for Kearns's sense of urgency about education reform grows directly from his experience at the helm of Xerox during what will surely go down in business history as one of the most remarkable turnarounds in the fortunes of any firm.[2]

Xerox's rise to prominence is one of the great success stories of American business. It began in 1937, when Chester Carlson filed the basic patent for what he called electrophotography. For the next nine years, he tried without success to sell his idea to a roster of some of the most famous names in American business. In 1944, he got the Battelle Memorial Institute to begin developing the process, but it was not until 1947 that Joe Wilson, CEO of the Haloid Corporation, a small company in the photographic paper business, decided to bet its future on Carlson's vision. The first Xerox copier, the 914, would not be announced until 1959, twelve years later. It had cost more than Haloid's total earnings from 1950 to 1959 to develop. And it was a wild success—arguably the single most successful product in our nation's history. Xerox hit the Fortune 500 in just two years, and reached the billion-dollar mark in sales faster than any American company had before. By the early 1980s it was one of the forty largest companies in the United States.

And then it fell out of bed. The parallel with the automobile industry is telling. For years, the Big Three auto makers had judged their prospects by looking at one another, all of them participants in a closed market that they had virtually to themselves. When Volkswagen and then the Japanese entered the low end of the market and did well, the Big Three were not worried, being willing to cede the low end of the market to the newcomers in the belief that the more profitable middle and high end was theirs forever. Only when the unbelievable happened and they were on the ropes did they come to believe that they were in trouble. By then it was too late, and their market share has steadily eroded ever since.

Xerox's slide began the same way. Though the Japanese had been challenging the firm at the low end of the copier market throughout the 1970s with increasing success, Xerox paid little attention. Their executives' primary concern was with IBM and Kodak, two premier American firms that had gone into the high end of the business, the latter with real success. But while Xerox looked the other way, the Japanese walked off with the prize. Between 1976 and 1982, Xerox's world-wide share of the copier business dropped from 82 percent to less than 20 percent. Though the company still dominated the high-volume copier market, it had been decimated in the low-volume, small copier segment of the market and very badly wounded in the mid-volume range, the source of 40 percent of its revenues and profits. But that is where the similarity to America's auto manufacturers ends. By 1983, the slide had been stopped. In 1984, Xerox had 36 percent of the mid-volume market, up from less than 20 percent two years earlier. It was not out of the woods, nor would it be for years to come, but its prospects were much brighter. To get there, Kearns had had to reinvent the company.

Time and again throughout the 1970s, individuals in Xerox had warned of the coming debacle, but no one had listened. Profits had actually continued to climb even as market share eroded. As Peter McColough, CEO through those years, put it, "Only when they saw it was necessary, that their jobs were on the line, other people's jobs were on the line, did they respond."[3]

The shock came when the firm began to take a close look at the Japanese competition. As the data came in, they told a frightening tale. The Japanese were producing machines at half the cost of comparable Xerox machines. Their price to the customer—including manufacturing, marketing, shipping, distribution, and sales—equaled Xerox's cost just to manufacture a comparable machine. Lower unit-labor costs accounted for only a tiny fraction of this difference. It took the Japanese half the design time and half the people to move a product from the drawing table to deliverable product. Most remarkable, the Japanese cost and time-to-market advantages had been achieved without compromising quality; in fact, the Japanese product was better matched with what the customers wanted. The first reaction to the initial data was disbelief. Teams of manufacturing executives and engineers were dispatched to Japan to disprove the first reports; they not only confirmed them but found that, if anything, they understated the Japanese advantage in virtually every stage of the business. The second reaction was despair. Many at top levels in Xerox believed it was impossible to catch up.

Kearns knew better. He had three good starting points: a team of executives just back from Europe who understood the Japanese threat and thought they could meet it; Tony Kobayashi, CEO of Fuji-Xerox in Japan, who had defied Xerox top brass during the 1970s to begin manufacturing copiers in that country and had gone on to win the Deming Prize; and a team of just seven people who had operated independently of Xerox's massive bureaucracy to design the Memorywriter and take IBM's lead in electronic office typewriters away from them. W. Edwards Deming, an American, had pioneered the development of the principles of quality. Unable to get a hearing for his ideas in the United States, he had found a ready audience in Japan. Adapting the Deming principles of quality management to Xerox's needs with a lot of advice from Kobayashi, Kearns used his new management team to drive those principles into the organization.

Ed Finein, a member of the engineering group that helped turn the company around, emphasizes four components of Kearns's strategy in explaining its success: competitive benchmarking, pushing responsibility down, and emphasis on quality and customer satisfaction.

Xerox got hurt because it forgot to measure itself against the competition— something it will never do again. The basic idea of competitive benchmarking is simplicity itself: to identify one's most effective competitors and achieve better quality at lower cost. The purpose is to be *dantotsu,* Japanese for "the best of the best." Kearns did not believe the Japanese were ten feet tall and he did not believe in excuses. He thought that if his people could figure out just how the Japanese did it, they could also figure out how to do it a little bit better.

But the power of the idea lies in the details. Everyone makes some sort of general comparisons with other organizations in the same business. Xerox goes much further. Every department at Xerox is expected to know what organization in the entire world is best at the function that department performs. And it is expected to measure the performance of that competitor in all of the relevant dimensions, find out how the competitor does it, and improve on it. Benchmarking is never finished; it is repeated over and over again, because the competition never stands still.

Actually, the word "competition" is misleading. Xerox and L. L. Bean, the Maine-based mail-order firm, are obviously not competing in the same market. One of the keys to the success of benchmarking as an organizational change strategy is that it is done not by a central department of professional "benchmarkers," but by each department for itself. The distribution department at Xerox identified L. L. Bean as the best distributor in the United States, on many indices. Managers studied Bean's operations carefully, discovered that it did not require full warehouse automation but instead used software designed to minimize the the time it took the "pickers" to fill the orders, and then rewrote their own software to get the same outstanding results.

Benchmarking is used to compare quality of product or service, the amount of time it takes to perform a function, the cost of various operations, the amount of indirect labor needed in relation to direct—or front-line—labor, and much, much more. It is used not only to describe where the other organization is now but, on the basis of the rates of improvement observed, where it is likely to be in five years. Benchmarking takes the mystery out of a competitor's success by revealing how the competitor does it, and it helps every department at Xerox set explicit targets for improvement in every dimension of its operation. It is a constant stimulus to excel, for every single person in the organization.

The second key to Xerox's turnaround was the move to push decision making downward in the organization. At the beginning of the 1980s, the company had enormous management and engineering bureaucracies in Stamford, Connecticut, El Segundo, California, and Rochester, New York. All decision lines went to the very top. Everyone could say no, but very few could say yes. Checkers checked checkers who checked other checkers. Because everyone was responsible, no one could be held responsible.

The benchmarking studies showed that one reason for the Japanese cost advantage lay in far lower ratios of managers to workers. The experience of the seven-person team that had beat IBM in the electronic typewriter business showed that lean and mean meant competitive. Kearns knew his problems lay in management, not with the workers. "Let's face it," he said, "the poor productivity of white-collar people puts blue-collar people out of work."[4] Between 1981 and 1983, the work force of 117,000 worldwide had been trimmed by 16,000, for a cost savings of $600 million a year. Most of the cuts had come from the ranks of management, engineering, marketing, and support staff.

But these savings, though important, were mainly a means to an end— pushing decisions down in the organization. Product groups were set up and chief engineers with the title of vice president put in charge of them. From that level down, performance objectives were set through the benchmarking process, and the managers at each level were given great discretion to decide how to use the available resources to get the job done without checking with those above them. For the first time, key middle managers could be held unambiguously accountable for the entire success or failure of a product because they had direct control over the entire product cycle. The engineering establishment was up in arms, holding that the decentralized administration would destroy Xerox's principal competitive advantage, its top-flight engineering capacity. But Kearns went ahead anyway.

Moving decision making downward did not apply simply to the top and the middle of the organization. The principle went right to the bottom, to include the front-line workers. Xerox's production workers had been members of the Amalgamated Clothing and Textile Workers Union since 1937. The union played a critical role in the corporation's early efforts to involve employees in the redesign of the firm. Turning tradition on its head, management invited its labor leaders in and gave them all the information they had on the nature of the challenge the company faced. They set up the competition's machines on the shop floor and gave teams of production people the benchmarking data. Before they shut down an uncompetitive facility or contracted out work, they gave the workers a chance to figure out how to save enough money to make the facility competitive, keeping the jobs in-house. And the ideas poured out. When new plants were built, shop-floor people were asked to participate in the design of the production operation to make it as efficient as possible.

"When we hired a production worker in the old days, we used to say crudely that we hired his hands and not his head," according to John Foley, then vice president of personnel. "Very frankly, what we are finding out is that there is an awful lot in his head."[5]

The third key to Xerox's turnaround was its commitment to the principles of quality management. Fuji-Xerox, half of whose shares are controlled by Xerox and half by Fuji Film, started out as a marketing arm for Xerox machines run out of buildings at Fuji Film, a company that had practiced Deming's methods of quality management for years. Fuji-Xerox saw the future coming in 1973, the time of the first great oil shock, six years before Xerox would face the music in 1980. Cash-starved customers in Japan turned away from the Xerox copiers to buy competitors' products at half the price. The company decided it had to build its own low-end machines if it was to survive, exceeding Xerox's quality and matching or beating Japan's prices. Tony Kobayashi, vice president of the firm and the son of Fuji's CEO, launched the New Xerox Movement, a determined effort to incorporate quality principles in the manufacturing program. His aim was to launch a competitive product in half the time and at half the cost of the typical Xerox product. Defying all the predictions of Xerox headquarters, he succeeded. He then challenged his staff to win the Deming Prize. Responding, they would punch out after a full day and come back for another eight hours on their own time, day after day. They won the prize, while increasing both profits and revenues.

David Kearns, the future Xerox CEO, made his first visit to Fuji-Xerox in 1975, and would return regularly thereafter. What he learned made all the difference when his time came to run the firm. Kearns confesses that he "did not understand the real meaning" of total quality control when he first talked to Kobayashi about the concept. "They meant running their company in a very different way. . . . As I understood more . . . that became an important motivator, a real knowledge base for change at Xerox."[6]

Kearn's version of the New Xerox Movement was to be called Leadership Through Quality. Many books have been written about the quality process, and we will not try to present a full summary here. What is important for our purposes is how Xerox defines quality and what it does to achieve it.

"Quality" means no defects at many American companies. But Xerox's definition of the term is much more powerful; there it means meeting the customers' requirements, no more and no less. Xerox employees all over the firm will tell you that it does not mean giving the customer a Cadillac at Cadillac prices if the customer really wants a Chevy. Quality by that more limited definition is not produced by weeding out the defective products at the end; rather, it is built in at every stage of product design, product development, and production. That means that quality is not the responsibility of quality inspectors; it is everyone's responsibility.

It sounds simple. Implementing it, as Kearns observed, means managing in an entirely different way. This is true in a myriad of ways. We will single out only two: defining the customers and making everyone responsible for quality.

At Xerox, anyone who depends on the quality of your work is your customer, inside the firm and out. Ed Finein tells an interesting story to illustrate this point. One of the firm's units is responsible for refurbishing machines that have been out on lease. Not long after the Leadership Through Quality program began, the operation in Chicago that was responsible for crating machines that had reached the end of their lease and shipping them back to Webster, New York, for refurbishing got a call from Webster. "We're not taking any more of your machines," the caller said. "There is more damage to the machine from your crating operation than from customer wear and tear." "What do you mean," said Chicago, "you're Xerox just like us." "But we're your customer," said Webster, "and you are not meeting our needs." Later, Chicago called back and asked meekly if Webster would take a few machines "on consignment."[7] Outside the firm, the customer is not just the person who makes the decision to buy or lease. When Xerox first systematized its customer requirements program, management was amazed to find out that the people who actually had to operate the machines in the copy rooms had a hard time doing it for reasons that would have been perfectly obvious if anyone had ever bothered to think about it before. If you do not know your customers' requirements—inside or outside the firm—and are not working hard to meet them, then you do not belong at Xerox.

A crucial part of Leadership Through Quality has to do with the way problems get solved in the firm and how meetings are run, two functions that turn out to be closely related. Xerox has standardized a model of the generic problem-solving process for use throughout the corporation. One must, for example, be clear about what the facts are before a problem is analyzed and a solution is presented. There is a standardized meeting protocol. Anyone holding a meeting is expected, for example, to state its purposes clearly, lay out an agenda with times allocated for each major agenda element, and state what the outcomes of the meeting are expected to be. The convener is expected to check with the participants for their agreement on the agenda, and to appoint a facilitator to keep the meeting moving as well as a recorder to make sure that it is clear what has been concluded and who is to do what when the meeting ends.

It sounds banal. But it means that it is all right to say to the boss in a meeting, "You're telling us what the solution ought to be before we have agreed on what the problem is and analyzed its causes. Don't we need to go back to step one?" When it works right, it provides a means for everyone's views to be solicited and heard, for collective action and individual responsibility. Normally dominant voices have to make way for the reticent. The boss has to listen to the line worker. It makes for an environment in which everyone, at every level of the organization, feels—and is—valued. It creates settings in which people can feel, and in fact, be effective. Leadership Through Quality is best understood not as skill building, although it is that, but as a powerful instrument to change the culture of the entire organization.

Xerox's commitment to Leadership Through Quality is enormous. Kearns and the people who reported directly to him began the process by participating in six-and-one-half days of training, led by Kearns. The group then took on quality management projects as part of their training, including improving Corporate Management Committee meetings and streamlining quarterly operations reviews. Then the group members did the same with those who reported to them, and so on down the line. Everyone in the firm gets at least forty hours of this training, which is over and above the training in sales, marketing, service, and manufacturing that people used to get and still do. In 1985, Xerox spent more than $9 million on trainers. In the three prior years, the employee time committed to this training had a value of more than $70 million. By the end of 1988, all hundred thousand Xerox people had been trained in the quality tools. Top managers at Xerox during the early 1980s thought that Kearns was absolutely crazy spending so much time and money on process training when the company was in real danger of going down. But Kearns persisted. This training, and, most important, the change in corporate culture that it was meant to bring about, was a primary response to the threat.

We asked Ed Finein what happened to managers who met or exceeded their targets, but failed to engage in the quality process. Isn't the bottom line the only thing that matters in the end? Why should it matter how you get there? Finein replied that managers who met their targets but ignored the process often missed their salary increases or had them reduced. In fact, if they did not get on board Leadership Through Quality, they did not last long at Xerox. If managers succeeded at meeting their targets by bullying their staff, they would not be making the most of their staff's capacity and they would not be committed to meeting the customers' needs, and they were told they would not succeed at Xerox. As simple as that.

Xerox won the prestigious Malcolm Baldrige National Quality Award, America's answer to Japan's Deming Prize, in 1989, the last full year Kearns served as CEO. It was a fitting close to a brilliant term of service.

The whole Total Quality approach can be viewed as a plan to capture the energy, allegiance, and commitment of a firm's entire staff—especially its frontline employees—by seriously engaging them in a conscious, disciplined effort to improve every facet of the firm's operation. This is a stunning reversal of the Taylorist methods of work organization we described in earlier chapters, a point to which we will return later. One of the implications of such an approach, however, is that, unlike Taylorism, it assumes the capacity of the entire work force—not just senior management—to contribute effectively to the redesign of the firm and the steady improvement of its products, processes, and services. In a country dominated by the legacies of Taylorism, that is not a safe assumption to make.

Motorola has the same kind of single-minded commitment to the implementation of the Total Quality approach as Xerox, and actually managed to beat Xerox to the Baldrige Award by one year. Here is what Bill Wiggenhorn, vice president of Motorola and director of education and training, had to say to the Joint Economic Committee on the subject of the skills of the Motorola work force in 1987:

> If you take one of our mainline factories in Chicago in a suburb called Schaumburg, we have about 7,500 people, roughly 3,200 or 3,300 are . . . production workers. One thousand of those individuals lack basic math skills—adding, subtraction, multiplication, division; 550 cannot comprehend English; 250 do not read above the first grade level; 2,200 people cannot think—do problem solving.[8]

These problems were not new. What made them serious was the move to Total Quality. When Motorola automated the Schaumburg plant, the managers were in for a big surprise. The thirty thousand computer terminals that were installed require the people who use them to read and write English. Before, only the managers had been communicating with the computers, doing the math, worrying about quality control. What the corporate executives did not know was that these managers had made it unnecessary for the front-line worker to have a good command of English. Now, Motorola's plan called for getting rid of most of the managers and having the workers solve the problems that arose themselves—in teams, interacting directly with the computers and doing their own quality control. If they did not do all that, they would never be able to match the quality benchmarks set by the Japanese, and the whole business could go down the drain. A great deal now depended on the skills of the ordinary worker. Congressman James Scheuer, who was chairing the subcommittee hearing, asked Wiggenhorn to compare the skills of these workers with their Japanese counterparts. Wiggenhorn replied:

> Well, almost every Japanese production worker would be reading at the twelfth grade level coming in. He could read that book [on quality control] and pass it on. Number two, they would be quite skilled in math. They would have already been used to working in teams [in school] so it's not a change in style for them. And they have been given problems to solve throughout their secondary school education.[9]

Like many other firms, Motorola found out that it had a serious problem with the skills of its front-line workers only when it was well into its program for restructuring for Total Quality.[10]

Years earlier, in the late seventies, Motorola's CEO Bob Galvin, had begun a company-wide program to train all employees in the use of new productivity tools, new technology, and teamwork, but it had failed at the plant level. Plant managers had brought in the new technology, but nothing else had changed.

Galvin decided the problem was at the executive level, and in 1979 set up the Motorola Executive Institute to provide a one-time course for four hundred executives that would give them an MBA in four weeks designed around the Motorola philosophy. That didn't work either, this time because no one at the lower levels of the organization saw any reason to change. Galvin pressed on, setting up the Motorola Training and Education Center in 1980, and naming himself board chairman of the center. The idea was to implement participatory management and improve quality tenfold in five years, goals almost identical to those of Kearns's Leadership Through Quality program.

MTEC's curriculum included statistical process control (which embraced the use of five quality tools), basic industrial problem solving (so the workers could participate effectively in the problem-solving process along with their managers and on the same terms, much as they would do at Xerox), how to present conceptual material (so workers could describe problems and propose solutions in sophisticated terms to engineers and others), how to conduct and participate in effective meetings, and lastly, how to set goals and measure progress. But MTEC was to be more than a training agency. It was not only to train people but to redefine the jobs that people were being trained to do. It was to be an agent of change.

But that, too, came to nothing. Few people signed up for the courses. No one had provided any motivation for them to do so. The top managers who came learned the materials and techniques quickly enough, but their behavior on the job did not change. Because of that, the people below them on the organization chart saw no reason to learn the new techniques. Even when they did, no one was interested in having them actually use them. There was no payoff.

Galvin realized that his own behavior was crucial (something that Kearns came to learn in much the same way). When he started paying more attention to quality reports than quarterly reports at review meetings, his staff paid attention. Another set of courses was introduced that dramatized for top managers what global competition was likely to do to the firm if quality did not become a top priority. Galvin and eleven top managers went through the training themselves and then issued special "invitations" to others to get them to attend. These courses were eventually supplemented by an annual seminar Galvin ran for his top staff. The effect of these initiatives, combined with the example set by the top, was to convey the sense of urgency and real priority that had been missing.

It all came together in 1985, when Motorola opened a new facility in Illinois to manufacture cellular telephones. The facility was to put all the new ideas about work organization together with all the accumulated training in quality techniques. For the first time, the front-line workers, organized in teams, were to be responsible for quality control, flexible manufacturing, and mentoring several thousand new hires.

That is when the firm discovered to its horror the data that Wiggenhorn later presented to the Joint Economic Committee. Less than half of the work force passed a test containing such questions as "Ten is what percent of 100?" They could not do much math because their reading skills were poor to nonexistent. These were intelligent, capable employees, many of whom had been with the firm a long time. They had been able to improve quality in the old plants because their supervisors did their reading for them. But that was simply not possible in the new plant. There were many fewer supervisors, as Wiggenhorn told Congress, and the intensive use of computer terminals meant that everyone had to read the screens and type in text and data. Motorola was in real trouble.

One of the biggest hurdles that had to be overcome was many workers' fear of formal education, of having to repeat the failure and humiliation they had experienced when they were in school. Galvin taped employees within a few years of retirement telling their colleagues why basic skills were important and expressing their own commitment to remedial education. He responded personally to letters from front-line employees asking if they really had to go "back to school." A policy was established that said that employees refusing necessary skills training would be fired, but that a place would be found for employees who participated and failed.

The next shock came when Motorola began to investigate the skills problems they faced at other levels of the organization. Time and again, they discovered that the skills they thought they had been buying when they hired people who had taken specified courses and received certain degrees were missing or very deficient. They had a massive "supplier" problem in education.

The firm therefore began to treat their educational suppliers just the way they had learned to treat suppliers of everything else. They began by making their customer requirements clear, which they had never done before, and then working intensively with those suppliers—from university presidents to grade-school teachers—to help them get up to the required standard, jointly developing curricula, sharing lab equipment, exchanging faculty, providing internships for faculty, and much more. A separate account was established to invest in educational institutions willing to work closely with the firm.

Eleven years after Motorola set out on this course, its education and training budget has mushroomed from $7 million a year to $120 million, far more than Galvin had ever imagined might be required.[11] In 1984, the company instituted a policy requiring managers to invest at least 1.5 percent of department payrolls in education and training. Wiggenhorn estimated that the actual investment in 1987 was about 2.4 percent and expected the figure to go to 3 percent. New front-line workers have to have at least seventh-grade math and science skills, soon to go to eighth- and ninth-grade. They have to be good at problem solving— alone and as members of groups. And they have to be prepared to do whatever it takes to reach Motorola's stringent quality targets—even if that means working fifty or even sixty hours a week.

These requirements came about, as we have seen, because the firm realized, as David Kearns put it, that a whole new approach to running the firm would be necessary in the new competitive environment. Workers had to have a conceptual grasp of their work, be able to fix problems as they arose rather than merely reporting them to a superior, and contribute to the continuous improvement of both the product they were manufacturing and the process by which it was produced. Survival—the capacity to produce very high-quality products efficiently—required both a fundamental redefinition of the role of the front-line worker and the capacity to perform effectively in that role.

In chapter 3, we described "high-performance work organization," the new approach to organizing work that enables employers of all kinds to make improvements in quality, productivity, and flexibility obtainable in no other way. At bottom, it is the antithesis of Taylorism, for it requires that front-line workers take many of the roles and responsibilities that Taylor would reserve only for management and professional staff—and it requires them, therefore, to think.

How, then, are high-performance work organization, Total Quality Management, and workers' skills related? What is the lesson we should draw from the experience of Xerox and Motorola?

When the Commission on the Skills of the American Workforce visited Sweden, Ira Magaziner, its chair, made arrangements for the members to meet for a day with key leaders of the Swedish government and their top advisers. During the meeting one of the hosts quietly observed that the successful firms of the future would not be those that concentrated on maximizing profits, acquiring the best technology, or keeping their costs down; they would be the firms that organized themselves for learning and for capitalizing on what they learn.

Benchmarking is a device that forces its users to learn constantly from the competition, from the very best in the world. Paying attention to the customer is a formula for learning from one's customers. Statistical process control is a bundle of tools for learning what stands in the way of higher quality and correcting the problems. Much of the power of the idea of quality circles comes from the potential for workers to learn from one another and from their own experience and for the firm to profit from their learning. Breaking down the traditional barriers greatly increases the flow of information and increases the learning that takes place. In the Taylorist model, learning flows in only one direction—from the top of the organization to the bottom. Indeed, the adversarial relationships in a Taylorist organization actually impede the flow of information in any direction, since workers and managers are likely to believe that their power is enhanced by monopolizing information. In the learning organization, information flows freely in all directions.

The point has been made that Total Quality and high-performance work organizations require very large corporate investments in continuing education and training. The point being made here is more subtle. The successful firm is the firm that organizes itself as a learning system in which every part is designed to promote and accelerate both individual learning and collective learning—and to put that learning to productive use.

Magaziner's insight is that the new forms of work organization will not work unless management understands that it is just as important for front-line workers to learn constantly and to put that learning to work as it is for management. By learning enough to take over many functions previously reserved for management, they not only contribute directly to great productivity improvements, but they also reduce the compartmentalization of the organization, which once again increases the organization's learning capacity. In all these ways, the learning organization makes possible gains in quality and productivity that are not achievable in any other way. And, ultimately, it makes it possible for modern societies to substitute ideas, skills, and knowledge for physical resources.

Ray Stata, president and CEO of Analog Devices, believes that:

> The rate at which organizations learn may become the only sustainable source of competitive advantage. . . . The "scientific management" revolution of Frederick Taylor took the traditional division of labor, between workers and managers, and gave us the "thinkers" and the "doers." The doers were basically prohibited from thinking. I believe our fundamental challenge is tapping the intellectual capacity of people at all levels, both as individuals and groups. To truly engage everyone—that is the untapped potential in modern corporations. Interestingly, just as [front-line] workers have gotten stuck as the "doers" in traditional organizations, managers have gotten stuck as the "thinkers." There is a tremendous tendency of people high in the organization to become remote from reality and the facts. All in the organization must master the cycle of thinking, doing, evaluating and reflecting. Without [that], there is no valid learning.[12]

But this view is not widely shared among American employers. Deming, perhaps still mindful of the rejection of his ideas for so many years by American managers, recently observed:

> With the storehouse of skills and knowledge contained in its millions of unemployed, and with the even more appalling underuse, misuse and abuse of skills and knowledge in the army of employed people in all ranks in all industries, the United States may be today the most underdeveloped nation in the world. If Japan be an example, then it is possible that any country with enough people and with good management, making products suited to their talents and to the market, need not be poor. . . . The problem is to find good management. It would be a mistake to export American management to a friendly country.[13]

Bill Brock, co-chair of the Commission on the Skills of the American Workforce, said when its report was released that "the good news is that there is no shortage of skilled labor in the United States. The bad news is that there is no shortage of skilled labor in the United States."[14] The 5 percent of American firms moving toward high-performance work organization is the same 5 percent that is moving toward embracing the Total Quality principles. Xerox and Motorola are among the best companies in the world, but there are very few such companies in this country. As long as that is so, there will be no real improvement in the education and training of our people, because there will be no effective demand for it.

Five percent is not enough. If 5 percent are struggling to create learning organizations that can compete on quality and productivity and 95 percent are competing on wages and hours, the United States will slip more quickly into relative poverty with every passing year, a course, as we have pointed out, on which it is already well embarked.

It is reasonable to ask what other countries have done by way of public policy to increase firms' use of high-performance work organizations, Total Quality techniques, and investment in the skills of their staffs. The answer, however, is frustrating.

As we saw in chapter 4, in Germany very strong government policies were largely responsible for moving corporate managements in these directions. Labor-dominated governments, elected following the Second World War, set wage rates very high and made it very hard to fire anyone. Firms were forced by this environment to seek survival strategies that favored solutions emphasizing high quality, high productivity, and high-value-added operations. In Japan, as we saw, the aftershocks of the same war engendered a very close partnership between government and industry that created different legislative programs but very similar business strategies.

This happened in Japan and Germany but not in the United States. There are no government policies in place here that would create strong incentives for firms to move toward high-performance work organizations, adopt Total Quality principles, or embrace the idea of the learning organization. On the contrary, the incentives run the other way. As our two examples show, it is very hard to do what Xerox and Motorola have done. It requires determined leadership over many years, entails endless false starts and backward steps, costs a great deal of money, forces one to deal with obstacles that cannot be anticipated in advance, and therefore raises the specter of considerable real risk.

W. Edwards Deming and others have shown conclusively that, in the long run, these measures are the surest way to save money, boost quality, increase productivity, and enjoy competitive success. But, as many have pointed out, there is no long run for most American business leaders. To the vast majority, it seems less risky and easier to do what comes naturally—meet the competition by seeking government protection, keeping wages down, contracting out, automating jobs entirely, exporting production offshore, or getting product from offshore and becoming simply a domestic marketing agent. These are, in fact, rational choices and, as matters stand now, an honest business consultant would be hard-pressed not to recommend them to a client in many cases. Such measures may save a firm in the short or even the long run, but they are disastrous for the country, for their inevitable consequence is lower pay, longer hours, and lengthening unemployment lines.

But, if the European solution of tough legislative programs enacted by labor governments is out, and the Japanese solution of very tight collaboration between government and firms is equally unimaginable, then what can the United States do?

This country can begin by committing itself to a policy of high wages and full employment. The root difference between us and our most successful competitors is that most of them have made these into overarching social goals, and we have not. These goals can only be reached by moving a nation toward high-value-added, high-productivity enterprises, and such firms can only be successful if they have access to a highly educated and trained work force and use advanced forms of work organization. This simple chain of logic is well understood by everyone in these countries, which makes it possible to enact a wide range of economic and social policies that would be unthinkable here.

The people of the United States would never choose to be poor, but they have never chosen to be rich either. If some American firms choose to compete by paying low wages, providing indifferent quality, achieving low productivity, and charging low prices, while others choose high wages, high quality, high productivity, and high prices, we have treated that as a largely private matter. That is because we have always assumed that the market will sort it all out, and, when it does, the best firms will survive, and the American people will do well. But we now know that in the new global economy, American firms can do quite well using the first set of strategies while the American people do poorly. It turns out that if we as a people have no preference with respect to business strategy, then we have no preference between being well-off or poor.

It is time for the president and the Congress to engage the nation in a debate about social priorities, and to pass legislation that clearly establishes full employment and high wages as the overarching domestic policy goals of the United States and sets forth a framework for achieving those objectives. In the rest of Part Four, we lay out our proposals for developing the human-resources system America needs to pursue a high-wage future. In Part Five, we sketch in the kinds of broad economic policies required. In the rest of this chapter, we make several proposals for policies designed to change the behavior of firms. The program described by all of these proposals taken together constitutes our framework for achieving the objectives we would have the country embrace. We begin with proposals intended to lead to the restructuring of American business for high performance.

Provide incentives to employers to pay high wages, improve productivity, and use high-performance forms of work organization—and disincentives to those who don't. The most straightforward approach to wages, of course, is to raise the minimum wage, thus driving general wage levels up and thereby providing an incentive to employers to develop high-productivity business strategies. This approach is discussed at some length later. Other, less direct, methods are also available to achieve the same objectives. In Singapore, for example, the government taxes employers with a high proportion of low-wage workers to create training funds from which all employers—including high-wage employers—can draw.

In the past, many states have tried to attract new firms or induce firms to stay or expand by offering free training, subsidized infrastructure and services, tax abatements, and so on. In the future, states could offer such inducements only to high-wage employers, which amounts to a tax on low-wage employers; or to high-productivity employers, which amounts to a tax on low-productivity employers; or to employers using high-performance work organizations, which amounts to a tax on employers using conventional forms of work organization.

The point is that whereas in the past, states have focused on the quantity rather than the quality of jobs, federal and state policy can and should shift to policies that favor firms that offer the kinds of high-pay, high-productivity jobs on which the future of this country depends. This does not mean picking winners and losers among industries. But it does mean looking at pay levels, productivity, and work organization as criteria for government subsidy and support. A low-wage strategy, by contrast, subsidizes inefficiency.

Provide incentives to employers to invest in the development of their employees. The Commission on the Skills of the American Workforce observed that most of the advanced industrial countries and many of the newly industrialized countries require employers to invest a sum equal to 1 percent of salaries and wages in the continuing education and training of their employees. The United States is the rare exception to this rule. It is hardly surprising that American employers invest far less in the continuing education and training of their employees than their foreign competitors do. The commission reported that the vast majority of American workers receive no formal education and training at all from their employers, beyond the absolute minimum required for safety and initial orientation.

The commission recommended that the United States require employers to spend an amount equal to at least 1 percent of salaries and wages on the continuing education and training of their workers, or if they are unable or unwilling to do so, to contribute to a Skills Development Fund operated by government, which would supply the education and training to the firm's workers. Firms would be required to spend the money on management and front-line workers in reasonable proportion to their presence in the work force. Only expenditures on programs leading to educational certificates granted by the state, industry-wide training certificates, or recognized degrees would count toward satisfying the requirement.

There is, as one would expect, considerable resistance in the business community to the introduction of such a requirement, on the grounds that it is a tax that would further disadvantage American employers in the competitive race by adding to their costs, and that it would allow the government to create yet another bureaucracy, this time to tell firms how to carry out their internal training function. It is not clear to us, however, why a requirement of this sort would make American firms less competitive than those in Singapore, Ireland, France, Germany, Sweden, and many other countries where training set-aside requirements have been in place for years. Nor is any great bureaucracy required; firms could simply certify on their tax return that they have used the funds in the manner required by law, and their auditors could check that they did so, just as they check other fund flows in the organization as a normal part of the audit procedure.

If, however, it proves impossible to institute such requirements here, it may be possible to create programs that would match private-firm contributions for such purposes with public funds up to a certain amount.

Establish a technical assistance program to move the management of all kinds of enterprises toward high-performance work organization. In June 1862, only a few months after establishing the Department of Agriculture, Congress passed the Morrill Act, setting aside federal lands in each state for the purpose of endowing colleges whose primary purpose would be to instruct citizens in agriculture and the mechanical arts. In 1887, the Hatch Act was passed, authorizing agricultural experiment stations, to be run in conjunction with the agricultural colleges.

Twenty-seven years later, in 1914, the first comprehensive legislation for agricultural extensions was passed in the form of the Smith-Lever Act. One of the service's directors, M. C. Burritt, described its objectives as follows: "It is the function of the Extension Service to teach people to determine accurately their own problems, to help them acquire knowledge and to inspire them to action, but it must be their own action out of their own knowledge and convictions."[15] Burritt was referring, of course, to farm people. He was apparently very much aware that they were hardly likely to take advantage of the enormous investment that the government had made in research and development of improved methods of agriculture unless they believed they would benefit by doing so.

The result of the Morrill Act and its successors was an American agricultural system that turned out a product of unparalleled quality with unmatched productivity at highly competitive prices—the most successful agricultural system the world has ever known. It is at least as important in the closing years of this century to introduce the idea of high-performance work organization to American managers and persuade them of its benefits as it was to interest American farmers in the advantages of hybrid seed corn and teach them how best to plant and raise it in the century's opening years.

In Maryland, field staff members of the state's economic development agency often refer firms to the productivity institute at the state university for an audit that tells a firm what the institute's staff thinks the firm could do to improve productivity, both by upgrading the technology they are using and by changing the way work is organized in order to make the most efficient use of the new technology. Many states now have college- and university-based technology centers charged with conducting research on new technologies and getting the results of that research out to firms. A growing number of federally funded laboratories do the same, though it is important to note that the United States spends far less than its competitors on the dissemination of new technologies.

What is needed is legislation that will weave these developments together into a seamless web of research, development, and technical assistance, the purpose of which, to borrow Burritt's phrase, is to "inspire to action" countless managers of enterprises of all sizes and types. Just as in agriculture, these actions must grow out of their own convictions, prompted by the knowledge that the new ways of doing business will benefit them directly and that their risk in implementing these new methods is greatly reduced by their ability to rely on technical assistance from people who know their industry and have assisted many others successfully in implementing the same techniques and methods.

The sources of assistance might be research universities, land grant colleges (the legacy of the Morrill Act), other four-year institutions, community colleges, industry associations, federal laboratories, and many others. The aid they provide should be coordinated with the state agencies responsible for economic development and related functions. Technology development and assistance should be coordinated with development of improved methods of organization and management, building on the Total Quality approach, and both should be developed in close collaboration with the people who will have to adopt the new methods. The program will have to embrace not just the fashionable fields of biotechnology and new materials technologies, but everything from fisheries to jewelry, from financial services to laundries.

Employers are like everyone else. If they think that people they respect are in favor of these new methods, they will be more eager to embrace them themselves. So governors and industry groups could help by offering recognition to firms that train the most or the best, that show the greatest productivity improvement, that lead their industry on indices of total quality, and so on. Industry journals and the general business press could help by publicizing such awards and featuring the firms that win them.

But the key is the extension system: the people who are out there every day going from firm to firm explaining what is at stake, what is to be gained by taking another route, what kind of assistance is available, what the firm will have to do, how long it will take and how much effort; and the people who actually do the audits, the training, and the hand-holding. Elements of such a system are in place in a number of states, but a full system has not been developed on a sufficient scale anywhere. If agriculture is in fact an apt precedent, and high-quality resources are deployed to get to a significant number of firms, then such a policy could affect the practices of many employers in a relatively short time. Development of such a program is probably the single most important policy initiative that could be taken to lead employers toward high-quality, high-productivity, and high-performance forms of work organization.

If this effort is actually mounted, and it succeeds, it will provoke a crisis, as the Motorola example shows: there will be a terrible shortage of the skilled workers crucial to the success of the new systems. And that is largely because public education may be the industry most in need of the new forms of work organization required to improve quality and productivity. That is the subject of the next chapter.

CHAPTER 8

Restructuring the Schools for High Performance: Tough Road to Excellence

For fifty years or more, every reform in American education, from the Master of Arts in Teaching degree to the new math, from parent participation to team teaching, has been based on the premise that the basic organizational and management structure need not change. The only important exception, educational vouchers, is a misguided attempt to strike at the heart of the problem, as we will explain in the next chapter. All of the earlier reforms in curriculum, teaching method, and school organization have ultimately disappointed their advocates. All have been rejected or watered down in the course of time by the larger system, which seems impervious to any real changes at all. It is the system that is the problem, and only basic changes in the structure of the system will fix it.

The most striking feature of our schools is that the quality of the students they graduate is mostly a function of the background of the students they enroll. Schools that enroll wealthy students produce accomplished graduates and those that enroll students from low-income families typically produce students with poor academic records. We think of the first set as good schools, but there is no reason to do so. A truly good school would be one that graduated students who are more successful than would be predicted by their social class.

Now here is the curious thing. One would think that schools with better results than could be predicted by the social class of their students would be widely imitated, that successful programs of any sort would be quickly identified by school boards and superintendents, copied instantly, and quickly improved upon. But nothing of the sort actually happens, as countless innovators, philanthropists, and government planners have discovered. Through decades of educational history in this country, programs of unquestioned effectiveness have spread very slowly, if at all. In fact, teachers and principals who have achieved such successes have often done so as renegades within their districts, and are given the cold shoulder by their colleagues and superiors.

The reason is not hard to find. Success in educating students is not reflected in the pay of teachers or principals, nor is it rewarded with opportunities for advancement in the system. These facts are merely indicators of a broader problem. School districts are not performance-oriented organizations. There is no bottom line and there are no rewards for achieving it. Superintendents are the only people in the entire system who can be fired without going through numbingly complex procedures. What a superintendent most fears is anything that will result in a controversy that will appear in the press and provide an excuse for a board member to threaten his or her control of the system or job security. The way to minimize such controversy is to make sure, first and foremost, that everyone in the system is loyal—to the person in the hierarchy above and, ultimately, to the superintendent.

Loyalty to the system, not contribution to student performance, is thus the primary criterion for success in the schools. That is why new methods of proven effectiveness are so often ignored. If implementing the innovation is likely to arouse the wrath of anyone inside or outside the system, it is quietly shelved, along with the person who promoted it. The system's primary obligation is not to its students, but to itself.

Imagine now that school districts were organized and managed in such a way that everyone in them was striving constantly to improve student performance. A system for doing just that is the subject of this chapter. It is the first of three keys to producing a world-class education system in the United States. The other two keys are the creation of systems of educational standards and of incentive systems that reward all the participants when those standards are achieved, the subject of chapters 8 and 9.

As we saw in the last chapter, the large, multinational American firms that have survived and prospered in the 1980s have done so by restructuring their operations from top to bottom, using highly skilled, highly paid labor, and wholly different methods for managing and organizing the work of the organization than they had in the past. By doing so, they succeeded in raising productivity levels greatly, producing a much higher-quality product while actually reducing their costs. This is very similar to the challenge American education faces: to make an enormous improvement in educational achievement at a modest increase in cost. The lessons our best firms have learned, we believe, hold the key to great advances in our schools.

The basic formula followed by these and other firms is simple. They started by being very clear about what business they were in, by getting their goals straight. They communicated those goals to everyone in the organization, and made sure that everything top management did reinforced those goals so that no one could forget them. They worked to find measures of progress against those goals that reflected what they wanted to achieve. They changed the incentive systems of the firm so that there were real rewards for performance and real penalties for nonperformance, and everyone had strong incentives to contribute to the company's goals. They made major investments in new systems to give the workers the skills, time, and information they would need to function in the new environment. Then they pushed a lot of decisions that had been made by middle and top management down to the front line, to those people closest to the production process and the customer. And they held those on the front line accountable for the results of their work, having gotten rid of as much as possible of the bureaucracy that used to be there to tell the lower levels what to do and how to do it.

In a nutshell, what they did was to treat the people on the front line like professionals, whether they were white- or blue-collar workers. This required, as we saw in the last chapter, driving a fundamental change in the culture of the organization through the whole firm. These measures gave the people on the front line the discretion to figure out how to get the job done. But this discretion came at a price. Management made it clear that they expected the people on the front line, like professionals, to be fully accountable for the results of their work. This approach provided a mighty motivation to the workers, engaged their energy and commitment, and enabled the firm to dispense with much of their vast—and expensive—bureaucracy.

It has not been easy for American firms to accomplish this transition. It is hardly complete in most firms that have tried it, and most have not attempted it at all. It has entailed fundamental changes in management roles and responsibilities, even greater changes in the attitudes and methods of union leaders, and equally great changes in such matters as the way work is organized, how operations are staffed, how information flows through the organization, and how budgeting is done. The greatest changes probably have to do with the culture of the organization: people's attitudes, values, and ways of relating to one another, things that are notoriously difficult to change. All of this has required enormous investments in training and continuing education for everyone in the firm.

What does all this have to do with schools?

Everything. As we have seen, schools in the United States have been organized on the old industrial pattern since the 1920s, each successive layer seeing it as its task to tell the one below what to do and how to do it. It was assumed in the schools, as it was in industry, that those on the bottom did not have the skills or knowledge to act independently in the best interest of employer or client. As a monopoly provider of education services, the system has had little incentive to improve the quality of the service or the efficiency with which it is provided. Efficiencies would produce lower revenues. No one was rewarded for meeting the needs of students, nor were there any penalties for anyone if they were not met. Teachers and other lower and midlevel staff members were mainly rewarded for loyalty to the system in general and their supervisors in particular.

Nothing has changed in these respects since the 1930s. It should surprise no one that such a system has produced rising real costs for decades but only modest improvement in student performance. This is an indictment not of the people who staff this system but of the system itself. The only way to get higher performance and greater efficiency is to change the system root and branch.

The first comprehensive blueprint for such a transformation was laid out in *A Nation Prepared: Teachers for the 21st Century,* released by the Carnegie Forum on Education and the Economy in 1986.[1] The report pointed out that the schools are among the most Taylorized of all American organizations, that teachers are treated like blue-collar workers in the old-style work place. In the future, it said, the quality of school staff needed to produce the highly skilled graduates the country now requires will be people who could qualify for the true professions. Access to those professions was long denied the college-educated women and minorities who had been the mainstay of our teaching staff for decades, but that is no longer true. Because the true professions are now open to these people, the best of them are hardly likely to select teaching as a career. Recruiting them to education now and keeping them there would require a transformation in the organization and management of public education, because it would be impossible without transforming the roles of teachers and the environment in which they work. De-Taylorizing the schools calls for the same kinds of changes that are being made by the best American corporations. *A Nation Prepared* laid out a series of recommendations for bringing about that transformation—a wholesale change in goals, governance, organization, management, curriculum, staffing, indeed in the schools' very ethos and culture.

The analogy to the restructuring of industry for high performance is straightforward. It begins with clarity about goals for the students: what the community expects students to know and be able to do when they leave high school. It requires the development of measures of student performance and a new curriculum that accurately reflects those goals. It assumes that many decisions now made by the state, the board of education, and the central administration about how to get the job done will be devolved upon the principal and the teachers, and that much of the intervening bureaucracy will go. It entails a major effort to get the highest possible quality of staff in the schools, and to support that staff by giving it the information and skills it needs to do the job. It requires development of a whole new set of incentives and accountability measures that provide real rewards for school staff whose students make real progress and real consequences for those whose students make little progress. In this scheme of things, principals and teachers are treated as real professionals, and as with real professionals, the rewards they get are a function of their ability to meet the needs of their clients.

At the 1986 summer meeting of the National Governors' Association, the governors formally endorsed the Carnegie report and released their own call for school restructuring, *Time for Results,* which had been produced under the leadership of the NGA Chairman, Governor Lamar Alexander of Tennessee. Governor Thomas Kean of New Jersey, lead governor for education of the NGA that year, was also a member of the Carnegie Forum Task Force and chairman of the Education Commission of the States, where, assisted by Richard Mills, then his education aide, he had made the professionalization of teaching his personal agenda. Kean and Mills, along with Alexander, played important roles in focusing the NGA members on the restructuring agenda. The American Federation of Teachers had endorsed the Carnegie report in June. The NEA, though stopping short of a full endorsement, had followed the lead of its president, Mary Futrell, in supporting many of its recommendations. Many other organizations were to provide formal endorsements during the summer and fall.

Through that whole period, states and school districts around the country were beginning to embrace the Carnegie report's recommendations. A few months after the report's release, Governor Booth Gardner of Washington State submitted a $500-million education reform program to his legislature, much of it based on the Carnegie restructuring agenda. Massachusetts created a "Carnegie schools" program. Governor Bill Clinton designed his own program for the state of Arkansas. Richard Mills left Governor Kean's staff to become chief state school officer in Vermont, developing a statewide consensus around the agenda he had helped develop for the Carnegie Forum. Iowa, Maine, Oregon, and many other states created restructuring programs. Most were designed as demonstrations or experiments involving only volunteer schools. None attempted to redesign the whole system of education at once, but each was a good beginning on a process that their authors knew would take years.

School districts around the country were no less interested. In San Diego, School Superintendent Tom Payzant formed his own version of the Carnegie Task Force, drawing on local leaders, and asked it to recommend ways in which the report might be implemented in that city. Joe Fernandez, then assistant superintendent and shortly to become superintendent of the Dade County public schools, joined Pat Tornillo, head of the Dade affiliate of the American Federation of Teachers, in an effort that was to make Dade a leader in the national restructuring program. Largely on the strength of the reputation he gained restructuring Dade's school system, Fernandez went on to become chancellor of the New York City schools, where he would adopt a similar agenda.

In the fall of 1986, the Rochester City School District in New York State and the Rochester Teachers Association announced a new contract that caught the country by surprise. The contract incorporated the salary recommendations of the Carnegie report, raising average teachers' salaries by more than 40 percent over the three-year life of the contract and making Rochester's teachers among the best paid in the country.

Though the nation focused on the salary increase, the contract's provisions went far beyond salary matters, incorporating many other recommendations made by the Carnegie Task Force, among them a career ladder for teachers designed to keep the best of them in the profession; an agreement to develop a site-based management system that would empower teachers to make many more of the key decisions about instruction than they had made before; a provision involving the teachers' union in working to improve the performance of weak teachers, and, when necessary, weeding out incompetent teachers; and an agreement to develop a system for increased teacher accountability for student progress. The framework of the Carnegie report could be found everywhere in the contract, but the detailed design of almost all these systems and many others had yet to be undertaken. All the implementation work still lay ahead.

But the outlook for implementation was very promising. Adam Urbanski, president of the Rochester Teachers Association, was highly regarded by his constituency and by the leadership of his national union, which gave him room for bold initiatives. Peter McWalters, the superintendent of schools, had a reform-minded, community-activist board of education behind him. A highly regarded high-school social studies teacher who had skipped almost all the usual steps in a meteoric rise to the superintendency, McWalters was no bureaucrat. He strongly identified with both the teachers and the needs of the largely poor and minority community whose children were in his care. Urbanski, a Polish émigré, had received a doctorate in history from the University of Rochester and then spent his whole professional career teaching in the Rochester city school district, rising to the presidency of the union. A charismatic leader, and, like McWalters, a deeply thoughtful educator, he was determined to lead his members out of the ranks of hired hands to the status of true professionals in the community. McWalters shared this aim, believing it to be a key to building schools that would work for students. Both were fully aware of the profound changes that would be required in labor-management relations.

A few weeks after the contract was signed Marc Tucker was asked if he might have any interest in moving to Rochester to help the community implement the restructuring program. With help from Carnegie Corporation of New York, Tucker was by that time well along in the process of creating a not-for-profit organization, the National Center on Education and the Economy, to work on national policy issues that the Carnegie Forum had not addressed. The prospect of combining technical assistance at the local level with state and national policy development was very attractive.

But it would be expensive. Jim Hunt, former governor of North Carolina and vice chairman of the new organization, called New York's Governor Mario Cuomo to ask whether the governor would be interested in bringing the new center to his state. Ten days later, at the beginning of January 1988, the governor called a press conference to announce that he was asking the legislature to appropriate $1 million in unrestricted support for the National Center to help make Rochester a restructuring laboratory for the state and the nation, and for the center's national policy development program. It was to be the first of many such requests by the governor.

The first thing Tucker did was engage Sonia Hernandez as the center's director of the Rochester restructuring program. A teaching principal in an elementary school in San Antonio, Texas, Hernandez combined a deep belief in the restructuring agenda with the political and organizational talent it would take to help move that agenda in an urban school district.

Tucker also paid a visit to David Kearns at Xerox's headquarters in Stamford, Connecticut, to seek Kearn's assistance in the Rochester restructuring effort. Tucker was convinced that the Rochester city school district could benefit greatly from the experience Xerox had gained restructuring its own operations for high performance. Kearns agreed to loan the National Center two Xerox executives who would join Hernandez on the center's Rochester team. They would be joined later by loaned executives from the Rochester Institute of Technology and Eastman Kodak.

In September 1988, center staff negotiated a contract with the board of education that would serve as a basic charter for the restructuring program in Rochester. It called for the center to provide assistance in helping the district formulate goals for student performance, come up with better methods of measuring student progress toward those goals, push instructional decisions down to the school level, develop new accountability systems for professional staff, and create systems of staff development that could support the entire program.

Hernandez worked through the fall and winter with school district staff and a district-wide committee to create a set of decision rules for the formation of site-based management teams in the school that would be responsible for the development of school-wide plans and have substantial authority to make many instructional decisions formerly made by the central office, the school board, and the state. Thomas Sobol, commissioner of education in New York State, had pledged expedited consideration of requests for waivers from state regulations and had appointed top level liaisons from the State Department of Education to follow though on that pledge.

It took months for the committee of top district administrators, union representatives, parents, and school representatives to agree on the rules that would apply to the formation of the teams and their responsibilities. Teachers, the school administration, parents, and, in the high schools, students would be represented, with the teachers in the majority. A complex method for ensuring that the actions of the team would be taken only as a result of a consensus among all the constituencies was decided on. The team's task was to reinvent the school, coming up with a design that represented the considered judgment of the members as to the best way to meet the needs of the students. If the standing rules of the district, the unions, or the state would prevent implementation of that design, they could apply for waivers.

The teams proposed by the schools would not be certified as meeting the criteria until the beginning of the fall term of 1989. Center and district staff, in the meantime, had come up with a design for an eighteen-month-long series of workshops, intended to help the team members function effectively in their new roles. Educators from all over the country who had been involved in similar efforts were brought in to share their experiences, and prominent facilitators from both education and business were asked to work with the teams to help their members develop the skills they would need to develop effective plans and carry them out.

But the teachers had little experience in planning and management and many were not at all sure they wanted to learn. Principals had just as little experience in sharing their decision-making authority and many were reluctant to do so. Few school staffs and parents had any experience in working closely together as colleagues and found that this takes a great deal of skill and good will, both of which take time to build up. The participants quickly found that a two- or three-day workshop is not enough. Sustained assistance is needed, but the school system's budget did not provide for it. The best American firms undergoing a similar restructuring have found that they need to raise training and development budgets from about 1 percent of salaries and wages to 4 percent or more, as we reported in chapter 7, but school districts find it very difficult to persuade the public that resources of that sort are necessary.

Some months later, the district developed a design for site-based budgeting, a process for decentralizing budget control from the central office and vesting it in the site-based management teams. McWalters and the board recognized that decentralizing control of instructional decisions would not mean much if those teams had little to say about how the school budget was used. The plan called for piloting the design first in a few schools, working the bugs out, and then implementing the system district-wide.

Pushing decisions down to the school level puts a premium on the quality of school staff. One effect of raising teachers' salaries so much and so fast was to reduce retirements to a trickle. Teachers who might otherwise have retired realized that their retirement pay would be much higher if they put in another few years at the higher pay levels and chose to stay. McWalters was very concerned. He knew that the system for recruiting, selecting, and hiring teachers was rudimentary at best—though no worse than that of most American school districts. When the teachers who had decided to stay started to retire, there would be a flood of openings, and the rickety system would be overwhelmed. Rochester could easily get less capable teachers than it had had before salaries were raised, and the entire plan would be imperiled.

In a Taylorist system like the public schools, it makes very little sense to invest heavily in the recruitment, selection, and training of front-line staff—in this case teachers. After all, they are interchangeable parts, not to be relied on for independent judgment, there to do as they are told. Teacher compensation systems are very revealing in that respect. After teachers reach about twelve years of service, they typically get only cost-of-living raises. After that point, the system reasons, it is cheaper to get two new teachers and just as effective. This is hardly the view one would take if one valued the professional competence of teachers as we value the professional competence of lawyers, architects, or accountants. It is the way we view counter workers in a fast-food restaurant. Few school systems have carefully defined the qualities they are looking for in prospective teachers, and few have developed even elementary procedures for judging how candidates measure up to those criteria. Very little is invested in the recruitment, hiring, and initial training of teachers compared to what the best American firms spend on their new front-line workers. From this we can reasonably conclude that teachers are not regarded as the key to the success of schools, all the rhetoric to the contrary notwithstanding—management is. But in a restructured environment, everything depends on the capacity of the teachers and school-level administrators to exercise independent judgment with a high degree of professionalism. So it makes all the difference who is hired, how they are initially trained, and what provisions are made for their continued development through their whole career in education.

Given the urgency of the requirement to build a new system for teacher recruitment, selection, and hiring, the loaned executives from Xerox went to work on that issue first, assisting the district's personnel director and the Career in Teaching Panel, created by McWalters and Urbanski to deal with issues related to the professionalization of teaching. That effort led directly to work on a companion problem, planning for the replacement of key administrators and their development both before and after their appointment to management positions. Teacher replacement rates, the data showed, would be more than matched by retirement rates among school principals. No American school district that we know of has a formal management development program, commonplace in American corporations, in which promising front-line professionals are identified and groomed over a period of years for positions of increasing responsibility in management. Everyone knew that the quality of school leadership would be as important as the quality of teachers in the restructured school system.

When the Xerox executives had arrived on the scene, they had spent their first few weeks putting together informal meetings with people at every level of the school district to get a feel for the issues. When they had finished, they reported to Tucker and Hernandez that morale seemed high and the quality of staff good, but the task seemed very daunting. Two things, they said, struck them most forcefully. First, though the district and the National Center were getting many of the necessary pieces of the restructuring strategy in place, the district did not seem to have a way to organize them into an integrated management plan. Second, when they compared the district at the beginning of its restructuring effort in 1989 to Xerox at the beginning of its effort in 1981, they said that the district faced every problem that Xerox had faced earlier, with two important differences that would make the task ahead even more difficult than it had been at Xerox. First, the district, unlike Xerox, was a public agency operating in a political fishbowl, making it far harder for the chief executive officer to formulate a plan and execute it. Second, while Xerox employees were willing to make fundamental changes in the organization because the alternative seemed to be bankruptcy and unemployment, no one in the district seemed to believe that anything would happen to them if the district's restructuring plan failed, and so there was no incentive to take the tough measures that would be needed. Each of these issues would prove central in the months and years ahead.

The Xerox executives' observation about the lack of an integrated management plan went to the heart of an important characteristic of school systems. Districts are managed to respond to ever-changing pressures from an endless round of unanticipated quarters, in no particular order. They are not mission-oriented agencies. Because of this, they typically lack the capacity to develop a plan for reaching a major target that is years away and then to manage their affairs step by step to reach the targets set by the plan. But that is exactly what is required to restructure a complex organization—a patient, determined effort to coordinate many separate initiatives over a long period of time into a well-orchestrated system.

When the Xerox executives asked to see the board's priority action list, it included dozens of items, only a few of which were related to the restructuring strategy, and these were scattered through the list, rather than organized as an integrated program of activities. Many of these action items did not have a person assigned to make them happen. The district had identified the need for a strategic management plan but did not have a management process in place for making the plan or executing it. The National Center's team therefore worked with McWalters and his top aides to help them establish responsibility for planning and policy related to restructuring and to put in place a management system that would establish priorities, assign tasks, allocate resources, track their progress, and make corrections along the way.

David Kearns's approach to restructuring depended heavily on creating a new organizational culture in the firm, a compound of new values and new skills. At Xerox the driving value is quality—defined as meeting customer requirements—and both this value and the skills required to make good on it are conveyed by the Leadership Through Quality program. McWalters's overriding value for his staff was conveyed by the simple and powerful statement that "All Kids Can Learn," and the companion goal of creating a school district in which the academic achievement of the students cannot be predicted by the incomes of their parents. The National Center team set about to help McWalters create an analogue to Leadership Through Quality that would have the same effect on district values, culture, and operating methods that its predecessor at Xerox had had there.

It has been slow going. Educators are deeply skeptical of the idea that education has anything of value to learn from business. They are put off by the notion that they are engaged in producing a "product" or that they have "customers." And they have a hard time seeing the relevance of the business conception of "quality" to the work that they do.

One of the major differences between a manufacturing firm and schools, of course, is the fact that the material with which the professionals work consists of people, namely students, not inanimate objects. McWalters's experience as a teacher had persuaded him that one of the major problems facing urban school districts is the belief on the part of many students that no one—no adults in the school at least—care very much about them or believe in their capacity to succeed. This is why McWalters, in his talks with staff, emphasized over and over again his belief that that "All Kids Can Learn." In business terms, McWalters believed that his first obligation was to his "customers," conceived as the students; to "quality," defined as meeting the needs of those customers; and to "zero defects," defined as a situation in which all students achieve at high levels.

But, just as in business, belief without action is of little value. Building on a successful program pioneered by the school in which he had taught, McWalters had negotiated a provision in the teachers' contract providing for a district-wide policy requiring secondary-school teachers to take personal responsibility for a group of students, keeping track of their academic progress in all their courses, and being in regular touch with their parents. But many teachers took the view that they had never signed up to be social workers. And many others agreed with the aims of the program, but feared for their safety when visiting their students' parents in their homes. Parents organized neighborhood groups to escort the teachers when necessary.

Moving from a system based on design standards to one based on outcome or performance standards obviously cannot be done until the performance standards are defined. In the fall of 1989, the board of education asked the National Center to engage the whole Rochester community in a year-long process intended to lead to a consensus specification of what the district's graduating seniors should know and be able to do.

Focus group sessions were conducted with teachers, school administrators, employers, students, parent groups, college professors, and admissions officers, leaders of community-based organizations and churches, and community political leaders. Louis Harris did a community-wide poll. Community forums were held. People were interviewed by telephone. In the fall of 1990, the center's report went to the board of education.

The report painted a rich portrait. The community's aspirations for its children were as high as those of any other community. Their expectations, on the other hand, were very low. Neither the employers nor most local college officials placed a very high priority on candidates having more than the most basic academic skills. Most disheartening, the actual standards used by employers and college officials in the community to hire graduates or admit them to college were so low as to be virtually nonexistent. Many college officials said that they had no admissions requirements, only preferences. If they were to insist on a level of high-school achievement that would ensure success in college, they would not have enough students to fill the capacity they had built in the roaring sixties and seventies. So they would take whatever they could get—often only a high-school diploma and sometimes not even that.

Employers gave the same report. Those hiring clerical help did not insist that applicants be able to spell, because they could not fill their positions if they did. Machine shops did not assess the academic skills of applicants because they were experiencing terrible trouble finding anyone who would even show up for work once enrolled in an apprenticeship program.

These actual practices of both employers and colleges sent the signal to youngsters in school that most could get a decent job or go to college simply by getting a diploma. They did not really have to know anything. Neither the colleges nor the employers seemed to realize their own complicity in the system that produced such poor academic performance in the schools.

The National Center recommended that the school district create a compact involving the business community and the colleges. The district would ask both to help define a new set of specific school-leaving standards, and then ask employers to give preference in pay and promotion opportunities to graduates who met those standards, and the colleges to give the same group preference in admissions and financial aid. This would provide a strong incentive for all students to work hard in school.

As this is written, the district is drafting such a set of standards for presentation to an external body of the kind suggested by the center. District staff know that if Rochester's students are to reach the new standards, they will need a radically different curriculum and greatly improved teaching techniques. That curriculum that the district is building will recognize the cultural diversity in the student body, provide a means for students to acquire the higher-order thinking skills that the modern workplace requires, and encourage students to integrate all the disciplines in the application of their knowledge to real-world problems.

The district has worked hard and well on these issues at the middle school level in the system, but this time there is an added dimension. The restructuring strategy calls not for central curriculum development, but for giving each school staff primary responsibility for developing a curriculum that will enable their students to meet the new standards. Much of the curriculum development effort will have to be based on a staff development program that helps school staffs build the skills they will need. This requirement merges with the need to train the staff in the use of the tools of a Total Quality management process—such things as common problem-solving techniques, data analysis, consensus building, and meeting skills—to produce in turn a need for resources for staff development that far outstrips the funds now available.

Clarity on student performance standards, of course, is of little value unless student progress toward those standards can be accurately assessed. Rochester is doing some of the best work in the country on the use of portfolios of student work to assess their accomplishments in the early grades, but because McWalters wanted a set of measures that would enable him to compare the performance of Rochester's students with that of students elsewhere in the country, he decided to have Rochester join the New Standards Project, a national effort to develop a whole new student performance measurement system that incorporates portfolio systems, described in the next chapter.

Following release of the report of the Commission on the Skills of the American Workforce in June 1990, Kay Whitmore, CEO of Rochester-based Eastman Kodak and a member of the commission, agreed to loan the National Center a high-level executive to lead the implementation of the commission's recommendations in Rochester. Whitmore felt keenly the business community's obligation to produce explicit standards for work readiness. In the absence of this, he said, business leaders could hardly hold the district accountable for poor student performance.

But much more than business involvement in setting school-leaving standards would be needed. Many firms would have to help build the science and math curriculum; set technical standards for apprenticeship programs; offer opportunities for on-the-job training; provide mentors, job opportunities, and personal support to disadvantaged students; and offer real rewards to students who work hard in school.

A group of Rochester community leaders agreed to provide start-up funding for the implementation program. To provide broad policy direction for the effort, the center assembled a committee composed of top executives from leading Rochester firms, business associations, and educational institutions. This group reviewed the agenda established by the Commission on the Skills of the American Workforce, and agreed on a broad set of goals for the effort, roughly matching the commission's agenda, but casting it in a form appropriate for this community.

At the same time, the Center formed a forty-four-member task force to design a school-to-work transition program for Rochester. This group included among its members middle-management officials of firms, public-sector employers, unions, community-based agencies, state and local government, local school districts, higher education, training organizations, and other agencies. Few of these people had ever worked together before. Their job was to hammer out an action plan to be presented to the Board of Education and the business leaders' group for their review and approval.

The plan they came up with embraces kindergarten through postsecondary education and training. It calls for sweeping changes in the schools and deep involvement of the business community at every point along the way. Its great virtue is that it shows why the whole community, not just the schools, must mobilize to get the job done. It portrays the tight relationships among three streams of reform that few now perceive to be related: school restructuring, school-to-work transition, and the reform of services to children. Skills are developed, it points out, not just in school, but at work, in the family, and in the community as well. Its thesis is that the community will not get young adults with the skills it needs unless all these streams are involved with and related to one another in an explicit way. It shows why employers, among others, must be involved from start to finish.

As spring of 1990 came to a close, the teachers' contract was about to expire. The central issue was accountability. There was real anger in the community on this point, many people feeling that the teachers had gotten their handsome raise, while the accountability for student performance that the community had been promised in exchange had been deliberately ignored. But there was matching anger on the part of many teachers, who felt that the community was unwilling to be held accountable for its responsibility to send kids to school who were healthy, decently housed, well motivated, and ready to learn. More than that, many felt that some parents were not willing to be accountable for their own children but were quite willing to hold the schools accountable for things over which the school had no control.*

The contract that was negotiated in the fall addressed the accountability issue in several different ways. First, provisions in the old contract that involved the union in removing incompetent teachers were strengthened. Second, an elaborate plan was included for evaluating individual teachers against the professional standards being developed by the new National Board for Professional Teaching Standards and compensating them based on that evaluation. Third, a mechanism was established for identifying schools that are in deep trouble, withholding raises from the staff of such schools, and, if necessary, dismissing them from their positions. These provisions supplemented a policy that had already been in effect giving parents and students their choice of secondary school in which to enroll. The proposed contract was to include a 33 percent pay raise for the teachers, spread out over three years.

The board of education approved the contract in a split vote and the teachers narrowly defeated it a few days later, a stunning surprise to all concerned. Urbanski considered resigning his position. The community, seeing the defeat of the contract as proof that the teachers were opposed to accountability, was

---

*The issue of accountability is very sensitive among teachers for all these reasons and many more. Most union leaders prefer to duck it, for understandable reasons. Urbanski is among the very few who have had the courage to raise it and make it the core issue in a contract negotiation. Some months earlier, Albert Shanker, the president of the American Federation of Teachers, had raised the same issue with his top union leaders. His views, much like those we express in this book, were made public in his article "The End of the Traditional Model of Schooling—and a Proposal for Using Incentives to Restructure our Public Schools," *Phi Delta Kappan* 71 (5 [January 1990]): 344. Shanker had been using his weekly column in the *New York Times* to promote the Carnegie report proposals regularly, with considerable success. Contrary to the conventional wisdom, the RAND Corporation found that restructuring was furthest advanced in the most highly unionized school districts. But his members proved rather unreceptive to his ideas about new incentive structures for American education.

outraged. No doubt some teachers do oppose accountability, but the defeat of the contract does not prove that the majority does so. A remark McWalters made to the board when it was considering the contract led the teachers to believe that very few would get the raises that strong evaluations were supposed to entail. Many were uneasy about being judged against the standards of the National Board, which they knew little about. Some were also leery of being judged by students and parents, also called for in the contract, when they did not know what the canons of judgment would be and believed they were being set up for retribution on grounds that might have little to do with their teaching ability. Forty percent of the teachers, many of them supporters of the proposed contract, were not present for the vote, but many of its detractors were.

The contract was renegotiated and put up for another vote. This time, 98 percent of the teachers were present, ratifying the contract by an unprecedented margin of 97 percent. But this time, the board rejected it—unanimously. As the community saw it, two key things had changed in the meantime, neither for the better. In the attempt to win the teachers' assent, some of the accountability provisions had been altered. But the main thing that had changed was the fiscal condition of the state and the district. New York State was projecting a six-billion-dollar deficit. The contract's projected teachers' raise, acceptable to most in the early fall, was now thought to be way out of line. The teachers were seen as insensitive and greedy by many outspoken community members. As many teachers saw it, however, they had agreed to pay raises that left them at salary levels still below those successfully negotiated by teachers in some suburbs—teachers who had students easier to teach—and they had agreed to accountability provisions which, though unsatisfactory to many in the community, far exceeded anything they knew about in any teachers' contract in the whole nation. Both sides felt angry and betrayed.

At the end of March 1991, the contract dispute had gone into a fact-finding procedure managed by the state's Public Employees Relations Board. During the process, provisions for parent participation in the evaluation of teacher performance and for relating teachers' pay to that performance were added, with the agreement of the teachers. But McWalters was estimating a budget for the coming school year of somewhere between $20 million and $30 million less than what the district estimated as needed to maintain the program in 1990–91, a cut on the order of 10 percent of the district's $317 million budget. That would mean substantial layoffs, and cutting nonpersonnel items to the bone.

For the board of education, the contract dispute had brought the recognition that the board was way out in front of the community. Little effort had been made to bring the community into the process of planning the reform program and, as a result, few parents or other community members understood what the board was trying to accomplish and how it was going about it. So, when community support was most needed, it was not there. A concerted effort would have to be made both to engage parents and other community members in the reform program more deeply and to develop a more sophisticated and multifaceted strategy for communicating the board's goals and programs to the public.

The Rochester experience demonstrates some of the complexity of the restructuring agenda in practice as well as some sense of the time it will take to implement that agenda. Many of the components of the Rochester strategy are still in the design stage. Others have not yet begun at all. Only a few are in the early stages of implementation. The district is only now figuring out how to weave all of the elements of the agenda into one seamless web.

Rochester is not the only pioneer. As the leaders learn how to do it, it will be easier and faster for those that follow. But it will never be easy. The Xerox team was right. Public-school staffs do not believe their jobs are in danger if the students fail to learn. One reason that progress is so slow in Rochester, as one governor put it to us in the context of his own state, is that there is no penalty if the professionals choose to sit on their hands.

The structure of incentives for the professionals is a crucial issue, one that is much more likely to be solved at the state level than locally. This issue is the topic of the next chapter, but for an approach that could not be better calculated to match a local effort of the kind we have just described, we need to look at the state of Kentucky.[2]

The story began in 1985 when sixty-six Kentucky school districts joined forces to file suit in the state's courts seeking to have them declare the state system of finance unconstitutional. Four years later, the Kentucky Supreme Court did just that—and much more. To the astonishment of the state and nation, it declared the entire system of education unconstitutional and gave the legislature one year to invent a whole new state system of public education.

Nothing like this had ever happened in the history of American education. In June 1989, the legislature created a twenty-two-member committee, chaired by the speaker and president of the Senate, to steer the work. David Hornbeck, a partner in the Washington law firm of Hogan and Hartson, served as principal consultant to the committee responsible for coming up with the new design of the program features of interest here.

All of Kentucky's extensive laws and regulations establishing the inputs to the education process had been abolished by the court decision. The reform act passed by the legislature abolished the old State Department of Education and the jobs of its entire staff, and created a new one. Unlike the old department, it had the primary tasks of developing clear student performance standards—through a new Council on School Performance Standards appointed by the governor—and new measures of student progress toward those standards, and of providing technical assistance to the state's schools. The department—and the legislature—were to get out of most aspects of the regulating business. Responsibility for deciding how students are to meet the student performance standards was given to the teachers and principals. The new law mandated formation of school councils made up of three teachers, two parents, and the principal. By

1995, the school districts must hand over control of the schools' budgets and programs to these councils. The law specifically gives the councils the right to determine the curriculum (within a curriculum framework adopted by the state), student assignments, staff assignments, the daily schedule, instructional practices, and the use of school space. They will even select the principals from lists supplied by the superintendent and select new teachers after the superintendent has made recommendations. Teachers recommended for dismissal by the superintendent can be fired by a tribunal composed of one teacher, one administrator, and one layperson.

The act mandated an early childhood program for disadvantaged four-year-olds; ungraded primary schools through grade 3; family and youth resource centers (one "in or near" every school with 20 percent or more poor students); a major state initiative on educational technology including development of a statewide fiber-optic cable system; continuing education for students who need time beyond the regular school day, week, or term; regional professional development centers; assessment centers for principals; an Educational Professional Standards Board; and an alternative route to licensing for teachers. It required that aspiring principals finish a certification program, go through an internship, and complete a principal's assessment program before they can be hired, and a similar procedure for candidates for superintendents' positions. The legislation reflects a carefully drawn coherent plan in which these features fit together like a puzzle.

But, for our purposes, the key provisions have to do with accountability. School staffs will be rewarded for increasing the school's proportion of successful students. The schools with the lowest proportion of successful students will be required to improve the most to receive a reward. These rewards will be shared among the whole instructional staff, who will decide by majority rule, school by school, how the rewards will be spent, though rewards used as bonuses will not be added to base salaries.

Schools that experience declines of up to 5 percent in student performance must develop an improvement plan and can get assistance from the school improvement fund. But schools that suffer declines in student performance of 5 percent or more will be designated "schools in crisis." In those schools, the staff goes on probation, with their tenure suspended. Their students are free to choose to go to successful schools. People designated as "Kentucky Distinguished Educators" will be assigned to these schools to evaluate the staff every six months and recommend retention, transfer, or dismissal. A State Department of Education S.W.A.T. team is empowered to shut down failing schools altogether.

The state board is empowered to develop similar rewards and penalties for instructional staff not assigned to specific schools and for entire school districts.

The legislature did, of course, address the original problem posed by the school-district suit—school finance. $1.3 billion in new taxes were voted by the legislature to fund the plan, with much of this revenue to go to property-poor districts. $15 million was set aside to reward successful schools in the first year of the reward program, with larger amounts to come as the program is fully implemented.[3]

The Kentucky plan clearly has many elements in common with the Rochester restructuring program. Both move from design standards to performance standards. Both move primary responsibility for instructional decisions to the school's staff in exchange for professional accountability for the results. Both provide for tough sanctions on the staffs of schools that are failing their students, while providing help to schools in trouble. Both combine school-choice policies with rewards and sanctions for school staff in their incentive plans. Both attend to the need to be clear about what the student performance standards will be. Both take unprecedented measures to assure a high-quality school staff and leadership. And both specify in detail who is to be involved in making school-level decisions.

The principles of restructuring laid out in the Carnegie report have been capturing the imagination of a widening circle of policymakers and other influential people. But the actual work of restructuring our school systems for high performance has barely begun. Only a handful of states and districts are seriously engaged with this agenda. National leadership from both the private and public sectors on a scale not yet seen is needed if it is to succeed. A concerted effort is required to restructure the nation's schools for high performance. A unified performance-oriented policy system for American education is required, from the federal government through state and local policy-making bodies to the individual school.

America's challenge is to restructure the entire system for public education, from the Federal government to the classroom. The principles on which such a system should be built are clear:

- Set clear goals for the students, benchmarked to an international standard;
- Find a way accurately to measure student progress toward those goals;
- Push the decisions about curriculum and other elements of instructional strategy, including resource allocation, down to the school level, and involve parents in those decisions;
- Reward school staffs that produce strong student progress and provide real consequences for those whose students fail to progress;
- Ensure that each school has the financial resources it needs to match the educational performance of any other school;
- Abolish all input rules and regulations except those that relate to health, safety, and civil rights, and those needed to organize the restructured system;
- Set high performance standards for the education professions; use those standards, not input standards, to control entry into and progression through the professions;

- Apply the Total Quality process for high-performance management and the techniques of high-performance work organization throughout the whole system;
- Set aside an amount equal to 4 percent of salaries and wages for the continuing education and training of the school staff, to enable them to acquire the skills and information necessary to do the jobs;
- Organize employers and colleges to reward students who perform to the high standards the system sets.

This agenda is not, of course, all that is required to turn America's schools into world leaders. In the next three chapters we will have more to say about the role incentives and national standards can play in the restructured system, and the urgent need to address the problems of poverty among children so that everyone can meet the standards we propose.

CHAPTER 9

Incentives: The Great Debate

Restructuring private industry for high performance is, as we have shown, very difficult. Restructuring schools for the same purpose is even more difficult, as Rochester's story amply demonstrates. Surely, there must be an easier way to accomplish the revolution. Many think they have found it in "choice"—the use of market mechanisms to provide powerful incentives to educators to improve their product or go out of the business. This option has powerful adherents—among them the Bush administration—who have been attracted by the idea's surgical simplicity and the notion that the improvement in performance that its advocates promise could be delivered at no additional cost to the public. The "choice" option therefore deserves careful examination to see whether it can really perform what its advocates promise.

The Magna Carta of the choice movement is *Politics, Markets, and America's Schools,* by John Chubb and Terry Moe, two researchers at the Brookings Institution.[1] Based on a study of a large sample of students in private and public schools, the authors conclude that the best way to improve the public schools is to subject them to the same market discipline that the private schools must live with.

They begin by asserting that the things that education policy usually focuses on—inputs to the process like spending, class size, teacher experience—have little if any effect on achievement test scores at the high-school level. Student ability and family resources have the greatest effect on measured achievement, but these things cannot be affected by policy. The only other factor that they found to have a major effect on student achievement is what they call "effective organization," that is, clear and ambitious goals, a strong academic program, teacher professionalism, shared influence, strong educational leadership, and staff harmony. The schools in their sample that had these characteristics were characterized by much professional autonomy and little bureaucratic influence. With rare exceptions, these were private and parochial schools, not public schools. It follows, they believe, that schools run by bureaucracies cannot be effectively organized and hence cannot succeed.

Chubb and Moe argue that "democratic control" is the enemy of "effective organization." This is because democratic political systems impose "higher-order values through public authority."[2] Since public officials cannot be sure that the people below them in the hierarchy will faithfully implement their decisions, they are forced to rely on "formal rules and regulations that tell these people what to do and hold them accountable for doing it." Unions add to the problem by

> protecting the interests of their members through formal constraints on the governance and operation of schools . . . that strike directly at the schools' capacity to build well-functioning teams based on informal cooperation. . . . [They] complain that the schools are too bureaucratic. . . . But they are the ones who bureaucratized the schools in the past, and they will continue to do so, even as they tout the advantages of autonomy and professionalism. The incentives to bureaucratize the schools are built into the system.[3]

Chubb and Moe acknowledge that there are effective schools in the public system, but they believe they succeed in spite of the system rather than because of it. With these rare exceptions, bureaucratic control—the implacable foe as they see it of successful schools—is the inevitable result of democratic control. The alternative is the market control that governs private education. In the private sector, schools must compete for the support of parents and students, who are free to choose among schools. In such systems,

> bureaucratic control [is] unnecessary. [Their] . . . primary concern is to please their clients . . . which leads them to favor decentralized forms of organization that take full advantage of strong leadership, strong teacher professionalism, discretionary judgment, informed cooperation, and teams. [T]he process of natural selection complements the incentives of the marketplace in propelling and supporting a population of autonomous, effectively organized schools.[4]

The solution to the schools crisis, Chubb and Moe then reason, is simple: Replace the bureaucratic control of schools found in the public sector by the market control of schools found in the private sector. This will get to the root of the problem. Nothing else will work, they say, because "the fundamental cause[s] of poor academic performance . . . are not to be found in the schools, but rather in the institutions by which the schools have traditionally been governed."[5] They are emphatic in their belief that choice—market control of schools—is the silver bullet of education reform.

> Choice is not like other reforms and should not be combined with them. Choice is a self-contained reform with its own rationale and justification. It has the capacity *all by itself* to bring about the kind of transformation that reformers have been seeking to engineer for years in myriad other ways. Indeed, if choice is to work to greatest advantage, it must be adopted without these other reforms, since they are predicated on democratic control and are implemented by bureaucratic means.[6]

Chubb and Moe's reform program begins by withdrawing authority from the existing institutions of public education and vesting it directly in schools, parents, and students. They would begin the process by having the states redefine what a public school is by setting forth "minimal" criteria that roughly correspond to the criteria now used to accredit private schools. Any private school that meets these criteria would be redefined as a public school, eligible to receive public scholarship funds through a "choice office" located in each district. Wealthier districts would be free to supplement the scholarships distributed by the state.

Each school would make its own admissions decisions, subject only to nondiscrimination requirements, and would be free to set its own tuition rate. Each student would be guaranteed admission somewhere, though not necessarily at a school of his or her choice, since many students could not afford the tuition at many schools. Similarly, schools could expel students based on their own standards, provided that such expulsions are not "arbitrary and capricious."

The states would be prohibited from specifying any particular organizational form for schools. They could continue to license teachers, but their licensing requirements would have to be minimal, limited to a determination that the applicants have a bachelor's degree and no obvious problems in their personal history. The states, furthermore, could not hold the schools responsible for performance. Accountability would be entirely a function of the choices made by parents and students. The states' role would be to make sure that the schools fully and fairly disclose their performance to their current and prospective clients.

The trouble with this picture is that the analysis that Chubb and Moe make of their own data is fundamentally faulty; other data show that private schools taken as a whole perform no better than public schools; and apart from their analysis, the reforms they advocate are more likely to reduce achievement in American schools than to improve it.

We will take their analysis of their own data first, following what we believe to be the most penetrating critique of *Politics, Markets, and America's Schools* to date, that of James Liebman, a professor at Columbia University Law School.[7]

Liebman's critique starts with a look at the role that student and parent "taste for education" plays in Chubb and Moe's analysis. Taste for education is, roughly, the equivalent of motivation to succeed in school and achieve at high levels. The point is important because, if private schools produce better results than public schools because they attract students and parents who have on average more taste for education than their public-school counterparts, then to that extent their relative success is not the result of school organization and freedom from bureaucracy, and Chubb and Moe's analysis does not hold up.

One could, of course, argue that this is a chicken and egg question. If private schools attract students and parents with a taste for education, it must be because of characteristics such as good organization and less bureaucracy that distinguish them from public schools. But there are other plausible hypotheses. Church-related schools, for example, might be attractive because of the value system they represent. Or parents hope that the high motivation of the other students will rub off on their own children. Higher achievement, in other words, is a function of both the characteristics of the school and the characteristics of the children who attend that school. The challenge for the analyst is figuring out how to apportion the reason for high achievement among the various factors that might account for it. One of the most interesting questions, however, is whether achievement in non-public schools is actually higher than that of students in public schools, after one takes into account the social class differences between those who attend public and non-public schools, or even if one does not do so. All these issues are discussed later. We begin where Chubb and Moe begin, with their attempt to show that the presumed beneficial effects of private education are not simply the result of selecting students who are more highly motivated to succeed.

In an attempt to eliminate the effect of taste for education as a factor in the analysis, Chubb and Moe use a statistical device that defines taste for education in terms of seniors' test scores as sophomores, on the assumption that this is a reasonable measure of student motivation. But Liebman points out that the motivation of college-bound students to succeed typically increases during the junior and senior years, as college admissions decisions draw near, and those of non-college-bound students declines, as the boredom of the last two years sets in. Curiously, Chubb and Moe ignore students' reports of the expectation of their parents that they will go to college, surely a crude but more accurate measure of taste for education than achievement scores in the sophomore year of high school.

Finally, and much more damaging, Chubb and Moe include such other factors as the proportion of students enrolled in college preparatory courses as measures of good school organization rather than among the measures of taste for education, thereby attributing to school organization factors that are more reasonably associated with motivation. The result is artificially to double the effect of school organization and to reduce the effect of motivation in their analysis by a corresponding amount. It is reasonable, as Liebman points out, to think that school policies have something to do with the choices that students make as to whether to enroll in college prep courses, but it is very unlikely that these choices have more to do with school organization than with parents' and students' taste for academics and for a college education and everything a college education brings.

When academic track is removed in the statistical analysis from the factors associated with school organization and added to the parent-student factors, Chubb and Moe's finding that school organization accounts for a substantial portion of student achievement crumbles. Parent-student factors end up accounting for 87 percent of the variation in student achievement, and school organization ends up accounting for only 14 percent of the school-related variation.

Liebman then looks into the (corrected) 14 percent of variation in achievement that is accounted for by "school organization" in Chubb and Moe's data. The critique here turns on the way Chubb and Moe measured effective school organization. According to them a school is well organized if (1) students report that the school has fair disciplinary procedures; (2) its teachers report that they feel responsible for the success or failure of their students, that they have strong influence over school policy, that they get along and cooperate well with each other, that administrative "routines and paperwork" only rarely intrude on their work, and that their principal has clear objectives for the school, values innovation and new ideas, and keeps the school apprised of where it is going; and (3) if the school's principal reports that he or she focuses more attention on students' academic excellence than upon basic literacy skills, attaches more importance to gaining control of the school than to career advancement, values the pedagogical more than the managerial aspects of the job, and employs excellent teachers.

Chubb and Moe would have us believe that these factors are determined by policy and that they in turn determine student performance. But Liebman suggests that the converse is more plausible: The participants in a school in which students are achieving at high levels are very likely to respond positively to questions such as those that Chubb and Moe ask than participants in a school where they are not, even if the objective situation in the two schools is actually identical. Students who are achieving at high levels and staying out of trouble are likely to express more confidence in a school's disciplinary procedures than students in a school where they are not doing well and in trouble all the time. Teachers and principals in schools where students are low achievers are far more likely to want to blame "the bureaucracy" for their failures than themselves; whereas teachers and principals in schools in which students are succeeding are likely to want to take credit for the success. We would agree with Chubb and Moe that what schools do accounts for a fair measure of student success or failure, but their measure of school organization seems to be less a measure of that variable than of students' and teachers' perceptions of success.

The suburban public schools and private schools (most of which are also in the suburbs) that Chubb and Moe like are largely populated by people who fled the public-school districts with the greatest educational problems, typically at great cost to themselves. By this measure alone, we can assume that these people have a greater taste for education than the people of similar means whom they left behind. We should hardly be surprised to find that performance is better in such schools when we find that the people who have the highest educational aspirations for their children congregate there, or that the people who patronize such schools are happier than those who do not.

In the end, as Liebman puts it, what Chubb and Moe have said on this point boils down to "two not very interesting propositions: that parent and student motivations affect learning, and that schools full of strong performers have happier clients and professionals than schools full of weak performers. . . ."[8]

Having demonstrated, to their own satisfaction at least, the primary importance of effective school organization in accounting for academic achievement, Chubb and Moe proceed to ask what factors might account for effective school organization. Here, they do consider the role of taste for education, but they do so in a curious way, measuring taste for education by parent contact with schools and student comportment.

It is hard to credit this. Families headed by two parents, only one of whom works—the kind most prevalent in the better-off suburbs—are obviously far more likely to have the time to be in contact with teachers than families headed by a single parent who is almost always working, the kind of family found most often in the inner city. It is also true that the typically white staffs of inner-city schools are often reluctant to visit the homes of poor minority youth and are often perceived by their clients as hostile and unapproachable. That hardly means, however, that these clients do not care about the achievement of their children in school. This measure of taste for education is more accurately a measure of family income and structure.

Chubb and Moe then attempt to isolate the effects of the presence or absence of educational bureaucracy on school autonomy. It is at this point that they try to demonstrate the superior virtues of the organization of private education. Interestingly, according to Chubb and Moe's own account, private control accounts, according to Liebman, for "only three-fifths of one-fourth of one-seventh of the posited causes of the outcome (achievement) [they] hope to foster."[9] That is 2 percent, hardly a firm foundation for policy-making.

What is most noteworthy, however, given Chubb and Moe's reliance on the private model of education in their argument for market control of education, is that they do not report any correlation between private control and student achievement. The reason is not hard to find. Over the years, try as they might, no researchers, when adequately controlling for other factors, have *ever* been able to find anything more than a very weak correlation between private control and achievement. Nor is it at all clear that private schools, taken as a whole, produce students with higher achievement, even if other factors, such as student motivation and social class, are not controlled. The 1991 report by the National Assessment of Educational Progress of achievement in mathematics, which for the first time published the data in a form permitting comparison of the performance of students in private education with those in public schools, is an important case in point.[10] There was no difference. When asked why they had never released the data in this form before, NAEP officials replied that they saw no need to do so because there had never been any difference, for as long as NAEP had collected such data.[11]

But Chubb and Moe leap over this singular omission in their analysis. Having demonstrated to their own satisfaction that effective school organization is a powerful cause of student achievement and that school autonomy is a powerful cause of effective school organization, and having established that private schools have more autonomy than public ones, they then go on to assert that market forces produce better results than democratic control because private schools function in the market and public ones are subject to democratic control. They offer no data on this point. That is, having offered us no evidence that private schools do a better job of educating students, they simply assert that the nation ought to abandon democratic control of its schools to embrace the market system that they assert controls private education, without even attempting to offer any evidence that it is the market that accounts for the autonomy they admire in the private schools.

Having revealed glaring methodological problems in Chubb and Moe's analysis (only a few of which we have summarized), Liebman turns to the next interesting question: Quite apart from the empirical evidence to support it, does the choice program offered by Chubb and Moe make sense on its face as a prescription for the future?

Imagine a truly free market, a market like the one in which carpets and soap are sold. Customers are free to decide whether to buy at all, and how much (including nothing) they are prepared to spend. But education is what economists call a public good; that is, expenditures on education benefit not only the individual who gets educated, but the society as a whole, because an educated citizenry, as this book argues, is the key to prosperity for all, and because an educated citizenry is also the bulwark of a free society. So the society compels everyone to participate and everyone to pay, whether or not they happen to be a participant at the time they pay. In a true market, the market functions to allocate scarce goods. Those with the highest incomes are expected to buy the best soaps and carpets; those with the least get the worst or go without.

But it is not in the society's interest to allocate public goods that way. Left to the discipline of the market, those with the lowest incomes can be expected to invest the least in their own and their children's education. But those with the lowest incomes are likely to require the greatest investment to realize their highest potential, so that society is least well served when the market is used to allocate education. With this rather straightforward reasoning, Liebman shows that Chubb and Moe have not simply done a poor job of statistical analysis, they have got the whole problem wrong.

To be fair, Chubb and Moe do not propose a completely unrestricted market. The state would establish a minimum "scholarship" amount and schools would be subject to antidiscrimination requirements. But the beneficiaries can take that "scholarship" to any school that meets Chubb and Moe's minimum requirements.

Bear in mind that those who now take the private-school option or move from the city to the better suburbs must now pay a substantial price for doing so. That price would be lowered by the amount of the "scholarship" in Chubb and Moe's plan, so that families with higher motivation and more financial resources would find it much easier than now to leave the city schools and climb the social ladder.

Many choice advocates, consistent with their free-market ideology, would leave schools free to charge whatever the traffic would bear. With more money available for what are now private schools, the better schools could be expected to raise tuition. Those with little means or low motivation or both would be left far behind, and the inevitable result would be much more social stratification in the schools than we have now.

But Liebman makes another, even more telling, point. Under any choice plan, schools seeking to do well in the market would be highly motivated to show that students who attended their institution achieved at high levels. Because the biggest contributors to achievement are family income and parents' education, the best way to establish a reputation for high achievement would be to screen clients based on parents' income and education. Those that did the best screening job would experience the fastest rise in achievement, and having done so, would be able to attract the most advantaged student body, in an endless upward cycle of profits, exclusion, and social stratification. If, in addition, prices were permitted to rise to whatever the market would bear, this process would operate with ruthless efficiency. The market, in other words, would do what it has always done best: allocate scarce resources on the basis of wealth. Our schools would be finely segregated, like any other consumer market, on the basis of class. The result would be, to use Liebman's apt analogy, a world in which it would be possible to sort schools by social class just as easily as one can now sort restaurants by social class, from McDonald's to Sardi's.[12] In fact it would be easier, because one can more readily imagine the rich patronizing McDonald's and the poor indulging in a night out at Sardi's than the rich sending their children for a year to an inferior school or the poor finding their way into a rich suburban school. The prospects of the poor would be truly desperate. It would be the end, as a matter of policy, to any aspiration that this country ever had that its schools would serve as the first line of defense in a strategy to provide equal opportunity to all.

Chubb and Moe, unlike the advocates of pure voucher plans, would restrict what schools could charge and customers would pay, for the reasons we have just put forward (though they would permit schools to select their students based on the income and education of their parents). By doing so, they restrict the ability of the disciplines of the market to produce what they most desire, because they reduce in comparable measure the ability of the suppliers of education services to attract customers by lowering the price or to improve services by increasing the price. It is hard in these circumstances to see how they can say that the public will get the benefits of the market when they would deprive the market of some of its most powerful incentives. The only incentive left to put fear into the hearts of the managers of poorly performing schools is that a competitor could attract customers by providing a better service at the same price. As Liebman reminds us, this was exactly the state of competition in the airline industry before deregulation, when prices were very high and the service hardly universally admired.[13] Even then, however, the airlines faced competition from other forms of public transportation, a possibility that the educational institutions in Chubb and Moe's plan would not have to worry about.

The irony, as Liebman sees it, is the way schools are likely to respond to an incentive system in which they must compete on quality rather than price. As colleges have known for a long time, the surest route to success when success depends on perceptions of high student achievement is to select students who already excel. Because the Chubb and Moe plan would permit schools to sort students based on parents' education level, it would not simply condemn those now unfortunate enough to be poor, it would operate to condemn their offspring for generations to come by consigning them to schools in which not only their parents, but the parents of all of their classmates, would be poor. Even without letting prices rise to whatever consumers will pay, the plan would inaugurate a kind of class-based society that this country has never had—the kind that many of our forebears left their homelands to escape.

Some advocates of the Chubb and Moe plan respond to these criticisms by saying that the market works well enough in higher education; why not use the same principle in the schools? But Liebman asks us to take a look at who actually uses the public subsidies (such as Pell grants) to go to Stanford and Yale, and who uses the same subsidies to go to the institutions that prepare beauticians and secretaries.[14] And consider what the students who attend these institutions get for the same public dollar. Who would choose to go to beautician school when they could go to Stanford? And who, in fact, gets to choose?

There are still other restrictions that the schools operating under Chubb and Moe's plan would have to face. The two researchers, the reader will recall, say that the schools would have to avoid discrimination; to follow due process in dismissing teachers and other matters, that they would have to abide by accreditation rules set by the state; to develop fee schedules that took "special needs" into account; to collect and make public information about their operations in a form decreed by the state, and much more. All this would require a complex regulatory structure—far more so than the private schools now have to face. It would almost certainly involve an important new limitation on freedom of choice, since it is very unlikely that the courts would permit parochial schools to qualify for the funds distributed under the plan unless those schools were run on a strictly nonsectarian basis. Moreover, to comply with all this regulation, those private and parochial schools that choose to take the state's funds under the plan would have to put in place the very thing that Chubb and Moe are most anxious to avoid—their own bureaucracy.

In the end, Liebman says, and we agree, that Chubb and Moe's plan "achieves neither equity, market freedom, nor excellence."[15] The route to improvement, he argues, lies not in more choice, but less. The trick is to find a way to get those who care most about education to fight for it, to exercise their voice in the public (democratically controlled) arena on behalf of excellence. Create disincentives for those in the public schools to exit to the private schools and make it less advantageous for those in the inner city to leave the poor and the powerless by exiting to the suburbs. Make it harder for those whose children should be attending neighborhood schools to impoverish those schools by enrolling their children in a handful of elite magnet schools. This could be done, he says, by making all schools magnet schools, by creating metropolitan school districts where there are now suburban rings around rotting urban cores, and by taking away the tax exemptions of private schools, thereby raising their prices. We agree, but we think there is much more to the matter than that.

In our view, Chubb and Moe are right in thinking that the schools would perform far better if decisions about how students are to be educated to a high standard are made in the schools, rather than at the upper levels of the educational hierarchy. They are right in thinking that school systems would be much more effective if they were less bureaucratic, if the decisions in them were made more collegially, if the goals were clearer and agreed on by the staffs, and if the programs were challenging for the students. But, as we have shown, their prescription for achieving this does not begin to bear the weight of even casual analysis. If markets alone produced organizations that had the features Chubb and Moe admire in schools, then firms operating in the market in the United States and elsewhere would have had them from the time the country was founded. In fact, the opposite is true. Most firms in the United States are still organized on the same highly bureaucratic, Taylorist lines as the schools whose bureaucracy Chubb and Moe despise. Markets do not eliminate bureaucracies and bureaucratic behavior; indeed, under certain conditions they encourage these things.

The one insight that Chubb and Moe bring to the discussion—though it is hardly theirs alone—is that incentives count. People tend to do the things that are formally and informally rewarded by the organizations in which they work. If you want to change people's behavior, then you must change the incentives that motivate that behavior. As things are, the real incentives that operate in most school systems combine to lower independent initiative, discourage people who want more than anything to improve student performance, and encourage those for whom the highest value is personal loyalty to their colleagues and their superiors in the bureaucracy.

Likewise, Chubb and Moe are right in thinking that the discipline that competition for customers brings would be useful in the education sector. To the maximum feasible extent, that discipline ought to be used within the public schools. But for all the reasons put forward by Liebman, the discipline of unbridled competition would destroy everything the nation hopes to achieve in its schools, and the forms of competition that are left are not strong enough on their own to drive the kind of improvement that is needed.

Rather, the way to think about creating nonbureaucratic, non-Taylorist schools is to begin with the approach discussed earlier—that taken by America's best firms as they developed their own strategies to reach high performance. The system has to get the goals clear, find a way to measure them accurately, transfer decisions about how to reach the goals to the people in the schools, provide positive incentives, give those people the resources they need to do the job, and then hold them strictly accountable for student progress. Chubb and Moe, of course, will have none of this. They are opposed to district, state, or national standards for student achievement and reject the idea that the district or the state should hold the school staff accountable for student performance. Without standards and without accountability, however, there is only the market, and the market, by itself, will not work.

So how could one create a system that combines market incentives and the restructuring experience of private industry into a single system containing the most powerful incentives for top performance? We offer the following plan.

Assume that the state government and the school board have developed comprehensive but parsimonious standards, such as are discussed later, for what a student should know and be able to do on graduation from high school, as well as satisfactory methods for assessing the progress that each student has made toward mastering these skills.

Imagine, then, that the superintendent and the Board of Education say to the staff of the district that they are free to work together to plan programs for students that, in their judgment, will enable those students to make rapid progress toward these objectives. Each staff group would have to offer the full range of activities for students required to meet the core objectives of the district over a period of years, but need not have that full capacity within the group. They might wish to buy some specialist capacity—say the teaching of music or of laboratory science—from some group of teachers that chooses to band together to offer that service to their colleagues. (These service groups might be located within the district or might be private and based outside the district.)

The staff groups would be told that they could get a prorated share of the district's resources for their program, provided only that they meet two tests: first, that they attract parents willing to enroll their children in the program; and second, that they go before a board of their peers who will make a judgment as to whether the program they plan to offer meets professional standards of education. If they pass both tests, they are in business.

The entire district would then consist of such entrepreneurial units, competing with one another for students. One program, say a Montessori program for early childhood education, might have several classrooms in each of several school buildings. Another program, say a secondary-school program organized around the study of technology from a technical, social, historical, and political point of view, might occupy all of one school building and part of another. School buildings would be simply physical facilities to be managed as services; the fundamental unit of organization would be entrepreneurial programs.

These programs would grow and shrink to the degree that they were able to attract students. The base budget of each program would be a function of the size of the student body, corrected by a weighting that took into account the characteristics of the students, so that non-English-speaking students or physically handicapped students, for example, would bring in more revenue than students who spoke good English or did not have a physical handicap.

Beyond the base budget, the school district would hold a substantial portion of the whole district budget in reserve, for distribution at the end of the year according to the success of each program in promoting student progress, measured against that year's state and district standards. A program that had produced major gains for the students would receive a substantial year-end bonus. The staff of that program would have the option of putting that money into their pockets or plowing it back into the program. They would have a strong incentive to do the latter, knowing that other programs would be reinvesting the funds and those that chose not to do so would be at a competitive disadvantage.

The district would decide on a student performance "floor" below which no program would be allowed to fall. In this way, parents and taxpayers could be assured that charlatans could not persuade unwary or inattentive parents of the merits of a poor program. Even more important, students left behind in a program that was losing out to the competition would not be in danger of getting a substandard education.

No program could discriminate on the basis of race, sex, handicapping condition, or limited English-speaking capacity. Nor could a program turn clients away because they did not meet any other entrance requirements, though a popular program could use a lottery to keep its total size down if it did not wish to expand.

Within very broad limits, each program staff would be free to devise its own curriculum, though its choices would be constrained by the student performance standards set by the state and district, and by the structure of the incentive system. In effect, the staff would be free to choose the means by which students would reach goals that others had set.

Each school could also add its own goals to those of the state and district. One early elementary-level program might work at acquiring a reputation as a place that served the needs of parents who worked a full day; another might concentrate on attracting parents who wanted a program reflecting Piagetian principles of child growth and development. One high-school-level program might offer a curriculum geared to meeting the needs of the local laser industry for highly skilled laser technicians, and another might specialize in the arts. All programs, however, would be operating in the context of goals that would apply to all students; none could turn out narrowly trained graduates whose prospects later on in life would be constrained by the lack of a broad education.

The job of the Board of Education, the superintendent, and the central office staff in such a scheme would be to set the goals, structure the reward system, disseminate information about student performance by program to parents and community members, set the standards for hiring school staff (though the management of each program would determine who actually taught in that program), distribute funds to the programs, maintain a robust staff development system, operate the physical facilities, and provide the necessary support services.

Some support services, like transportation, would be centrally funded and centrally controlled. But others, like curriculum and instructional support, would be services purchased by the programs in the field. Those programs would have the choice of buying those services wherever they wished, so the central district service would go out of business if it were not delivering a service of a quality and at a price that was attractive to program managements.

In inner cities experiencing substantial student movement between schools, this plan would not work unless the district had a policy requiring students to remain enrolled for a full year in the school in which they began the year. That would mean that the district would have to be prepared to bus students from wherever they might move to after the beginning of the year back to the school in which they originally enrolled. This is a real cost of the structure we have laid out, but it can be justified on grounds having nothing to do with the merits of our proposals. In any case, the choice feature of this proposal would require that the district be prepared to transport any student to any school in the district, so the specific requirement to provide transportation to students whose families move in the course of the year would be only one aspect of the increased transportation requirement.

Perhaps the most important objective of this whole proposal is to create program staffs that would behave like entrepreneurial units. They would have very strong incentives to operate at maximum efficiency, to find out what their clients needed and to meet those needs, to strive constantly for quality, and to produce real gains for their students. They would be to present-day schools what Federal Express is to the United States Post Office.

All students would benefit, but none more than the minority and low-income students who today fare so badly under the current system. If the incentives were structured, as they should be, to provide the greatest rewards to the staff who produced the greatest student progress, then the most able professional staff members would prefer to work with those who needed their help the most, because that would be where the greatest progress would be possible.

This plan would both require and produce profound changes in the culture of American schools. Successful implementation would demand great managerial and political skill as well as creation of staff development systems that simply do not yet exist in the schools. But, in our view, the benefits to be gained in improved system performance could be no less profound. There is every reason to believe that the gains in performance would be comparable to those achieved by Japanese managers who took over failed American automobile plants and, with the same workers who had been there before, turned them into highly successful enterprises.

This is hardly a complete prescription for vaulting the United States to the top ranks of world education performance. Unlike Chubb and Moe, we believe that the failure of this country to be numbered in those ranks has to do, among other things, with the prevalence of poverty among children, our failure to organize social services properly and connect the delivery of those services to the schools, our failure to manage our education institutions well, and the inadequacy of our arrangements for school-to-work transition. But incentives are crucial, and this plan would work a sea change in the incentives that operate on school people. It includes the incentives afforded by choice within the public system, but it does not rely exclusively on them. It would turn our schools into entrepreneurial organizations, and the people in them into seekers after high performance.

Several features of the Kentucky plan described in the last chapter would do much the same thing. But neither the Kentucky plan nor the one just offered exhaust all the alternatives that should be considered as the nation thinks about changing the incentives that operate on school people.

We mentioned earlier one powerful approach to the use of public choice—the creation of metropolitan school districts in which students could enroll in any public school in the metro area, with free transportation to that school from any point in the enlarged district. In addition we would support a feature of Minnesota's choice plan that enables any student sixteen years old or older to enroll in any public postsecondary institution that will accept that student.

Ted Kolderie has suggested the idea of charter schools—schools chartered directly by the state that meet all the criteria other public schools have to meet, and are able to compete for students with the district in which they are situated, provided that such schools not be able to select students based on ability or parents' income.[16] Such schools could not discriminate. They would receive the same funds for each student they enrolled as the district in which they were located; that money would be transferred from the district with each student who transferred.

Kolderie has also suggested that the states should open up the possibility of chartering in the same manner, and subject to the same restrictions, organizations operating as public schools that would offer to run entire systems of education within current school districts, there being no reason on the face of it why a school district should have a monopoly on public education within its enrollment area.

Kolderie has gone further, pointing out that there is no logical reason why school boards should have to operate the education system in the districts for which they have policymaking responsibility. They could operate with a staff of half a dozen people whose task would be help them set standards and draw up requests for proposals from organizations that would like to offer their services under contract. The winners would have to meet performance targets set in the contract. Bidders could offer to take on the entire responsibility for the educational program in the district or only a part of that responsibility. Kolderie has suggested a variation on this theme, drawing on the example of the modern department store or supermarket, which typically runs certain departments with its own staff and contracts with outside firms to run others. School districts could do the same thing, contracting out the operation of particular schools, particular grades, or particular subjects. In each case, the contractors would have to serve all the students and their families, but they would be compensated in relation to the improvement in student performance that they produced.

These ideas are meant to be illustrative. They hardly exhaust the range of possibilities for changing the organization of public education to strengthen the incentives operating on school professionals to improve student performance. None of them are silver bullets, sufficient by themselves to produce the achievement levels that are required, but any one of them would produce substantial improvements over current performance. All, for that reason, are well worth considering.

CHAPTER 10

Building a System
Driven by Standards

Let us assume for the moment that the average American student has the same innate abilities, the same genetic capacity to learn, as students elsewhere in the world. Let us also assume that our teachers and school administrators are as intelligent and care as much about their students as teachers elsewhere. A visit to a school in any major foreign nation will show no major differences in curriculum or teaching techniques from the United States. What, then, could explain the difference in outcomes?

There are two primary reasons for the difference: student motivation and student poverty. As we saw in the last chapter, student motivation, when it is considered at all in the United States, is likely to be viewed as something that policy can do nothing about. As for poverty among children, it is rarely at the heart of the debate about education policy, when it is discussed at all.

American students need only get a high-school diploma to enter directly into the job market or college, except for the small proportion of students—less than 20 percent—who expect to go to selective colleges. In fact, as a practical matter, most of the work-bound and an increasing number of the college-bound do not even need a high-school diploma. Again as a practical matter, one can get a high-school diploma in most districts if one shows up in school most of the time and does not cause any trouble. The states that do impose some sort of performance requirement for graduation rarely set that requirement above seventh-grade equivalency. The result is that for the vast majority of American students, there is no incentive to do any more in school than simply show up and do just enough to get by.

There is an important corollary to this observation. Because the United States has never spelled out what students need to know and be able to do to succeed, teachers and boards of education have no guideposts for their own efforts, and parents have no way to determine whether their children are learning what they should be learning to be successful when they leave school.

This lack of relation between success in school and success later in life explains a great deal of the mystery of why similar curricula and teaching techniques can lead to such different results in our country than they do in the others. Real success in school takes hard work. If the students have no reason to work hard, they will not learn much, no matter what curriculum is used or what teaching techniques are employed.

The issue here is standards—what they are and how the system uses them to motivate student effort.

American education is not without standards. States specify the number of courses in particular subjects that students must take with a passing grade to graduate, the number of days in the school year and the length of the day, the courses that teachers must take to get a teaching license, and maximum class sizes for students of various ages. Districts specify the textbooks to be used, the length of school periods, and the scope and sequence of instruction in the various subjects to be taught. The federal government specifies class sizes for students with various handicapping conditions, the way in which aid is to be distributed to disadvantaged students, eligibility formulas for aid to illiterate adults, and much, much more.

But these are all standards of a particular kind. They are input standards, in the sense that they define the inputs into the process of education. Many states have shelves of laws and regulations literally a yard or more in length, defining the inputs that are to be used in the education process. Most say almost nothing at all about outcomes: what students should know and be able to do at the conclusion of each phase of their education and training.

Lewis Branscomb, the chair of the Carnegie task force and former director of the National Bureau of Standards, compares the situation in education with the distinction in engineering between design standards and performance standards.[1] Imagine a county manager who needs a bridge built and wants to get bids from companies seeking a contract for the job. There are two ways the manager can specify what is required. The first is to give the bidders the design specifications, annotated drawings of the bridge that specify in detail the design of the parts, the materials from which they are to be made, their manner of connection, and so on. The second way is to provide performance specifications: the distance it is meant to cross, the peak load traffic it will have to carry, and the length of time it will have to last before it is replaced.

Branscomb points out that performance specifications are always to be preferred over design specifications. Not only is it quite possible that the contractor will fulfill the design specifications only to find that the bridge does not do the job it was intended to do, but the use of performance specifications will almost always result in better designs and lower costs. That is because when performance specifications are used, the customer gives the bidders a very strong incentive to come up with innovative designs that will be more cost-effective than the competition's designs, or than any design the customer might have thought of. Design standards, on the other hand, stifle innovation, and set the cost at the lowest possible cost for only one design, that handed out by the customer.

American schools operate on design standards set by legislatures, state school boards, chief state school officers, local school boards, superintendents of schools, and central office staffs. The standards are remarkably uniform, they stifle innovation, and because so many individuals and bodies set them, no one can be held responsible for the failure of the system to produce results.

The bridge-building example is instructive. Bridge building is nearly an exact science. One can predict with near certainty the performance to be expected of a particular conventional design. The same, however, cannot be said of design standards in education. No matter how tightly the curriculum and the school and the classroom organization are specified, the variations to be expected in student background and learning styles, and in teachers' instructional methods and styles, combine to make the result for any given student quite unpredictable. A great deal of the art in education consists in matching the treatment of an individual student with the particular characteristics of that student. The more detailed and specific the policymakers make the design standards, the less freedom teachers have to make that match.

As matters stand now, teachers and principals cannot be held accountable for student performance outcomes for two reasons: they have never been clearly specified, and in any case, they are responsible not for student performance outcomes but for following the rules laid out in the design standards. If following those rules does not produce the desired result, that is somebody else's problem, not theirs.

Design standards and Tayloristic organizations go together like pieces of a puzzle. People who are conceived of as not much more than order-takers are told just what to do and how to do it by people who are thought to know far better than the front-line worker what the goal is and how to achieve it. In the last chapter, we described another way to conceive of schools and school districts as organizations: give the teachers and the principals the freedom to decide how to get the students to achieve clear student performance standards and reward them when they succeed. Our conception of how to restructure the workplace depends on replacing the whole system of educational design standards, from course specifications to time-in-the-seat requirements, with a system of performance standards. Furthermore, we believe that performance standards can be used as a framework for reforming not just the schools, but the whole system of education and training.

If such a restructuring were put into effect, the United States could not only match the European education systems in quality but surpass them. The European systems combine design standards and performance standards. On the one hand, they use examinations to set student performance standards. On the other, they typically tell the teachers what curriculum to use and specify many of the other inputs into the process, just as we do. Though teachers in Europe are typically more highly respected than in the United States, their work environment is often almost as Taylorist. They use performance standards not to free up the professionals to decide how to get the job done, but rather as a screening device to sort students into various futures, depending on their performance. This has the beneficial effect of providing powerful incentives to students to study hard, but it fails to provide the productivity improvements that will come with restructuring the schools as workplaces. We propose to use examinations to set student performance standards, just as the Europeans do, but not to sort students into various futures. Instead we propose to use the standards to motivate all students to achieve at high levels. And we also propose to use the same standards as the touchstone of the restructured education system, thereby both freeing and motivating school staff to do the very best job they can. If the United States combines such a system of performance standards with the restructuring agenda, and greatly reduces poverty among its children, it can have the finest educational performance in the world.

The system of standards we have in mind has four components: The first would qualify a person to go on to a college preparatory program or enter a program of technical and professional studies. The second would prepare people for jobs that do not require a baccalaureate degree. The third is a system of teacher qualifications. And the fourth is a set of standards for both entering and leaving college.[2]

Students meeting the first standard would receive a Certificate of Initial Mastery, in most cases by age sixteen. The certificate would be set at the highest standard in the world for students of this age.

The Commission on the Skills of the American Workforce made this recommendation in its report.[3] The members of the Commission had been struck by the power of the examination systems used in Europe and the Far East to motivate students to study hard in order to get good jobs and get into college. They also noted that in most of the advanced industrial countries, sixteen is the age at which students decide to pursue a path either toward the baccalaureate degree or of technical and professional preparation for jobs that do not call for a baccalaureate degree. They believed that that pattern, with modifications that permit students to elect college after choosing professional and technical preparation, would make a lot of sense for the United States. Most American students who do not plan to go to college spend their junior and senior years marking time. Why not make good use of that time pursuing technical training?

In the summer of 1990, the National Center on Education and the Economy, which had created the Commission on the Skills of the American Workforce, combined forces with the Learning Research and Development Center at the University of Pittsburgh to begin design of a project leading to a national examination system that could be used as the basis of awarding nationally recognized Certificates of Initial Mastery. The New Standards Project, directed by Marc Tucker, president of the National Center, and Lauren Resnick, codirector of the Center in Pittsburgh, began work in December 1990. It is funded by the John D. and Catherine T. MacArthur Foundation and the Pew Charitable Trusts.

The object is to create a national examination system in which states, districts, and even schools can select from many examinations, but with the passing level in all of these examinations set to the same standard. Eventually, a National Education Standards Board will set the standard, establish the criteria for examinations that will be accepted by the system, and judge whether any given examination meets those criteria. In this way, the nation could have a unified examination system without requiring everyone to use the same test.

The examinations would consist of three main components: performance examinations, assessments of student projects, and assessments of the contents of a portfolio of student work. The performance examinations would take place over a period of hours or days. Projects might take weeks or even months to complete. Portfolios would be made up of students' best work over their school careers, including the results of projects. The work on portfolios and projects would be similar to the tasks set by the scout merit badge system, permitting students to accumulate "badges" over a period of years, working at their own pace and selecting their own performances against a set of published criteria, just as the scouts do.

Having a high standard for all students means the end of the American system of placing students with different levels of measured ability in different tracks, a system that formally begins in secondary school, but really begins in the earliest years of the public education system. All students would have a curriculum that would focus on the skills of thinking and problem solving, and on the capacity to apply what one knows to the messy, complex problems found in real life. The curriculum would call for real mastery of bodies of knowledge as well as these global process skills. The examinations would assess not only what the student could accomplish working alone, but also the capacity to function effectively as a member of a group. The subject matter would encompass reading, writing, listening, and speaking, as well as mathematics, the sciences, history and the social sciences, the arts, and work skills, but the examinations would place a premium on the capacity to integrate knowledge from many of these disciplines in solving problems.

The typical American approach is to use tests and examinations as sorting devices, as we have noted. An exam is given once and the scores of those who take it are distributed along a curve. In order to have "winners," there must be "losers." The New Standards Project takes a fundamentally different approach.

It calls for an examination system that sets a high standard of mastery for all students, and permits students to take the performance exams whenever and as often as they like until they pass them and to accumulate "merit badges" at their own pace. Some "merit badges" might be optional, but those that are not must be passed at least at the level set by the examination system, and that level would be the same for everyone.

The American approach to student performance standards up to now has allowed the achievement level met to vary for each student while fixing the period of time in which the level must be met. We award the diploma based on a student's having completed twelve years of schooling, irrespective of what has been learned. The New Standards Project would turn this arrangement upside down, fixing the standard of achievement and allowing the time taken to reach that standard to vary.

Intermediate versions of the performance examination are being developed for roughly the end of elementary school and the end of middle school. Students passing the final examination and completing all of their required "merit badges" would receive the Certificate of Initial Mastery. Most would do so at the age of sixteen, though some might do so, say, at eighteen or twenty-one. Students who possessed the certificate would be eligible to go to work, enter a Technical and Professional Certificate program, or begin a college preparatory program. Which option they chose would be entirely up to them. In such a system, all students would have a strong incentive to take tough courses and to study hard in school.

It is critical that everyone—teachers, principals, parents, and students—know just what is expected of them. The developers of the project therefore envision an "open" examination system, in which the content standards—what a student is expected to know and be able to do—are widely publicized and most of the tasks in the performance examinations as well as many responses judged acceptable are released as soon as the examinations are over. The secrecy normally associated with examinations would be gone. Students would be working toward a clear objective with clear criteria for success.

Clear objectives for students need not lead to a national curriculum. Properly used, the examination would be part of the school restructuring strategy described earlier, which places decisions about what to teach and how to teach it in the hands of the professionals in the schools. With the objectives for students clear, school staff would be free to decide for themselves how to help students reach them, producing much more variation in the curriculum and in teaching methods than we have now, and the staff would be held accountable for the results of their efforts. The framework that is used to define the objectives for the students would also guide the professional preparation of teachers, the development of curricula at the school level, and the techniques used to teach. No single element of this system, including the examination system, is likely to produce the desired improvement in student performance unless the others are also implemented.

It is crucial that the national examination system reflect international standards of performance. It is very unlikely that that will happen if all fifty states and the territories have to agree on the standard. The idea of a national examination system also is likely to encounter a great deal of resistance if the effort is perceived as being led by the federal government. But it is equally important that the development program be perceived to have the kind of legitimacy that comes from strong participation on the part of key officials from general government and education. For all these reasons, the New Standards Project has assembled a volunteer group of seventeen states and six large school districts which collectively enroll more than half the students in the United States, to guide the initial development effort. All the members have committed themselves to the general principles just outlined, and, in particular, to setting the standard for the examination at a world-class level. The project's governing board of sixty-three people includes, among others, governors, teachers, union heads, business leaders, chief state school officers, leaders of prominent advocacy organizations, school board members, representatives of higher education, school superintendents—a broad cross-section of the American people.

The New Standards Project is now assembling standards frameworks and assessment materials from all over the world, including the United States, and determining which of them bear some reasonable resemblance to the criteria elaborated above. These include the pioneering performance assessments being developed by Arizona, California, Connecticut, Kentucky, and Vermont; the content frameworks prepared by Maine and many other states; the standards produced by the National Council of Teachers of Mathematics; an innovative framework developed by the government of Holland that has gained worldwide attention; and the work of many other national government agencies, states, disciplinary associations, and school districts. Those materials and the evaluations of them are being shared with a group of teachers, central office personnel, superintendents, chief state school officers, governors' aides, state and local school board members, and others. Project staff are consulting with a wide variety of organizations and constituencies, seeking their advice and working toward a broad consensus. Later, the governing board will decide what the assessment standards will be. This model is neither bottom-up nor top-down, but rather both at once.

The project team expects to have initial performance examinations in mathematics and language arts completed by the 1993–94 school year, and the core performance examinations in all the basic subjects at all three grade levels ready for use within seven years. But it may take several years beyond that before student performance on these examinations can be used as the basis of entry to jobs or further education.

The reason has to do with simple justice. Current tests operate as a formidable barrier to minority and low-income students. The New Standards Project proposes to create a high standard that virtually everyone would be expected to meet. On the face of it, this would pose an even higher barrier for minority and poor students. But that need not be the case.

Minority and low-income students have been very badly served by a system in which very few people expect them to do well, and which rewards them for what is in fact mediocre performance. An examination system that simply sorts students by measured achievement would greatly reinforce the inequities that already exist, but a system that sets a high mastery standard for all students and then lets everyone sink or swim would be even more unfair. The challenge is to create a system that sets a high standard and is structured to enable all but the most severely handicapped to reach it.

The New Standards Project has taken the position that a system in which students are rewarded for achieving a high mastery standard requires a new social compact with the students. Students' examination performance should not be released to colleges, employers, or any other third parties unless those students have had a fair shot at reaching the standard. That means, among other things, a curriculum that will plausibly prepare them for the tasks set by the examination system, teachers who have been trained to teach that curriculum well, and the other resources required to assure that those students have an opportunity to reach the standard. A social compact of this sort implies, among other things, a whole new approach to equity in school finance.

The proposed system would improve the chances of poor and minority children in other ways as well. The students, their parents, and their advocates will be armed for the first time with clear information about what they have to do to succeed, how well they are doing as they progress through school, and a clear standard by which to judge the adequacy of the school curriculum. Students, for the first time, would not bear the whole burden of meeting that standard, because the professionals would be held accountable for student progress. The measures themselves would not be limited to timed performance tests, but would include opportunities for students of many different cultural backgrounds to select their own projects and tasks to demonstrate mastery, making it possible for them to choose performances that play to their strengths.

As we have noted, students who need more time to reach the standard would have the time they need. In saying that, however, we do not simply mean that they will not have to get their certificate at a particular time. One of the peculiarities of the American system is that all students are expected to spend the same amount of time in school in any given year, no matter how well or badly they are doing. We would change that. In our view, one of the principal uses to which funds for the disadvantaged should be put is using them to extend the school day, the school week, and the school year. Rather than using them to "enrich" the current school day, which means pulling them out of their regular classes for remedial work, they should be left in their regular classes. If they start falling behind, they should be given extra work after the regular school day. If that is insufficient, they should come to school on Saturdays. If that still does not do the trick, then they should have a full summer program. Here again, time should be treated as a key resource, enabling those who need more work to keep up with everyone else. In addition, if children from low-income and minority backgrounds are to meet the standards, bridges will have to be built between the culture of the schools and the culture of the students, an issue that is discussed in detail later on.[4]

But even with this extra time and a determined attempt to reach out to these students, it is likely that many will not be able to succeed in regular schools. In a later chapter, we propose a system for recovering school dropouts, by providing an alternative path to the Certificate of Initial Mastery for students who seem unable to achieve it in regular schools.

In the fall of 1990, the President's Advisory Committee on Education recommended that the nation create some form of national examination system, adding its voice to that of the Commission on the Skills of the American Workforce. Several other groups came forward in the following months with much the same recommendation. At about the same time, the Secretary of Labor's Commission on Achieving Necessary Skills, chaired by Bill Brock, began work on development of a specification of the skills that are needed by high-school graduates for success in the workplace, a specification that would be needed to develop an examination leading to a Certificate of Initial Mastery.

In the same period, the National Education Goals Panel created expert groups to make recommendations concerning what should be measured to determine progress toward each national goal and the measurement methods to be used. Governor Roy Romer, the panel's chair, developed an overall schema for a national assessment system that could guide the work of the panel and the advisory groups. In his conception, the system would have two primary components. One, built around the National Assessment of Educational Progress, would be responsible for monitoring the progress of the nation toward the goals set forth by the governors and the president. The other would be a national examination system, which would consist of many examinations set to a common standard, along the lines proposed by the New Standards Project. The same criteria of what students should know and be able to do that would guide the examination system would also be used to monitor the nation's progress toward the goals.

As 1989 drew to a close, few would have dared to predict that the United States would be moving as fast as it now seems to be doing toward some form of national examination system. But there are many shoals to cross. Perhaps the biggest danger is succumbing to the inevitable pressures to create a simple system as quickly as possible—a system that actually sets the nation back. We believe there is a straightforward set of principles that any national examination system must adhere to if it is in fact to lead to much-improved student performance:

1. The purpose should be to raise the performance of virtually all students to world-class standards, not simply to measure student performance. This will mean raising the top as well as closing the gap between the best and the worst student performances.

2. Student performance measurement systems should be used to make sure that virtually all students reach the same high standard of performance when they graduate from high school, not to sort students out.

3. The standard of performance to be met should be the same nationwide, though many different examinations should be available to measure student performance.

4. The examinations should use performance examinations, projects, and portfolios to assess the capacity of students to apply what has been learned to the complex problems they will encounter as citizens, family members, and workers.

5. The examinations should provide students with many ways to demonstrate their competence, enabling them to take advantage of the strengths of their particular cultural backgrounds and experiences. The examinations and their administration should be free of any cultural or racial bias.

6. The system should be open and public. The public should be broadly involved in setting the standards. Those standards should be widely disseminated, along with examples of student performance that meet the standard. The examinations should be designed so that teachers can teach to them.

7. When the examination system is implemented, other mandated testing requirements should be eliminated or greatly reduced, and responsibility for the selection and use of any other tests should be vested in the school staff.

8. The education system must be restructured to give school staff much more authority to make the key decisions as to how to help students reach the new standards. Those professionals must be given the information and other resources they need to build effective programs. School professionals should be accountable for the results of their work, and much of the local and state regulatory framework within which they must now work must be eliminated. Parents must also be made effective partners in the education of their children.

9. There must be real consequences for students arising out of their performance on the examinations; but school staff must also be subject to

rewards and penalties arising out of the performance of students for whom they are responsible.

10. If students are to be held to a high standard of performance, and if much depends for them on meeting that standard, then a new social compact with the students is required. Specifically, high stakes should not be attached to student performance on the examinations until all students have a fair shot at reaching the new standard of performance. This means, at a minimum, that all students will be taught a curriculum that will plausibly prepare them for the examinations, their teachers will have the training to enable them to teach it well, and there will be an equitable distribution of the resources the students and their teachers need to succeed.

In the conception of the Commission on the Skills of the American Workforce, once a student has acquired the Certificate of Initial Mastery, he or she could choose a college preparatory program, go right into the work force, or enter a program designed to culminate in a Technical or Professional Certificate. These certificate programs would combine formal education and on-the-job training in a unified curriculum. The nature of that curriculum is discussed later. Our purpose here is to describe how the standards would be set for the Professional and Technical Certificates.

There is, of course, an existing system of postsecondary training, including everything from union apprentice programs, mostly in the building trades, to innumerable degree and certificate programs in our community colleges. More than half of those people who go through elementary and secondary education, however, participate in none of these, and therefore enter the work force with virtually no vocational skills. For the roughly one-quarter of our high-school graduates who go on to some form of postsecondary training not designed to culminate in a baccalaureate degree, the standards for that training, with the exception of the trades apprenticeships, are input standards, not performance standards. Where there are performance standards, they are unique to one institution or state.

Contrast this situation to that in most European countries, where fully 85 percent of the students who do not obtain a baccalaureate degree participate in an apprenticeship program lasting anywhere between two and four years. Such a program typically culminates in a written examination and a project evaluation—that is, the apprentices have to meet a performance standard to achieve journeyman status and get their certificate. The standards for the apprenticeship programs are set jointly by the employers and the unions, and are the same throughout a country. Moreover, the countries that are members of the European Community are now beginning to calibrate their standards, much as the New

Standards Project proposes to do for the Certificate of Initial Mastery here. Thus a student will know what score earned on the journeyman's examination for computer repair and maintenance earned in Ireland will be needed to get a journeyman's certificate in Germany and vice versa. The European Community has started to share these standards with other countries outside Europe, particularly developing countries around the world.

We have made a case that the economic future of the United States depends mainly on the skills of the front-line work force, the people whose jobs will not require a baccalaureate degree. Success, then, depends on developing a program to prepare close to three-quarters of our work force to take on tasks in restructured workplaces that, up to now, have been assigned mainly to the college-educated. Bank tellers will have to know about the full line of the bank's products, from zero-coupon bonds to tax-deferred annuities and checking-account lines of credit, and be able to steer the customer to the right product. People who work on automobile assembly lines will have to know how to use flexible-automation systems, program computers, use the methods of statistical quality control, and do production scheduling. The salesperson in the carpet store will have to know not only the characteristics of the various synthetic and natural fibers from which carpets are made, the strengths and weaknesses of different fabrication and weaving methods, and the pros and cons of different stain-resisting treatments, but also the fundamentals of retail sales and marketing. The idea that Americans just turning nineteen or twenty would come to the job knowing all this might sound like the stuff of fantasy, but it is increasingly common in many European countries. If it does not happen here, America will simply be unable to attain the rates of productivity growth and to deliver the quality that we must achieve.

The starting point for building such skills in the American work force is development of universal standards for Professional and Technical Certificates that embody the standards that employers envision as necessary in restructured work places to do the work that will have to be done.

The obvious answer is to use the European standards. There is a very strong argument for doing just that. The best of the European standards represent years of work, which we would otherwise have to duplicate. They also represent the state of the art in those countries that are furthest along in restructuring their work places for high productivity and quality. American companies that implemented the European standards in their training programs would also move forward on learning how to reorganize their work places for high performance.

But that is precisely the problem. It is not clear that most American companies could use the European standards, because American companies are so highly Taylorized. This is not just speculation. When the State of Illinois explored the possibility of using the European standards in the machine-tool industry, they found that very few Illinois machine-tool firms were using the high-performance work organizations on which the European standards were based, so they could not do the training. This is hardly surprising. When the Commission on the Skills of the American Workforce was conducting its research in Germany, it encountered German machine-tool makers who said that they could not sell their top-of-the-line machines in the United States because American workers could not be trained to use them.

Here then, is the catch. We may not be able to use European training standards because American firms are organized on outdated principles, and there is no one to do the training. Yet we cannot organize on the new principles without qualified workers.

There are two possible ways out. The first is to implement the European standards in the United States slowly, beginning with those industries that are making the most progress toward the new forms of work organization. The second is to start with our own, lower apprenticeship standards, and work our way up over time to something approximating the European standard.

There are many starting points for the second approach. The Perkins act recently passed by Congress, contains a provision requiring the states to devise performance standards for vocational education. A number of states are prepared to put significant effort into meeting this requirement. The American Banking Association, among a number of business associations, is interested in establishing performance standards for key jobs in the industry. Some industries that are hard-pressed to find competent entry-level front-line staff, like the aircraft industry, are reaching out to community colleges to help them develop both training programs and industry-wide standards for those programs.

The MacAllister Commission, established by former Secretary of Labor Dole to implement the third recommendation of the Commission on the Skills of the American Workforce, decided in the fall of 1991 to take the lead in engaging employers in the development of a system of standards for technical and professional training, in collaboration with the Departments of Education and Commerce. As we shall see, it is essential that the standards reflect the needs of firms using high-performance work organization. If that is not done, if the standards end up mirroring current work organization in the United States, then the current Taylorist work organization will be encased in concrete for years to come.

The industrial-technical assistance program proposed in chapter 7 could be managed so as to give a high priority to those industries implementing the new training standards. In this way, changes in work organization could go hand in hand with changes in technology and changes in training. Using this strategy, not all industries would have to be changed at once—an impossible task—but only over a period of years, by stages.

Just as performance standards can be a powerful tool for improving student performance, they can be used in much the same way to improve the quality of teachers and teaching. Yet until recently the standard for certifying teachers was not a performance standard at all. Teachers' colleges applied to the state for the right to offer programs leading to a teacher's certificate. If the program of studies they wished to offer was approved by the state, then, in effect, the institution could not only offer the program, but use the authority of the state to grant the certificate. Prospective teachers, then, had only to complete the program with passing grades to become certified teachers.

In the late 1970s, Philip Schlecty did a study of teachers' preparation and subsequent careers. Using scores on the Scholastic Aptitude Test as a measure of academic competence, Schlecty discovered that applicants to teachers' colleges were among the least able of college entrants. Among those who entered teachers' colleges, the least able went on to finish, the others having transferred to other programs. Of those who finished teachers' college, the least able actually became teachers. Of those who became teachers, the least able were still teaching after seven years.[5]

Following release of *A Nation at Risk* in 1983, governors and legislatures came under great pressure to do something about poor student performance. Many included in their programs measures to weed out teachers whose basic skills were below what could be expected of the average college-bound high-school graduate. The measure most frequently used for this purpose was the National Teachers Examination, published by the Educational Testing Service of Princeton, New Jersey. One could view this test as a performance test, but the standard set was embarrassingly low. People with good reading ability who had never taken a course in education and had never taught in school could pass the test easily. It is basically a reading test and a test of general knowledge, certainly not a performance test of professional teaching competence on a par with such professional licensing tests as the bar examinations or the architectural registration boards.

In the fall of 1984, Albert Shanker, president of the American Federation of Teachers, made a speech at the National Press Club that astonished many observers of the education scene. Shanker proposed that a system be set up to establish tough professional standards for teachers and certify teachers who could meet the standards. Up to that point, everyone assumed that teachers would be opposed to any form of evaluation of their competence, a rather sensitive subject in American education. Yet here was a union head proposing just such a step.

Shanker would be asked to join the Carnegie Forum's Task Force on Teaching as a Profession early in 1985. When the Carnegie report came out in 1986, it would feature a proposal for a National Board for Professional Teaching Standards which would award certificates independently of the states. A year later, the board was established. James Hunt became its chair, Marc Tucker its president, and Albert Shanker one of its members. The research work needed to begin development of the board's examinations was actually begun before the Carnegie Forum released its report, with a grant by Carnegie Corporation of New York to

Professor Lee Shulman at Stanford University. Shulman's work changed the thinking of the entire field on the subject of teaching standards. The board expects to confer its first certificate in 1993 following five years of development of standards so as to produce advanced forms of teacher assessment in all the fields and specialties required.

The intention of the board is to produce a series of performance examinations for teachers set at a truly professional level, a level that professionals in other fields would acknowledge met a standard of competence in teaching comparable to the standard set, let us say, by the examinations that one must take to be certified as a cardiologist. Teachers so certified would be in great demand in school districts and states that cared greatly about their relative standing in the education status hierarchy. Districts in cities and towns where the real-estate values depend on being known as having the best schools would bid up the price of board-certified teachers. Everyone would want to be certified in order to get the salaries such teachers could command. In time, the level of competence of the teaching corps would rise greatly and the respect in which teachers were held by the rest of society would rise commensurately. All of this would happen without any legislation being passed.

The biggest public controversy that the board has thus far faced had to do with a very basic matter. Should candidates for certification be judged solely on the basis of how well they do on the performance examinations or should they be required in addition to have graduated from an accredited teacher preparation program? Needless to say, the teachers' colleges demanded that the latter criterion be used. Fortunately for the nation, the board did not agree. If they had, the teachers' colleges would have been guaranteed in perpetuity their monopoly on teacher preparation, which has served the country so badly up to now. Why should it matter, the board felt, what courses candidates for certification took at a teachers' college if they can show they can perform at a very high level of competence in the classroom?

This was less of a threat to the teachers' colleges than might be assumed, because the board also ruled that candidates for board certification must have been teaching for several years before they would be considered. Since the states typically require that their teachers attend a teachers' college in order to get their license, those colleges seemed safe enough.

But, in our view, the basic logic used to decide the board certification issue applies with equal force to ordinary state certification.

To see how that might work, we need to review Connecticut's Beginning Educator Support and Training Program (BEST). BEST had its origins in Connecticut's $300 million Educational Enhancement Act of 1986. In the act, the legislature provided both a large increase in teachers' salaries and funding for a whole new system of teacher professional standards and professional development. The purpose of the latter, according to Gerald Tirozzi, Connecticut's commissioner of education, was to make sure that Connecticut got its money's worth for the higher salaries. Eight million dollars were set aside to create the assessment and professional development program.

The legislation created a three-stage certifying process for licensure: teachers would get initial, provisional, and professional educator certificates. A performance examination would be required for each stage.

Initial certification requires passing the Connecticut Competency Examination (CONNCEPT), a test of essential reading, writing, and mathematics skills. This is needed to enter a Connecticut teacher preparation program and as a prerequisite for the next stage of certification. The candidate for initial certification also has to pass an examination (called CONNTENT) in the subjects in which he or she planned to teach.

The next one to two years are the heart of the system. Once on the job, teachers hold an initial certificate good for a year, during which they participate in the BEST program. Each newcomer is paired with a mentor teacher, who acts as a role model and a resource. The mentor teacher is expected to help the new teacher focus on and master the fifteen Connecticut Teaching Competencies—everything from "Demonstrates knowledge of the subject to be taught" to "Encourages and maintains the cooperative involvement and support of parents and the community." Sometime during the first year, teachers will be assessed several times against those competencies by a team of highly regarded educators from outside the teacher's district, and will receive detailed feedback from the team. Each member of the visiting team will have received fifty hours of very demanding training. They do not use a checklist for the assessment, but render an overall judgment on each of ten broad indicators of effective teaching, based on extended conversations with the candidates and observations of their work in the classroom. The training makes it clear to the assessors that the creators of the BEST program do not believe that there is one best way of teaching; rather there is a uniform set of criteria that can be satisfied by many approaches. Participants—both the assessors and the assessed—have often said that this is the most rewarding professional development experience they have ever had. Candidates who do not pass this first assessment are given another year to develop the necessary skills, with the help of their mentor. Those who do are given their provisional certificate, valid for eight years. Districts are not permitted to hire teachers who have failed to get their provisional certificates.

A few years ago, Pat Forgione, then director of Connecticut's Division of Research, Evaluation, and Assessment (now Commissioner of Education in Delaware) and Ray Pecheone, Project Leader of the BEST Assessment Program, began development of a highly innovative structured interviewing technique for the assessment, still under development, that outside observers like Lee Shulman find very impressive. Connecticut later joined forces with the California State Department of Education, another leader in the design of advanced state assessment systems, to share the burden of the development effort.

Cynthia Jorgensen, the former manager of the BEST program, points out that it is having a major effect on teacher education in the state.[6] No preparation institution wants to develop a reputation for producing teachers who fail the assessment. In many respects, the BEST program bears a striking resemblance to the New Standards Project. Both are designed to set a performance standard that is either met or not. Both allow candidates to take the time they need to pass, because the purpose of both is to enable as many people as possible to succeed, not to weed people out. Both rely primarily on the exercise of judgment by assessors, not on checklists or multiple-choice tests. Both provide strong incentives to the home institution to provide the support required for ultimate success. Both concentrate on what the candidates can actually do with what they know. Both provide a strong incentive to work hard to achieve the necessary competence. Both are intended to have a strong effect on the curriculum used to prepare the candidate, but neither dictates what that curriculum will be. And both lodge responsibility for assessment outside the institution in which the candidate works or goes to school.

We would make only one change in the Connecticut program for teacher certification, but it is crucial. We would eliminate any requirement that candidates for a teacher's certificate attend a teacher preparation institution. We believe that they should have a bachelor's degree in a field relating to the subject they will teach, because it is essential that our teachers be broadly and deeply educated.

In the mid-1980s, when Thomas Kean, a former history teacher, was governor of New Jersey, he was so frustrated at the inability or unwillingness of the state's teacher education institutions to do what was necessary to produce highly qualified teachers for the state that he created the alternative routes program, a means by which highly able liberal arts graduates could enter the teaching profession without having first attended a standard teacher preparation institution. Accused by the education deans of lowering the standards for teachers, Governor Kean said he would match the abilities of the alternative route teachers against those of the traditional graduates any time.

But why should we need alternative routes at all? Governor Kean was right. The only thing that matters is what teachers actually know and can do. If it is possible to make a good independent assessment on those points—and the BEST program shows that it is—then why not abolish all formal training requirements for teachers and base certification entirely on measured competence? There is no doubt that there is a great deal one has to learn to become a competent teacher, and much of it cannot be learned on the job. So abolishing the formal training requirement would certainly not abolish teacher education. What it would do is open up the market for teacher education and put the established institutions under enormous pressure to produce teachers who are highly qualified by criteria over which the institutions themselves have no control. No single measure the country could take would have such an electric effect on the professional preparation of teachers. School districts, unions, independent teachers' professional associations, and many other organizations would offer programs, singly or in combination with one another and with established institutions. Teachers' colleges would become far more sensitive to the needs of their clients than ever before. The criteria established by the National Board for Professional Teaching Standards and by the states through programs like those of Connecticut and California would provide the means of weeding out ineffective preparation programs.

This may sound like a form of choice program for teachers, and in fact it is, to the extent that it would employ the incentives of the market. But the objections we raised in the last chapter to the program proposed by Chubb and Moe for the schools do not apply here. No one has a right to a free, high-quality teacher education program. The crucial advantages of the common school have no parallel here. The direct relation between the criteria for preparation and the criteria for employment that would make the market in teaching work is absent for high-school students. Applicants for entry into teacher education programs are in a far better position to judge the merits of the programs to which they apply than are either elementary or secondary students or their parents. In the end, we believe, this proposal would not destroy our teacher education institutions. To the contrary, it is likely greatly to strengthen them. All the necessary technical elements are in place. There is no reason not to enact the needed legislation now.

American higher education is one of the least accountable institutions on the national scene. Partly as a result of this, the measures used to determine admission to college are deeply flawed, and the virtual absence of leaving standards except for those entering postgraduate programs makes the contribution of our colleges to the skills of their graduates a matter of profound mystery.

We will deal with the matter of admissions first. The measures most widely used by college admissions officers in making their decisions are high-school grades and the Scholastic Aptitude Test, both of which are said to be reliable predictors of college performance. It is curious that high-school grades should be so reliable, but this fact is very revealing. Schools have notoriously different grading standards; a "B" in one high school does not mean what it means in another high school. So why should they both be good predictors of future performance? Because most students who want to get into selective colleges will do what they perceive they have to do to get into the top, say, 20 percent of their class and no more. When they get to college, they do the same thing—enough to get the degree they want, and no more. The grade is in fact a measure of the effort a student is prepared to put in to demonstrate satisfactory performance. Report after report shows that college students are far less interested in learning something than they are in getting the credential they are after, regarding it as a ticket to the job they want. The grading system motivates minimum satisfactory effort. When these same students arrive at most colleges, even highly regarded ones, their teachers find that the same psychology usually takes hold. The students, arriving as poorly prepared for college as they were for high school, make it clear how much work they think it reasonable to put in and refuse to do more. The professor, resigned to the low skills of the class and reluctant to set a standard only a few will meet, grades on a curve, just as the high schools did. In the end, very few students have to work very hard, either in high school or college.

The Scholastic Aptitude Test is designed to measure aptitude, not achievement. One is not supposed to be able to study for it. Many cram in the weeks before it is administered, but in fact, the SAT has virtually no effect on what students study through their school career or how hard they study it. The very idea of using an aptitude test for college admissions would strike many people in the rest of the world as absurd. What difference does it make if one has high aptitude, if one is not prepared to work hard to learn?

Apart from the College Board Achievement Tests, required by relatively few colleges, there are no real performance examinations used to determine college admissions. Because of this, high-school standards are low, students are not motivated to study hard, and they are poorly prepared for college.

As we see it, the colleges should abolish the use of the SAT for admissions and rely mainly on the College Board Achievement Tests for that purpose. The Achievement Tests might have to be modified for widespread use of this kind, but the basic approach they embody is absolutely sound. Each of these tests is based on a framework of assumptions about what students of the subject concerned should know and be able to do. Because of this, it is an examination that can be studied for. Because it is a uniform standard, it can be used to make valid judgments about a student's accomplishments, independent of the grading standards used by the school the student attended. The introduction of such a system will have a profound effect on the high-school curriculum. Furthermore, if the Achievement Tests were designed explicitly to build on the competencies examined for the award of the Certificate of Initial Mastery, then the United States could have a seamless web of standards, progressing in steps through the stages of the new school examination system right through college entrance.

To make the system fair and constructive, students should be allowed to take the Achievement Tests as often as they like, and should be given feedback each time, so as to improve their performance. Here again, our object is not to weed people out, but to construct a system in which as many people as possible can succeed.

This is not to say that students' high-school grades should not count or that the comments of their teachers should be ignored. These are important and, taken together with the test data, should convey a picture of the student as a person that will reveal information of great value to admissions officers, particularly in a close decision. Some students, for example, may have achieved an otherwise unacceptable score under conditions so adverse as to suggest that, once in the more favorable environment of a residential college, they would do quite well. That said, however, making examination results of the kind we propose the keystone of the admissions systems could, all by itself, go a long way toward producing major gains in the quality of people admitted to college. It would not simply raise the standard for admissions, which can be done easily with the present system, but also greatly increase the motivation of high-school students to take tough courses and study hard enough to achieve at much higher levels than they do now.

But the problem lies not just at the entrance into college. It is equally present at the gates leading out. Much has been written in this book about the importance of establishing exit performance standards for high-school students and for students in technical and professional programs that do not culminate in a baccalaureate. All of this applies, as well, to the baccalaureate. No one now knows what baccalaureate holders know and can do, except in a handful of institutions that either have volunteered to create an exit examination or whose state authorities have required them to do so. Even in those cases, the avowed goals of each institution are uniquely stated and so are their measures, making it impossible to compare the effectiveness of institutions on any common measure. Because future employers have only the names of courses taken and the grades received, they have no way to determine what an applicant actually knows or can do, and must rely solely on the general reputation of the institution or department, a notoriously inaccurate criterion. Most ratings of colleges are made on the basis of the views of professors and administrators at other colleges, hardly a substitute for a clear measure of individual student competence.

What we would do is very simple. We would require colleges to affiliate with other institutions with goals they perceive as similar to theirs so as to create final examinations using common measures of the competence of graduating seniors, and ask them to set scores on those examinations below which they will not award a diploma. We would require the candidates for graduation to take these examinations and give them the option of taking any other examinations they wish so as to demonstrate their competence to prospective employers or graduate schools.

In this way, no college would be forced to examine students against goals they do not embrace, but the goals that colleges do have would have to be explicit, and the public would be able to judge how well both the students and the institutions perform against them. With such a method, employers and graduate schools would have a good measure of the competence of applicants for admission and for jobs. Because of this, and because the goals of their college education would be clear, students would know what to study for and would have a strong motivation to learn, not just to get the credential, which is hardly the same thing.

Because a particular institution's performance could be judged against the performance of other institutions that shared the same goals, legislatures and higher education authorities would for the first time have an objective method for judging the relative effectiveness of colleges that receive state aid. Clearly colleges that take in a high proportion of poorly prepared students would not be expected to produce the same results as those that mainly serve highly advantaged students. On the other hand, colleges serving similar populations could be expected to produce comparable results, and those that did not could be asked why this was, and what they planned to do about it. The difference, of course, could be in the resources available to the institution, which would then constitute an argument for more equitable funding. Student scores for colleges serving heterogeneous populations could be broken down and the scores for students from similar backgrounds could be compared among colleges for the same purpose. These now largely unaccountable institutions could be made far more accountable with relative ease, without compromising the particular character or integrity of any institution.

The systems of standards we have proposed are not independent of one another or of the other proposals we make for building a world-class education and training system. They both constitute a seamless web of standards in themselves and serve as the keystone of the whole human-resources system. They are designed to promote excellence in achievement, the overarching goal; real effort on the part of the learner, without which no real improvement in achievement is possible; opportunities for everyone to succeed, without which no system is defensible; and true accountability on the part of those who provide the services, an inescapable requirement of public policy—however often ignored.

Everywhere in this book, we make the case for a fundamental redesign of our institutions, to make them more responsive, more effective, and more efficient. New standards alone will not accomplish those goals, but the goals cannot be accomplished without new standards.

CHAPTER 11

The Family

Jack is fourteen, the oldest of three children in the family. His mother is on welfare. She is twenty-eight years old, having had her first child when she was fourteen. Jack's father cannot be found. The other two children in the family were each fathered by a different man, neither of whom is around either. Jack's mother has a live-in boyfriend, who is unable to get a job and lives off her welfare check. Jack and the boyfriend do not get along. Frequently, Jack's mother and her boyfriend just take off for weeks at a time, leaving Jack to take care of his brother and sister as best he can. There is a lot of fighting in the house. Occasionally it gets so bad that Jack leaves, finding some friend who will take him in. Neither Jack's mother nor any of her changing partners has graduated from high school. School left such a bad taste in Jack's mother's mouth that she gives him no encouragement to stay or finish; she is so fearful of the school authorities that she will not go to the school or be his advocate in any way that requires talking to school staff. After years of being told in myriad ways that he has no future, that he can only fail, Jack has become a real problem at school. Not only are his grades in the basement and his attendance record spotty at best, but he is hostile and defiant and the cause of ceaseless disruption in school. It is hardly surprising that he trusts no one. Many of the school staff would be a lot happier if Jack would just leave, and do not conceal that from him. Jack cannot wait to get out.

Families are the quintessential learning system in any society. They are the crucible in which our attitudes and values are shaped, our aspirations generated, our expectations formed, and our relation to the larger society determined. They teach us the value of hard work and investing in the future, or the pointlessness of work and the hopelessness of the future. It is in the home that we learn the contours of our native language, to distinguish colors, to count. Families provide the richness of shapes, colors, objects and a myriad of other things that either stimulate learning and brain development or, when they are lacking, fail to do so. They are the social units responsible for feeding and housing us when we are young, for attending to our health and happiness. It is in our families that we learn to love and be loved, or to distrust and hate. Our families teach us, as we grow up, that we are valued and worth valuing, or that we are unloved and worthless. And the people in the neighborhood and larger community share in all these responsibilities, forming a human community of adults that has its own role to play in supporting children as they grow and develop—healthy or stunted. It will do the country little good, therefore, to restructure schools unless we make families better learning systems and include families as integral components of restructured schools.

Most youngsters have the good fortune to find themselves surrounded by adults who care and have the emotional and financial resources, as well as the time and energy, to create an environment that fosters learning. Others—like Jack—ran out of luck before they were born.

Jack is a composite portrait of the typical student enrolled in one of the programs we describe later in this chapter. He is a stand-in for millions of children growing up in poverty in the United States. Some, of course, have families that manage to provide all the love and support and conditions for learning that many children in middle-class families enjoy, despite their lack of money income, and some children somehow find the inner resources to make it even in families that function very poorly. And we know children from better-off families who share many of Jack's problems—the unintended victims of a deteriorating family and community structure that leaves growing numbers of middle-class children emotionally abandoned by their parents, their community, and their schools, defeated before they begin, angry and resentful, unskilled and without much hope of making it in a society that has little use for them and lets them know it.

Real and important as the needs of middle-income children are, however, they pale in comparison to the problems faced by poor families. The children of poverty are far more likely than other children to be denied the caring and support from the adult world that is the indispensable condition of the self-confidence on which human development depends, and we are paying a heavy and growing price for that failure in transfer payments, crime, and lost productivity. We should hardly be surprised when many of these children grow up as criminals, deadbeats, shiftless workers, and "welfare cheats." Society has broken its contract with them and they see no reason to honor their contract with society. Why should they? No nation that turns its back on its children the way we do in the United States can hope to build its future on the human capacity of its adults.

Many Americans of good will have thrown up their hands at this problem, believing that nothing that has been tried has worked, that the problem is intractable, that the problems of our families, and especially of poor families, lie beyond the reach of policy and programs. Some of those same people, however, were among the most outspoken advocates of aid to the Kurdish and Shiite people who fled the Iraqi government troops after Operation Desert Storm, and who demanded that this country assume responsibility for rebuilding the shattered social structures of that unfortunate country following the war. Why should we be able to do half a world away what we have given up on accomplishing right here in our own communities?

We propose that the United States face this problem head-on, building a national system of family and youth policy to serve as a firm foundation for an economy based on the quality of our human resources.[1] There is nothing utopian about these proposals. Many countries have had national policies of the kind we propose for decades, and there is little doubt that such policies work. Similarly, the changes we propose in community structure to support young people's growth and development are based on real programs that have been shown to work and work well in communities and states right here in this country. Nothing needs to be invented. Nothing needs to be researched. All that is required is the political will to tackle the problem on a large enough scale to make a difference.

When we think of how families ought to be, we think mainly of the families we grew up in or the stereotypical families we see on television, and when we think of those families, we tend to think that families were always that way, at least until recently. But that is hardly the case. For millennia, families were largely self-sufficient work units. Father and mother worked side by side, usually in or near the home, and their children were always about, joining in the work as soon as they were able. Sons worked with their fathers and daughters with their mothers. Almost all values and skills were learned in the family setting. Neighbors and friends were there to help out when necessary. A sense of self-worth came naturally, as did a sense of one's place in society.

The growth of cities and then the Industrial Revolution changed all that. Fathers left the home to work for money wages. More book learning and technical skills were required for many kinds of jobs, and these things were learned in school. Gradually a set of social institutions developed to provide for the young many of the services that had formerly been provided in the home. With the upheavals caused by the Industrial Revolution, real poverty came to many families that were no longer in a position to grow and make what they needed, and the larger society created charitable institutions to provide what it could for those in the most dire need. In the early part of this century in this country, real income rose very quickly, as we have seen. Small family farms went into decline, the country moved to the city, family size became smaller (both because the extended family living under one roof disappeared and because parents had fewer children), and the modern image of the family consisting of mother at home, father at work, and two children playing in the yard was born.

As productivity increased and labor unions acquired power, child labor, formerly an asset to both parents and children when done in the home, became socially undesirable and formal schooling was extended. As the nature of work changed from requiring mainly physical strength near the home to requiring the ability to manipulate symbols in an office, store, or factory, the work that adults did became more of a mystery to their children and more time had to be spent at school doing things quite unrelated to children's own sense of their place in the world.

Gradually, children became less of an economic asset and more of an economic liability (one of the reasons for smaller family size), and were progressively cut off from the adult world, increasingly unable to contribute to the family and thereby acquire the skills, habits, attitudes and, most important, feelings of self worth that had been theirs in earlier ages. Thus was born the youth culture of modern times. Parents and community groups developed organized sports programs, staffed the scouts, funded community swim programs and the "Y," organized church events and youth social activities, and spawned a bewildering variety of summer camps for their kids. Middle-class mothers organized most of these activities, staffed many of them as volunteers, served as their children's advocates with the growing array of community agencies, and supported them in countless other ways through the day. As their children became young adults, upper-class parents took them for college tours and helped them fill out applications. Blue-collar families took their offspring to their union hall, introduced them to friends who could offer them their first job, and did whatever else was necessary to help them get started.

This pleasant picture did not, of course, fit all families. Black mothers, for example, who moved to the big cities of the North in the years following the war had no choice but to seek paid work, often at two or more jobs. Working as domestics or, if they were lucky, as schoolteachers in segregated schools, they made do as best they could, unable to offer their children many of the benefits that most middle-class children could take for granted. These black women were not alone, but, for the most part, the picture just painted fit the majority through the fifties and into the sixties.

The period from the end of the Second World War to the present has seen a sea change in the structure of American families and equally fundamental changes in the capacity of many families and communities to provide the support to children that had been taken for granted in earlier decades. The changes in family structure that have taken place in the last few decades are not bad for children in and of themselves, but have disastrous consequences because, as a nation, we have failed to build adequate support systems for families in which both parents are employed, and to provide a path out of poverty for single mothers who do not have the emotional and financial resources and time to provide their children with what they need (a child born to a single mother in the United States is five times as likely to be poor as a child born to a married mother). This country never put formal policies in place to provide for children's needs, as many European countries have done. Many married women were at home attending to those needs. Now that both parents work outside the home, many of children's most basic needs are unmet.

The question, of course, is what to do. One answer lies in high policy: basic changes in law that would ensure that families are able to support their children and have access to decent health care. But it may take some time to catch up with what other countries have long since done along these lines, so the second answer has to do with more immediate policy steps we can take to mitigate the worst effects of poverty among children. Finally, there are the things that must be done in any case to rebuild the fabric of our communities so that children are once again surrounded by adults who care about children and provide the web of support to them that they need to believe in themselves and their future.

Families, the most important human-resource development agencies in any country, are in considerable trouble in the United States. The problem is not, as is commonly assumed, mainly because more women are employed. Mothers working outside the home for pay can provide greater economic security for their families and better role models for their children (especially their daughters), and make important contributions to society. Work outside the family has become a major way in which women acquire a sense of identity, organize their lives, and gain a sense of self-worth.

The main family problems are due to the fact that too many households have members who work full-time for wages below the poverty level, too many children are born into poor households, too many women have inadequate prenatal care for themselves and their babies, too many fathers do not support their children at all, too many children are born to unwed mothers who are unable to care for them, and too many mothers transmit drug addiction to their children. On all of these indicators, the American experience is much worse than that of any other major industrial country.

Divorce rates have doubled since the 1960s, and the United States has by far the highest divorce rate in the world. About half of all first marriages and 60 percent of all second marriages end in divorce. In the middle of the 1980s almost a quarter of all families with children under age eighteen were maintained by a single parent, usually the mother. Divorce, of course, is always an emotional crisis for families, but researchers have been unable to find, on balance, any serious long-term emotional consequences for children of divorce, per se. Divorce does, however, have serious economic consequences. Because most children stay with their mother after divorce, and most divorced women's standard of living falls precipitously following divorce, their children suffer enormously as a consequence. In the first year after divorce the average mother's living standard drops 30 percent while the father's might actually increase 10 to 15 percent.[2]

The 1980s saw a dramatic increase in the proportion of children living with only one parent. The latest census report shows 15.3 million children living with only one parent, and 1.9 million living with neither parent. Among whites, divorce was the principal reason. Among blacks, the majority (54 percent) of single parents had never been married; the same was true for 33 percent of Hispanic parents.[3]

The United States also ranks very low on important health indicators, despite the fact that it spends a larger percentage of national income on medical care than any other major industrial country. On one important measure of health care, infant mortality, the United States ranked nineteenth in the world in 1989.[4] The rates are very high for minority children. According to Marion Wright Edelman, president of the Children's Defense Fund, "In 1986, a black baby born in Indianapolis, Detroit, or in the shadow of the White House was more likely to die in the first year of life than a baby born in Jamaica, Chile, Panama, Rumania, or the Soviet Union."[5]

Between 1980 and 1988, on average, 7 percent of all American babies had a low birth weight, a very good predictor of later health problems and learning disabilities. Twenty OECD countries had lower rates, including Norway (4 percent), Japan (5 percent), and Germany (6 percent). Moreover, 12.5 percent of black Americans, on average, had a low birth weight during the same period. This was a higher rate than for Cuba, Panama, China, Iraq, Peru, South Korea, Lebanon, Syria, and Mexico, among others, and more than double the proportion for Japan or Germany.[6]

Health and poverty problems are especially serious for teenage pregnancies— another area where the rate for the United States is the highest for any industrial country. In America every year about one-tenth of all teenage girls or about one million a year, get pregnant. Because the vast majority of teenage mothers live in abject poverty, they are unable to meet the most basic needs of their children. Almost half of teenage mothers receive no prenatal care at all. The absence of prenatal care and adequate nutrition greatly increases the health risks to teenage mothers and their children, particularly for having low-birth-weight babies.

The primary causes of these health problems are the heavy incidence of poverty and the absence of universal health care in the United States. America is the only major country without a national health system.

But the health and education problems of American children are also closely related to the inadequacy of housing for poor families. While incomes for the poor have stagnated or declined in the last ten years, housing prices in the urban centers have skyrocketed. The result has been a terrible squeeze. For a single parent under twenty-five heading a household, housing cost 46.2 percent of income in 1974, but had risen to 81.1 percent by 1987. Those over twenty-five paid 58.4 percent of their income for housing in 1987, up from 34.9 percent in 1974. These dramatic increases in share of income paid for housing reflect more than rapidly increasing housing prices. From 1980 to 1988, there was a staggering 81 percent decrease (in real dollars) in federal government funding for low-income housing. The combined effect of stagnating incomes, swiftly rising housing prices in the open market, and the gutting of the federal low-income housing program has been either to leave almost nothing for food, medical care, and clothing for many families, or to make the street the only available home.[7]

Finally, there is drug addiction, among the factors most seriously affecting the quality of our human resources. Drug addicts' capacity for work and learning, as well as their ability to support their families and maintain their health, are often crippled or severely diminished. Though addiction afflicts all racial groups at all income levels, it is closely associated with unemployment, poverty, the deterioration of family structures, school problems, deteriorating neighborhoods, and failing child-support structures. Among low-income children and young adults, selling drugs is far more lucrative than the legitimate jobs open to them and represents a much surer payoff, whatever the risk, than the slim hope offered by working hard in school. Young children are drawn into the trade at very early ages by dealers who find it advantageous to use them because of the light penalties given to minors if they are caught. Thus the very compassion society shows to the young leads to their early and often irrevocable involvement in this deadly commerce. In addition, the violence associated with the drug trade has doubtless contributed to the fact that homicide is the chief cause of death among young black males.

The problem of child poverty in America is getting worse. Children as a group are becoming poorer, but the problem is particularly acute for minority children, who will provide most of the relative increase in our work force for the rest of this century and into the next. Nearly half of all black and a third of all Hispanic children are poor. By 2000 a third of all children will be black or Hispanic; their number will increase by 25 percent between now and then compared with only 0.2 percent for whites. Over a fifth (20.6 percent) of all children were poor in 1987.[8] If present trends continue, by 2000 sixteen million American children, or one in four, will be poor.

Though the problem of poverty among children is worse for minority groups than for whites, no one should assume that it is confined to minorities. In fact, the poverty rate among white American children is higher than the overall rate for any other major industrial country. Despite five years of economic recovery, the poverty rate for all Americans increased from 11.4 percent in 1978 to 13.1 percent in 1988. About 32 million Americans were poor in 1988, seven million more than in 1978. The poverty rate for blacks rose from 30.6 percent in 1978 to 31.6 percent in 1988, and the number of poor blacks rose to 9.4 million, up 1.8

million from 1978. The Hispanic poverty rate was 26.8 percent in 1988, up from 21.6 percent in 1978. Almost 5.5 million Hispanic Americans were poor in 1988, 2.8 million more than in 1978.[9]

The implications of this for human-resources development are fairly clear. By tolerating the highest rate of poverty among children within the industrialized nations, the continued growth of that poverty even in times of relative affluence, and the progressive failure of the social services and supports that are intended to alleviate the effects of poverty, we have crippled the capacity of those very people who will grow up to provide almost all of the increase in America's work force. A large and increasing proportion of the people on whom our aging population will depend in the years ahead to operate an advanced-technology economy are growing up under conditions making it almost certain that they will suffer from poor physical and intellectual development all of their lives.

There is a simple arithmetic that applies here. We have argued that in the future, those societies that succeed in maintaining high-wage, full-employment economies will have high-technology, high-skill economies. The children of poverty we have been describing will be quite unable to qualify for the jobs that will be available if the society as a whole succeeds, because they simply will not have a high enough level of skills to justify an employer paying those high wages. They are therefore likely to become dependents of the larger society, on welfare or in jail. But a high-skill, high-technology economy by definition requires a very high level of investment in both skills and technology. It will not be possible to generate the funds required for those investments if a large proportion of the income that would otherwise be invested must instead be used to sustain a large proportion of the working-age population on welfare or in jail. No advanced economy could possibly succeed under such conditions, nor could it compete with others that did not have to do without the productive services of so much of its working-age population. National policies that produce a work force composed increasingly of people who grow up poor, ill-housed, in poor health, badly nourished, and convinced that the cards are stacked against them hardly constitute a program to provide the nation with the finest human resources in the world. The inevitable consequence of permitting this enormous waste of human beings is the steady decline of the national economy.

The old joke has it that the reason that people are poor is because they have no money. A great many of those who are not poor do not believe that. They think people are poor because they are lazy, that any self-respecting person who is willing to work can lift himself out of poverty. The truth is that most of the poor do work, but that a single person working full-time for the minimum wage cannot support a family of any size above the official poverty line. In fact, two adults working full-time at the minimum wage will make only $17,677 after taxes, assuming they take full advantage of the tax laws—$1,037 less than the poverty level for a family with four children. A single parent of two children working full-time at the minimum wage will collect $9,878 in pay after taxes and federal benefits, $1,054 less than the poverty line.

What reader of this book would care to try to support a family of two adults and four children on $20,860 a year? Or two children and oneself on $9,878? Remember that minimum-wage earners are likely to have no health insurance at all. A few visits to the emergency room (you do not have a family doctor) for the normal things that happen to children could easily take 10 percent of your annual income; a real illness could easily wipe out all of it. It is best not to go at all unless the problem appears to be life-threatening. Every other choice you have to make is agonizing. Pay the rent and there is not enough to eat. Buy T-shirts and jeans for the children and there is not enough to pay the rent. There never was enough to even consider buying a car, so every trip beyond a walk means taking a bus or a cab, with more money out of pocket. Nor is there anything for a babysitter, so you either have to work part-time, which means even less income, or you leave the children with someone you really do not trust. There is no question of finding some place that will help them develop the skills they will need to be ready for school; the issue is finding some place where they will not be in physical danger. The stress is unrelenting, so you bark at the children all the time, though you tell yourself that it's not their fault. Millions of Americans live like this every day.

Most other industrialized nations dealt with this problem decades ago by instituting a system of child allowances—payments to all families with children, whether poor or not, that increase with the number of children they have. This is done out of the simple recognition that healthy, well-developed children are a vital national asset and that the family is the best caregiver there is. The United States is among the very few industrialized countries that do not have such a system of child support.

But we once took measures whose effect was similar. During the Truman administration, Congress modified the income-tax system to provide a personal exemption for dependents. In 1948, when the personal exemption was first introduced, it was set at $600, and median family income was $3,182. If the personal exemption had kept pace with inflation, it would be worth about $8,260 today, but of course, it has not. One could argue, therefore, that the best approach to the problem of family poverty would be to correct the personal exemption for inflation. But that is far from an ideal solution. The value of the exemption is greatest for the better-off families in the higher tax brackets who need it least, and it is of no use at all to to the struggling families we just described, who pay little or no taxes.

The income-support program recently recommended by the National Commission on Children makes real sense.[10] Our recommendations closely follow theirs:

- *Create a $1,000 refundable child tax credit for all children through the age of eighteen and eliminate the personal exemption for dependent children.* This would apply to all children, irrespective of the income of the family, as with child-allowance systems in most other countries. It also means that families who owe less taxes than the credit for which they are eligible get the difference back in cash. In proportion to total income, then, this system would bring the biggest benefits to poor people. But the middle class would benefit substantially, too, and everyone with children would get something. This proposal is the heart of the income-support plan. In terms of what other countries do, it is hardly extravagant. It does not equal the cost of correcting the personal exemption for inflation. But it has the great advantage of making an enormous difference to the children who need it most, which correction of the value of the personal exemption would not do.

- *Fully fund the earned income tax credit.* The earned income tax credit was established by Congress in 1975. The idea was to correct the situation where people on welfare who go to work typically lose benefits worth more—potentially much more—than what they can make working in low-wage jobs. When fully phased in, the credit will provide its maximum benefits to working people whose income is almost exactly at the poverty line, gradually declining in value as family income rises, until there is no benefit at all for families making $24,159 or more. Congress has expanded the program several times since its inception. The recommendation of the commission is that Congress appropriate the full amount that has been authorized for expenditure over the next few years, rising to $11.8 billion in 1994, at which time the maximum credit will be $2,030.

- *Improve child-support enforcement and provide a government-insured benefit when absent parents fail to meet their obligation.* Only one single parent in four actually receives the full amount of the court-ordered child support. The National Commission on Children recommended a four-point plan: (1) get the states to record both parents' social security numbers when their children are born, (2) set child-support payments based on a uniform statewide schedule, (3) use automatic withholding to collect child-support payments, and (4) set up a government fund to pay the difference between what is collected and the court-ordered amount when the payments fall short. This is both fair and efficient. The first three provisions are already incorporated in the Family Support Act of 1988, though this has not yet been fully implemented. The fourth remains to be enacted.

- *For parents who are willing and able to work, but cannot find jobs, provide community employment opportunities where feasible and appropriate.* This is not a recommendation for a new federal employment program, but rather something that the states can and should do, using federal funds that they already have, provided that the federal government issues the appropriate waivers from the regulations now governing the use of those funds.

- *Raise the minimum wage to bring a family of four with one wage earner up to the poverty line.* This recommendation was not made by the National Commission on Children on the grounds that it would make American enterprise less competitive, create a hardship for small employers, and increase inflation. That decision may have been politically wise, but it does not augur well for the American economy. America cannot have it both ways. We cannot be a rich country while paying low wages. Even tiny Singapore places a surcharge on the contribution to the national training fund required of employers paying low wages, with the policy objective of making life uncomfortable for employers who add relatively little value to the goods and services they produce. The Singaporans know that if they want to become a high-wage economy they must provide an incentive to employers to restructure their operations so that their workers are more productive and can contribute more to their economy. We need to learn the same lesson. It should be a matter of high priority to create economic conditions that make it inviting for employers to invest more in their people and in the equipment that those people use. That is the only way for the entire country to prosper. Because raising the minimum wage will lead to greater productivity over the long run, it will not make the American economy less competitive or increase inflation. In fact, it will do exactly the opposite. It is also the case that a higher minimum wage will provide an incentive to work for those whose alternative is welfare. The driving principle of any income-support program should be developmental, that is, it should provide incentives, skills, and opportunities for self-support through earned income. If this recommendation were to be adopted, the earned income tax credit would no longer be necessary and the cost of the refundable child tax credit would be reduced.

These recommendations represent a key change in national policy—a shift from means-tested programs to programs that are available to everyone, not just the poor. Means-tested programs by their very nature lack broad support because they benefit only a small portion of our people, and a politically weak segment at that. The children of the poor are somebody else's children, not ours. Like it or not, the country will not do what must be done for its children until everyone's children benefit. When all the features of the income-support program are taken together, it will be seen that, while they provide support for all families, they provide the greatest benefits for the families that need the most help. That being so, low-income families are likely to receive more than they would receive if the funds were targeted exclusively on them. That is sound politics and sound public policy.

The debate also rages on national health insurance. In recent years, the costs of health care have soared as increasingly sophisticated and powerful technologies have appeared on the scene and the population ages. Every segment of the complex health-care system has attempted to shift these rising costs onto other segments. Health-care providers try to shift the costs to the insurers. Insurers try to shift the cost to employers by increasing premiums, to individuals by refusing to insure those who pose greater than average risks, and to doctors by capping reimbursements for specified procedures. Employers try to shift costs to employees by increasing the proportion of employees who work less than full-time and therefore have no benefits at all, and by increasing the proportion of costs that must be borne by the employees and reducing the benefits for those who do work full-time. As a result, a rising proportion of workers have no insurance at all and benefits continue to decrease for those who are insured. Those who suffer the most are poor children, low-income mothers, and pregnant women.

Virtually all of the parties among whom these costs are being shifted are at the limit of what they can pay, which makes it both necessary and possible to consider alternative methods of financing health care that would not have received a hearing in this country until very recently.

The national health-insurance system that is most widely admired by American analysts is the one used by Canada, a unified system in which there is only one health-insurance agency—the national government. Every analysis has shown that the Canadian system costs far less and provides more health care— and far more preventive health care—than the American system by a wide margin.

One would think that the clear and unchallenged advantages of the Canadian system would easily win the day in the policy debate. But this has hardly been the case. There are two powerful sources of opposition: the private health-insurance industry, whose clients would disappear, and people in the upper half of the income distribution, whose access to expensive procedures would be rationed, and who would have to wait, often for a long time, for such procedures when they do not face life-threatening health problems. Though everyone recognizes that something must change if the present system is to avoid collapse, no one, it seems, is willing to give up anything they now have.

To solve this problem, in the summer of 1991, the National Governors' Association and the National Commission on Children, separately recommended a mixed system in which employers would continue to deal with private insurers (subject to certain provisions intended to improve coverage) and those not covered by employer-provided insurance would be insured by government.

The plans recommended by the National Governors' Association and the National Commission on Children would both greatly improve the present condition of poor children. They may be the best practical resolution of the political problems involved in producing a universal health-insurance system, given the current circumstances. In addition they would require less public funds than a Canadian-style system, since employed people would be covered by private insurers. But both will cost billions of dollars more a year in total than a Canadian-style system, money that could be put to far better uses. Even more important, such a system perpetuates the American penchant for creating special, segregated social programs for the poor. Our very strong view, as we said earlier, is that all social programs work better both for the poor and for everyone else when they are for everyone, not just for the poor. The United States can no longer afford a health-care system in which no one gives up anything, and does not need yet another system in which the poor are treated differently than everyone else.

We therefore urge policymakers to create a system of national health insurance modeled on the Canadian system.

Unfortunately, adequate income and good health care are not alone sufficient to sustain children who will be ready to take full advantage of school when it starts. In Europe and the United States many mothers as well as fathers are now in the paid work force. For a great many mothers, this is not a question of choice, as we have seen. Either they are single parents living on one paycheck, or the value of real wages has fallen so far that both husband and wife must work to sustain even a minimal standard of living. But this is not just an issue for families living in poverty or close to it. Parents today spend 40 percent less time with their children than did parents in 1965—seventeen hours a week, compared to thirty hours a week.[11] This one fact speaks volumes about the reduced capacity of families as effective learning systems.

The question is, who will take care of the children? It is not, of course, just a matter of custodial care, though that is a crucial first issue for millions of families. Beyond that, there is the issue of whether there are adults around who will provide real love and affection when it is needed, and who will be there through the day to develop all the capacities on which continued formal learning will depend.

Most of the advanced countries of Europe have addressed this issue by requiring employers to provide paid leave for working family members to take care of their children, as well as free day care and high-quality child development services for young children. The first requirement ensures that parents can be with their very young children, and the second ensures that these children have high-quality care from others when their parents must be at work. In the United States neither of these requirements exists.

Clearly, we must legislate them both. Only the United States, among seventy-five leading industrial countries, is without a national policy providing incentives for or mandating that parents be given time off to give birth to and care for an infant.[12] The Bush administration argues that such matters should be left to bargaining between employers and their employees. But there is no evidence that this approach will solve the problem. Fewer than 20 percent of employers with more than fifty employees offer any form of maternity leave and just 5 percent of those with fewer than fifty employees do so. Only half of those that offer such a benefit guarantee a job at the same level when the employee returns, and seniority and continuation of health benefits while on leave.

The lack of family-leave in the United States is, of course, due to the determined opposition of employers, who argue that they cannot afford it, and that any government requirement to provide it will make them uncompetitive. But they have failed to explain why employers in so many countries that have successful economies can somehow afford it without going bankrupt or becoming uncompetitive.

This position also ignores the proven returns to employers that have voluntarily adopted strong family-leave policies. The report of the National Commission on Children cites the example of Merck & Company, a large pharmaceutical manufacturer, where a family policy that includes partial pay, the continuation of benefits, and substantial overhead costs nevertheless produces a net savings for Merck of $12,000 on average for each of the employees who takes advantage of it.[13] Moreover, Merck's attrition rate is half of the industry average, another benefit to the company that it attributes in significant measure to its family leave program. But there are few Mercks. As the figures just cited show, other firms will not follow unless they have very strong incentives from government to do so. The value of the Merck example is that it shows that such incentives will benefit not only American workers, but also the firms for which they work. The biggest benefit, however, will come to the society as a whole, in the form of children who are more secure, more confident, and better cared for by their parents.

The nation has made more progress on the issue of child care and development than on family leave. The 1990 Congress passed legislation establishing the child care and development block grant program, which for the first time created the basis for building a truly national child care and development system. But there is a long way to go to equal the programs that many other countries have had in place for years.

What parents need is affordable quality day care that provides a good developmental program for their children as well as a safe environment. What they have is something else. What is available to most poor family heads is someone in their neighborhood who will take the children in for the day and feed them. That caregiver is more likely than not to be unlicensed, untrained, and unreliable. Organized day-care centers are typically not much better. Because the average day-care worker made only $5.35 an hour in 1988 (equivalent to an annual wage below the poverty line for a family of three),[14] those workers are poorly educated and trained and the centers that employ them experience a very high rate of turnover—as much as 40 percent a year.

One might ask why it should be necessary to pay people much more than the minimum wage to take care of our children. Surely all we need is people who will care about the children, make sure they do not get into trouble, and keep them from harming themselves—in other words, glorified babysitters? But a large body of research shows that children who grow up to do well in school and in life need much more than that. They need a structured environment full of materials that will stimulate their brain development, and adults who will encourage the informal learning on which later formal instruction will build. In addition, they need a social environment in which they can build confidence in themselves and trust in others, and learn patterns of relating to others that are constructive rather than destructive. Building such an environment takes real skill and the people who do it, the record shows, are much more likely to do it well with good training.

It is very important to improve greatly the education and training of caregivers, but training alone will not solve the problem. Few would take the time or spend the money to attend such programs as long as the pay continues to be so low. In addition, the problem of high turnover rates in the centers that are now available is not just a problem for the centers, but for the children as well—it is very important for young children to form strong attachments to the adults who care for them. If the pay were increased to the point required to attract and keep people with the necessary training, a great many low- and middle-income parents could not afford the care without a substantial subsidy.

Finding good day care and developmental programs for children is no more a problem uniquely affecting the poor than is the problem of the lack of family leave. Both afflict the middle class too. Just as with health insurance, a comprehensive national policy that is not means-tested, addressing the needs of everyone irrespective of income, would receive wide support and fill a need which, if not met, will continue to frustrate any concerted attempt to produce the quality of human resources the United States must have to build a world-class economy. We therefore believe the United States should require employers to offer paid family leave and should move as rapidly as possible toward a system of free or heavily subsidized high-quality child care and development.

Enactment of the comprehensive family and youth policy we have in mind is not likely to come easily or soon. What is essential to do right now is to fully fund two federal programs that have proven their worth to every observer, but fall far short of covering everyone who is eligible for the services they provide: the Head Start program and the Special Supplemental Food Program for Women, Infants, and Children (WIC).

Head Start is a comprehensive program providing health, education, and social services to low-income children, mainly between the ages of three and five. An analysis of two hundred evaluations of the program conducted in 1985 shows that it produces cognitive gains and improvement in self-esteem, motivation to learn, health, and social behavior. Head Start graduates are less likely to fall behind in school or to be placed in special education programs.[15]

Estimates of the proportion of eligible children actually participating in Head Start differ. The administration, using one set of calculations, found that 53 percent of eligible children received the program's services in 1990. Congress, using another set of assumptions, found that only 30 percent participated in the same year. In its most recent reauthorization of the Head Start Program, Congress authorized the expenditure of enough funds to provide at least two years of the program for all eligible children by 1994. Adjusting for inflation, and using an estimated cost of $3,640 per child, the program would cost about $7.66 billion in 1994. This money, though authorized, has not yet been appropriated. We strongly urge that Congress appropriate the full amount authorized for expenditure on the Head Start program for 1994, and that part of the funds be used to increase the pay of Head Start teachers.

The WIC program provides highly nutritious food and nutrition education to low-income women who are pregnant or breast-feeding and their children to age five. Because it is tied to other health services, especially prenatal care, immunizations, and pediatric care, the program has resulted in major decreases in the rate of premature and low–birth weight newborns among the poor and in better health for infants and young children. The cost-benefit ratio for the program is staggering. The average program cost for a pregnant woman is about $250; the cost of maintaining a low–birth weight infant in an intensive care unit is many times that per day. Even so, appropriated funds only permit serving four million out of the seven million who are eligible. We recommend that Congress appropriate the additional $1 billion a year that would be required to fully fund the WIC Program.

In the summer of 1991, Congresswoman Pat Schroeder, chair of the House Select Committee on Children, Youth and Families, issued *A Plan of Action for Families: Response to a National Emergency,* the key component of which was KIDSNET. KIDSNET is a multiyear plan allowing a phase-in of funds before the year 2000, sufficient to enable the Head Start, WIC, and childhood immunization programs to meet the needs of all eligible children. The proposal would amend the Budget Enforcement Act to declare full funding of these programs to be emergency actions, and therefore outside the restrictions of the act, until the whole eligible population receives services. When President Bush asked the Congress to appropriate money outside the restrictions of the Budget Enforcement Act for the Persian Gulf War, Schroeder led a successful move, approved by a vote of 243 to 180, to amend the legislation to declare also a state of emergency for children, thereby authorizing KIDSNET. The Senate agreed to the amendment. In the event, Congress adjourned without actually appropriating the funds, but, as Schroeder observed, "Finally, Senators and Representatives are beginning to understand that tending to the health and education of our children today has profound ramifications for the well-being of America's economy tomorrow."[16]

The measures we have recommended in this chapter, though benefiting the middle class substantially, would also go a long way toward eliminating poverty and its effects among children and their families. The welfare program, much reduced in size, could once again be devoted to fulfilling its original purpose, to serve as a resource for the disabled and for those experiencing temporary hardship because of short-term unemployment caused through no fault of their own.

We do not have in mind the creation of a welfare state—defined as the support of those who do not wish to work by those who do—but rather of a system in which work is rewarded and in which children have the support they need to grow up strong, healthy, and ready to learn. A system with universal health care, income supports for children, universal child care, and family leave is not very attractive for loafers. One cannot live off health care, child care, and family leave, and the child-support payments we have recommended would not by themselves maintain a family at or above the poverty level. So they would provide a strong incentive to work, unlike our current welfare programs, which have a corrosive negative impact on the incentive to work. Though expensive, these policies would be no more costly than the equivalent programs many other countries have now and have had for years, which enable those countries to pay much less for what we call "welfare" than we do. Creating such policies is not a matter of compassion, but rather of self-interest. We have little choice if we expect to develop an economy that will maintain our current standard of living.

CHAPTER 12

Rebuilding the Community Fabric

The policies just described are essential, but their enactment will not by itself ensure success. What matters as much as the policies themselves is whether or not they and many other programs come together in a strong fabric of community support. In part, this is a matter of more efficient administration, the kind that results in effective integration of those programs so that the whole adds up to more than the sum of the parts.

But success requires far more than making sure that children who would otherwise be diagnosed as learning-disabled have access to someone in the health community who discovers that they need eyeglasses and makes sure they get them. Among its other appalling effects, poverty operates to deprive many of its youthful victims—especially those also subject to racial discrimination—of a belief in themselves, in their capacity to succeed, no matter what they do. These youngsters believe the system is stacked against them, that they cannot succeed, that they, like their parents and the other adults around them, are losers. They refuse to study hard and invest in academic success at school because they "know" that no amount of effort on their part is going to bring the same rewards it brings to other children. They look for companionship to other children who, like themselves, have been rejected by the larger society, and they make their way in defiance of the rules set by that society.

To solve this problem, young people must be put in an environment in which the adults in their lives tell them in countless ways—by their actions, not just their words—that they matter as individuals, that they have what it takes to succeed, that there will be someone who cares enough to be there when they are needed.

Many decent people in the upper ranks of our society are quite willing to acknowledge that poor families are hard put to it to make ends meet, but wonder why we must make a special effort now that was not made for the waves of immigrants who arrived in the United States no less poor and who nevertheless managed through sheer determination to make it into the middle class. Is there, they ask, anything really different about these times? Are poor children really in worse shape than their predecessors who succeeded without any special help? This is not an unreasonable question and it deserves a better answer than it usually gets.

In the years just before and after the turn of the century, immigrants finding their way to our great cities came to very different places than those the poor live in today. The social-service system we have today did not exist. In its place were two things now largely missing: the ward politics of the machine and a social structure of which only a fragment is now left. The old ward politics had its horrors, but among its virtues was its need to deliver real and valuable services, from jobs to medical help and emergency food assistance, to poor people in exchange for their votes. The bargain was simple: you take care of us at election time and we will take care of you for the rest of the year. There was nothing bureaucratic or impersonal about this. The machine, in the person of someone you were likely to know quite well, delivered its own version of integrated social services to your door. Not all groups were well served by this system. There were no nutritionists figuring out what your family should eat nor any professional job counselors giving vocational test batteries. The system was terribly corrupt. But it was also very personal and very responsive in a way and to a degree that we can only marvel at today.

It was also true that most immigrant communities, huddled together in the city's core, included people who were well educated as well as those who were not, people with entrepreneurial skills as well as those who had none, people with strong skills as well as those who had few. Most able-bodied men and many women were employed and slowly made their way up in the society. Because of this mix, and because the means of earning a living were at hand, young people had adults throughout the neighborhood to whom they could look up, with whom they could identify, and who could offer them a hand as they sought to make good on their aspirations. However poor these communities were in funds, they were typically strong in spirit and their desire for a sense of community in a strange land gave a special force to their need for community expression. As the means became available, they built churches, savings and loan associations, social clubs, youth clubs, summer camps, sports associations, and much more. The corner grocers, butchers, and bakers took an interest in the young people and reported wayward behavior to their parents. They gave them jobs and took them under their wings, teaching them the trade. As labor unions were formed and gained strength, they provided another vehicle through which the newcomers could lift themselves and their children up.

Later, in the reform era, much of this changed. We have already described the impact of the reformers on the governance, organization, and management of city schools. Much the same thing happened to the organization of social services, which was also professionalized and bureaucratized. The ward heelers gave way to social-service professionals administering legislated programs in a system that has grown steadily more complex, fractionated, and impersonal up to the present day.

Up until the Second World War, there were plenty of jobs in the city that required little or no education or skills—simply a strong back and a willingness to work hard. Many of these jobs were held by members of unions strong enough to command good wages, enough not only to make ends meet but to propel the families who held them into solid middle-class comfort. But since the war, such jobs have been disappearing from the American economy at an ever-increasing rate. They have largely left the inner city altogether. With them has gone the ladder out of poverty for the urban poor.

The result for blacks has been perceptively described by William Julius Wilson.[1] Blacks arrived in our great cities in the largest numbers just as those cities were about to convert from major manufacturing and distribution centers to nerve centers of the service economy. Toward the end of this process, between 1970 and 1984, the city of Boston, for example, lost forty-four thousand jobs requiring little or no education and gained sixty-seven thousand jobs requiring higher education. Those manufacturing jobs that did not move offshore went to the suburbs or even farther from the central core. The social structure of the urban ghettos was shattered. Unemployment rates among black males soared. Rates of crime and drug use rose sharply, a measure of the desperation and hopelessness among young people who could not find jobs. Young women, having no incentive to marry young men they would have to support, did not marry at all, but chose to have children, causing the rate of out-of-wedlock births to soar.

Educated blacks were able to escape, leaving behind a new kind of underclass, a group of young people who, unlike their predecessors, had no link upward to adults in the productive society. The grocers, bakers, and butchers were gone. The churches moved away with their middle-class parishioners or were abandoned. Central city YMCAs, progressively abandoned by middle-class inner-city residents who were fleeing to the suburbs, attempted to survive by converting the swimming pools that neighborhood children had used into gymnasiums for executives on their lunch hours and eliminating their outreach programs; some were forced to close altogether. As the unions declined along with the industries that had been best organized, they no longer offered a way out. As the Reagan revolution proceeded during the 1980s, tax rates climbed and taxpayer revolts forced local authorities to cut back on summer job programs, recreation services, and local training programs for the young and their families. Gradually, the urban poor were cut off from the larger economy and society to a degree without parallel in the history of the United States. The stress on families and children in these enclaves is now unrelenting.

The best cure for the problems of the inner city is a healthy economy in which the residents are full participants. We said in the last chapter that there is no better way to empower poor people than to enable them to get and hold good jobs, to become as solidly middle-class as the immigrant groups who occupied their neighborhoods before them. The question is how to achieve this.

Two things, at least, are necessary. The United States must create a full-employment, high-wage economy, a challenge we deal with elsewhere in this book; and the residents of the inner city must have the skills, attitudes, and habits that will enable them to get and hold the jobs that such an economy will provide.

In the long run, the policies described in the last chapter will greatly alleviate the problem of providing the basic means by which families can form effective learning systems and the society can assure that children arrive at school ready to learn. But for now and for the foreseeable future, the best hope lies in making far better use of the resources now available by changing the way current programs work and weaving them together into a web of support for the most troubled families that will enable them to once again become effective learning systems for children. There is no doubt that this can be done. In this chapter we draw on a burgeoning literature to show how new approaches to social-service delivery are making a big difference in American communities right now.

Homebuilders

Lisbeth Schorr has compiled the most complete and compelling set of examples of successful efforts to break the mold of bureaucratic social-service programs, showing how creative and determined people can combine and redirect the resources now available to make a real difference in the lives of poor people.[2] One of the most striking examples in her book is the story of the Homebuilders program, started by Catholic Children's Services in Tacoma, Washington, in 1974.

Catholic Children's Services were faced with a dilemma. If they took children out of a disintegrating home and put them in the foster-care system, those children were highly likely to be shuttled from one foster home to another. Their prospects thereafter were very bleak. On the other hand, if the agency tried to prop up their families with the inadequate resources that were available, the children's lives would be in danger.

The new Homebuilders Program assembled a team of professionals in social work, psychology, and counseling who took on cases of family crisis referred to them by child welfare, juvenile justice, and mental health agencies, which would ordinarily have resulted in the removal of the children from their homes, and provided "intensive care" for these families in crisis. A team member takes on only three cases at any one time. The object is first to get the family back on its feet and then to enable it to function effectively in the long term. Team members have direct access to the full resources of the social-service system, the courts, and the schools. And the help is immediate—a team member is on the scene within twenty-four hours of the first call for help.

Schorr describes the story of one family helped by the Homebuilders program. There had been a long history of child neglect. Four children had previously been placed in foster care. The kids were frequently truant from school, "ashamed of their appearance and ridiculed by classmates." The family had been involved with many social-service agencies, each of them telling the mother what to do, and none of them providing much real help from the family's point of view.

Homebuilders "got a refrigerator, mattresses, sheets, blankets, and other basic necessities . . . and helped the mother scrub the walls and floors." By responding to these immediate needs, they built up enough trust so that they could teach the mother to set realistic goals and accomplish them, such as learning how to obtain food stamps and enrolling in a vocational education program in budgeting and food preparation. Winning the confidence of the children, the team worked with the school staff to improve attendance and got the children jobs. Within a year, "the children were doing well in school and were helpful at home, and the eldest child, previously intent on leaving school at sixteen, had decided to continue."[3]

Ninety percent of the children helped by Homebuilders are still with their families. At a cost of $2,600 per year in 1985, the program showed a five- to sixfold return on every dollar invested. The benefits to the children were incalculable. With strong support from the Edna McConnell Clark Foundation, an intensive family preservation program based on the Homebuilders model has now spread to more than thirty-five states.[4]

What accounts for this spectacular success? "First," says Schorr, "the families are highly motivated." They know that if they do not overcome their problems, their children will be taken away from home. Second, because the team comes to the home, the family members are not faced with having to travel, often long distances, to wait in long lines for "services" that seldom come and are rarely what they actually need. Having the team member in the home is much less threatening, much more useful, and much more likely to build trust. Third, the intensive care approach means that the social worker has much more time to do what is actually needed and that help will come when it is needed, not on the schedule of some remote agency. Fourth, the staff have access to a wide range of social-service resources and can provide the right service at the right time.

Even more important, the team becomes an effective, knowledgeable advocate for the family in a highly complex, rule-bound system that is often impenetrable by people who do not understand it and do not know how to negotiate it. Fifth, the team members have access to a wide range of help beyond the usual social-service agencies that can often prove crucial and to which the family often has no access at all. Mainly, though, the "system" becomes friendly and genuinely helpful. It provides real people who are there when they are needed to do whatever needs to be done, more like trusted family members than the social-service bureaucracy with which families in crisis are usually faced. The Home-builders program, in short, represents a way in which modern society can organize itself to provide an effective substitute for the extended informal support community that once was available to families in trouble, but is no longer.

Sinai Hospital's Department of Pediatrics Program

Lead poisoning, a problem faced by many young people living in dilapidated housing, can cripple a child's capacity for learning throughout life. Lisbeth Schorr tells the story of what Dr. Barbara Howard, a pediatrician at Sinai Hospital in Baltimore, did about it.

Howard took Schorr to visit a classroom at the Cold Spring Headstart Center. The three- to five-year-old children in that classroom had come from all over the city, referred by the city health department. Three months earlier, they had been screaming and hitting each other, the effects of the lead that had poisoned their bodies. The meals the children had been fed in the Head Start center were carefully planned by nutritionists to compensate for the effects of the lead and for the diets that most lead-poisoned children get. The program was also de-signed to provide some of the structure that is missing from the rest of their lives and the stimulation that their impoverished circumstances rarely provide.

The children's mothers were in a session in a nearby room with a nutrition aide from the University of Maryland Cooperative Extension Service. They would use what they were learning about nutrition to plan and prepare a meal for their children at the center and then apply what they learned at home. But more was going on than nutrition education. These mothers were also engaging in discussions about everything from child development to methods of removing lead from the home. And they worked as aides in the classroom, applying what they were learning about child development and gaining the practical skills that they needed in the home.

Using funds from Head Start, various nutritional and lead control programs, Howard had put together a support system that took into account the multiple problems faced by the children of the poor and their families. The changes this program had made in both children and parents were very impressive. Six of the children in the first "class" in the program had been classified as retarded or borderline retarded. Of these six, three had moved into the normal IQ range by the program's second year. The great majority entered the program nonverbal, overly active, disorganized, and uncooperative. Within two years, they had calmed down and begun to relate well to other people. Their verbal and motor skills had improved substantially, and their blood lead levels had decreased.

This all sounds very sensible, like the sort of thing that a caring physician ought to do when confronted with a problem that requires a solution that goes beyond one's own technical expertise. But Schorr shows that this kind of initiative is very rare, that physicians, like most professionals, do what they are trained to do and no more, whether or not what they are trained to do actually meets their clients' needs. She cites the case of the emergency-room doctor who was presented with a baby who was being brought in for the fourth time in two months suffering from diarrhea and dehydration. Schorr asked whether there were any signs in the previous visits that the baby was not being properly fed or cared for. He said that there were, but he had just treated the baby and sent her home. It had never occurred to him that an appropriate medical response might have included sending a social worker, or a public-health nurse, or any other competent professional to the home to find out what the situation was and set it right.

This doctor behaved like the vast majority of professionals, but such behavior causes the symptoms, whether dehydration and diarrhea or the impaired mental ability caused by lead poisoning, to continue to show up, get worse, and become overwhelming. Dr. Howard, however, treated the patient and not just the symptom, and, in doing so, saved both people and money.

Yale University Child Study Center

When James Comer, Professor of Child Psychiatry and Director of the School Development Program at Yale University, was growing up in a working-class community in East Chicago, Indiana, he noticed an important difference between himself and the other black children who were not able to make the leap into middle-class America that he later made.[5] None were poor. All of the fathers worked in the local steel mill. But two of Comer's friends wound up in jail, one died prematurely from alcoholism, and a fourth was in and out of mental institutions. Why did Comer's life turn out differently? He thinks "it was simply because my parents, unlike those of my friends, gave me the social skills and confidence that enabled me to take advantage of educational opportunities."[6] His parents became friendly with his teachers, read books, took him to the library, and did other things that signaled to the young man that the teachers were good people and that academic skills were expected and valued.

Comer observes that life for most poor black children is more like that of his childhood friends than his own. All children tend to form a strong bond with their parents which powerfully affects their own values, attitudes, and behavior. When the values, attitudes, and behavior of the family and the adults in the school are much the same, children tend to do well, but when they are very different, as is typically the case with schools serving the poor, then the children naturally choose those of their parents. But the school, unwilling or unable to reach out to the children on their own terms, demands conformity with its rules and its culture. Alienated and rejected, the children fight back by denying the importance of school. In this way, the pattern of school failure is established early and rarely turned around.

In 1968, Comer and his colleagues at Yale decided to take on the Martin Luther King School in New Haven to see if they could help the staff and parents address these problems, and, by so doing, improve student performance. The school ranked thirty-second out of thirty-three in standardized tests of the basic skills. Fourth-grade students were nineteen months behind in reading, and eighteen months behind in math. Apathy and conflict and other behavior problems were the norm. Staff and student attendance were both poor. The parents were "dejected, distrustful, angry and alienated."[7] In 1977, they started work at a second school, the Katherine Brennan School, serving a housing project, with similar problems. Both schools are 99 percent black; 90 percent of their students are below the poverty line.

Comer and his colleagues developed a strategy for reducing the cultural gap between parents and school staff based on parent involvement at three levels: shaping school policy, participating in activities supporting the school program, and attending school events.

Parents participate in making school policy through membership in a school management team. Directed by the principal, a representative group of parents and teachers, along with a child development specialist or support-staff member, develops a master plan for the school with specific objectives, goals, and strategies in three areas: school climate, academics, and staff development. The clear focus for all is student achievement. The parents take primary responsibility for school climate, but are involved in all the decisions, which are made by consensus. Among other things, the parents work with the staff to develop a curriculum and activities for the students that will enable them to master the social skills expected when they graduate, including such things as writing invitations and thank-you notes, serving as hosts, maintaining a checking account, and planning concerts.

At the next level, parents participate by working ten hours a week at minimum wage—and often for additional time as volunteers—as teacher assistants. Only parents can serve in these roles, thereby building a bond of communication, trust, and understanding among themselves, teachers, and students. These parents form the core of the larger school parent group. They immerse themselves in the academic and social programs of the school, and devise workshops to increase their knowledge and skills.

At the third level, the larger parent group sponsors school parties, opening and closing day events, and occasions when the whole community can take pride in itself and its accomplishments. Some tutor while others form student activity groups.

In all these ways, the project finds ways to replicate the environment in which Comer grew up, where the values of his teachers were much the same as those of his parents, both teachers and parents respected one another, and the learning taking place in school and in the home was complementary rather than conflicting. In many respects the method is to arrange a situation in which parents and teachers come to see the other's world, to enter into that world, and in the process to develop real empathy and understanding. In time, the teachers, school psychologists, child development specialists, and parents become a team, setting goals together and working together to achieve them on behalf of the students. Parents, more trustful of the teachers and better informed about what was expected of the students, can much more effectively work with their children at home to support what the teachers are doing in school.

By 1979, with no change in the general composition of the student body, fourth-grade students in the Martin Luther King School were performing at grade level. By 1984, the fourth-grade students in both schools ranked third and fourth highest on the basic skills test used by the district. Attendance rates at King were either first or second in the city, and there were no serious behavior problems.[8] Attendance at school events mushroomed from 15 to 20 parents to 250 and sometimes as many as 400—in a school enrolling only 300 students.[9] The program is now being introduced into all New Haven schools and is being tried out in schools elsewhere around the country, with results similar to those achieved in New Haven.

Here again, we see the contrast between professionals delivering their service in a bureaucratic framework, and, on the other hand, an effort to bring the professionals together with their clients in an environment in which the clients' needs, rather than those of the professionals, drive the way the program is structured and the services are delivered. The clients are seen as real people, not as the objects of service delivery. The result is that the service is restructured. Results are what counts, not following the rules. Because this is so, the problem for the professionals is redefined, and the clients, rather than being seen as passive recipients of a predefined service, become partners in the enterprise.

The Wegman's Work/Scholarship Connection Program

On January 13, 1987, Wegman's Food Markets of Rochester, New York, held a joint press conference with the Rochester City School District to announce a new program. Wegman's had for years offered scholarships on a competitive basis to its own employees, but very few students from the inner city had been able to qualify because of their poor academic performance. Wegman's executives wanted to change this. They intended to work with the Rochester City School District to identify young people fourteen to sixteen years old who appeared to have high potential but who were in real danger of dropping out of school. It would offer these students part-time supermarket jobs, on the condition that, to keep these jobs, they would have to stay in school and make steady progress. If they did so, and qualified for college when they graduated, Wegman's would guarantee them a scholarship making up the difference between what they could get from other sources and what they needed to attend college. Once enrolled, and as long as they were making a real effort to succeed, the youngsters would get a lot of help from the company along the way.

Wegman's does not ordinarily employ students under the age of sixteen, but it knew that they would have to make an exception in this case if it was to get to these students before it was too late, since most students the company wanted to reach drop out as soon as they legally can. The question the designers of the program faced was how to help these youngsters succeed against all the odds.

The program manager is looking for students who, ranking high on these indicators, are identified by the district as highly likely to drop out but who, despite that, appear to have significant promise in the eyes of their teachers and school administrators. Candidates are told that they are expected to maintain a good attendance record, and to cooperate with all the adults involved in the program, both at school and at work; that they will be responsible for getting all the legal documents they need to work; and that they will have to abide by all the rules and regulations at work that any other Wegman's employee has to follow. Students who are signed on provisionally in their first marking period are dropped if they cannot meet these conditions.

The student selects a member of the school staff to serve as his or her school sponsor. This person is the school link to the program staff and is committed to providing personal support to the student while at school. The sponsor keeps track of how the student is doing in all courses, stays in touch with the teachers of those courses, consults with the administration and teachers when problems arise, and provides academic and personal counseling for the student.

We mentioned earlier that Wegman's has for years had a scholarship program for its employees that has mostly involved students from outside the central city. Many of these scholarship students are now assigned as tutors to students in the Rochester Work-Scholarship Connection Program. They are in regular touch with these students, giving them help on their school subjects and also with their study skills. Functioning as friendly coaches, they help find an approach to school work that will help their charges succeed, whatever it takes.

The jobs provided to the participants in the program are part-time, as clerks at the checkout counter, stockers, and so on. How much time they work depends on how well they are doing at school. Participants who start to fall behind in school are given no work at all, although other forms of support continue, and cannot regain their jobs until they start to make progress in school again. All of the employees in the supermarket, from department managers to coworkers, know that they have an obligation to help the participants succeed at work.

In addition, each participant is assigned a mentor, a volunteer staff member who, once again, serves as a coach and advocate, providing training for the job, letting the student know what is expected of employees, helping out when difficulties arise, and providing encouragement when the going gets tough. The mentor, selected by the Work-Scholarship Connection Program staff on the store's recommendation, provides the link back to the program staff for the participant at the employment end of the system.

A full-time Youth Advocate is employed for every thirty students in the program. The Youth Advocate is responsible for coordinating the entire support system for all of the assigned students, keeping track of performance on the job and at school, and checking with parents. Youth Advocates select the school sponsors, tutors, mentors, and the other people at the work site who provide support to the students, train them for their roles, and weld them into a team. They run workshops and plan group activities, deal with the various social-service agencies that affect the students' lives and serve as the students' advocates with those agencies, and are there when simple problems arise and when real trouble comes. It is they, more than anyone else, who assume bottom-line responsibility for helping the student to succeed against the odds.

Here is how Peter McWalters, Superintendent of the Rochester City School District, summed it all up:

> The Wegman's Work-Scholarship Connection demonstrates in a microcosm the broad-based approach that requires the whole community to support the education initiatives taking place in the district. . . . The Wegman's Program makes the work-school connection real—a responsibility that must be shared by all Rochester businesses. . . . At Wegman's, they [the students] are not only learning "the job," they're learning something about what it means to work in a culture, the work ethic and collegial responsibility to get a job done. *That's* curriculum.[10]

But there is, in fact, much more than that involved. These youngsters were failing in school in large measure because there were few if any adults in their lives who seemed to care about them and believed in them. This program provides work skills and helps students develop solid academic skills. But much more important, it also wraps a web of human support around these students that gives them a reason to develop those skills and the confidence they need to persevere when the going gets tough. The Work-Scholarship Connection is, more than anything else, a human connection.

The design of the program has some interesting features. The advocates are in a position to cut through the school bureaucracy when necessary because they are located not only at the school but also within a few yards of the superintendent's office. Those same advocates can go directly to the social-service agencies, deal directly with parents, and intervene on the job. Troubled students can get help and see the results almost instantly in a world that is otherwise almost wholly unresponsive. Nothing builds hope or engenders trust—two crucial ingredients of success—faster than a system of this kind.

The results speak for themselves. Most members of the very first group of students are now eighteen or older. Twelve of the group of thirty finished high school, and all but one of the graduates are now in college, assisted by scholarships from Wegman's; fifteen dropped out; and the rest are still in high school. If current trends continue, two-thirds of the students recruited by the program will get a high-school diploma and most of those will continue on to college. According to the school district's analysis, few, if any, of these students would have graduated without the program, and none, of course, would have gone to college.

But these statistics do not tell the whole story. These students now have confidence in themselves that they never had before. They know what is expected of them in the workplace and can live up to those expectations. They have met a group of adults who believe in them and who continue to provide personal support and encouragement even when they are enrolled in college. They have found an alternative to the culture of alienation, and many are not only encouraging their friends to take advantage of that alternative but have dedicated themselves to working with others when they are out of school and have the resources to help. They have the courage to set goals for themselves and the discipline required to reach those goals, whatever it takes. They have learned to control their anger, to work out their differences with others without the explosions that have so often short-circuited their progress in the past. All of these capacities amount to more than work and academic skills. They are the means by which these students have gained control over their lives and over their futures, the foundation on which they can build successful lives.

New Beginnings

Each of the programs we have described thus far is an island of success in a sea of failure. Throughout this book, we have stressed the lack of effective systems in American life. San Diego's New Beginnings program shows how many of the islands of success can be brought together to form an entire system that works for a large metropolitan area.

Jake Jacobson, director of the San Diego County social-service system, one of the largest in the United States, described the origins of New Beginnings to one of the authors of this book.[11] The costs of the schools and of all the social-service systems in San Diego were spinning out of control. Key county officials, facing an increasingly impossible budget situation, looked for a way out in a radical departure from the bureaucratic delivery system over which they had been presiding for years.

Jacobson observes that each manager's costs is another manager's savings. For example, each additional dollar invested by the criminal justice system in education and training saves the welfare system money when released offenders get jobs instead of going on welfare. Conversely, a successful intervention with a foster child will save the criminal justice system money. In essence, he points out, all of these systems are dealing with the same clients. Each, however, delivers its service independently of the other, and none has an incentive to increase its costs even if doing so will save another agency two or three times that amount. Each agency operates just like the doctor we described earlier, treating the symptom he was trained to treat, and doing nothing about the underlying cause of the problem, so that the symptom keeps reappearing. The results of this program- and funding-driven system, in San Diego and elsewhere, are huge administrative costs and a very low success rate.

There is only one way out, Jacobson says. All the agencies will go down together unless we pool our data, look at the flows of dollars and assistance, and analyze the community's problems as a whole. That way, we can get at the problems at their roots, before we have to cope with their results at far higher cost. Analysis of the criminal justice data for Washington, D.C., for example, showed that a very small fraction of the children in the community account for a very large fraction of the total crime. Why not find out where those children live and under what conditions, and focus substantial attention on those neighborhoods in a comprehensive attempt to address the underlying problems there? It is the same principle that animates the Family Preservation Program, but focused on a crucial group in the community rather than a single family. This is just an example, Jacobson says. Whatever the analysis shows, the point is that all the agencies need to pool their data, use them to work out a shared plan, then pool the people who are eligible for aid, and, finally, integrate the delivery systems to get at the root problems in a systematic way.

As the San Diego team designed their program, they thought carefully about the factors that had contributed to the failure of similar programs elsewhere. One of the most common, they found, was that other communities had conceived of what they were doing as a "project," organized outside the mainstream of agency life and funded by "soft money"—typically foundation funds or special short-term government grants. While such a project was underway, agency line managers had typically viewed it as temporary and peripheral—somebody else's project—so that it rarely got strong support when the outside money was there and usually died when the money was withdrawn. Jacobson told us that the San Diego agency heads decided to use their own regular agency funds for everything but the extraordinary costs of the transition. They also decided that the management of the system change could not be assigned to project managers outside the regular management structure. The day-to-day management of the effort has been assigned to senior officials of each participating agency as a key part of their regular responsibilities. They know that they are not managing a project off to the side, but are responsible for restructuring the basic ways in which their agency functions and relates to other agencies as well as clients.

The founders of New Beginnings also knew that they would need the strong support of the key policymakers and the general public in their communities, that what they had in mind could not be accomplished in the shadows of agency work. Between July 23 and July 25, 1990, all of the collaborating agencies—the City Council, the Board of Supervisors, the Community College Board, and the Board of Education—unanimously adopted a Statement of Philosophy for New Beginnings, committing all the dozens of agencies and major programs for which these bodies are responsible—with combined budgets totaling more than $3.5 billion—to an explicit and unified set of principles. Among other things, the statement describes the family as the community's primary caregiver, and its support as a primary objective. It calls the fragmentation of the social services and education system a major problem, identifies early intervention to help families as a key strategy, and declares that only "an integrated services system involving all these agencies and the full resources of their professional staff can meet the complex needs of children and families in our community."[12]

New Beginnings has begun its work by identifying a school and its community that have all the problems that the coalition proposed to address. The object is to use this initial effort as an opportunity to develop and pilot an approach that can then be applied throughout the county. Hamilton Elementary School is located in East San Diego, which has the highest housing density, the highest crime rate, the second highest rate of child abuse, and one of the lowest average incomes in the county. The students have the highest mobility rate in the school district. Nine percent of the students are white, 24 percent are black, 24 percent are Indochinese, and 39 percent are Hispanic. They speak more than thirty first languages. Student performance on all the measures of basic skills is very poor.

The work at Hamilton began with a case study coordinated by a social worker over a three-month period during the winter of 1989–90. This initial data-gathering effort documented the needs of the families, their eligibility for services, the barriers to receiving those services, the effects of case management services on about twenty high-risk families, and issues having to do with communication between the school and a range of social-service agencies.

Each agency assigned a staff liaison person to work with the school and with the social worker conducting the case study. Their assignment was to help Hamilton staff gain access to agency services, increase the agency staff's awareness of the school's needs, find out what the barriers were to better agency service to school and students, and identify changes that might be made to improve agency service delivery.

Meanwhile, off-duty County of San Diego Public Health nurses were conducting interviews of about fifty Hamilton families, so as to understand the needs of the families and the reasons that those needs were not being met by the agencies that were supposed to be serving them. They documented the effects of the case management services being coordinated by the social worker, and worked to improve the communications among the families, the school, and the social-services agency staff.

At the same time that the families were being interviewed, another set of interviews was taking place with selected staff members from agencies that worked with Hamilton families. These interviews examined family needs from the agency point of view, those things that frustrated the staffers' ability to meet those needs, and their views about how to improve communication between the agencies and families.

Another group was going through the data held by the schools and the social-service agencies, matching data from these sources for the Hamilton families. Large fractions of the families were known to one or more of the agencies and qualified for various public programs. Forty-seven percent of the students identified by the district as at risk were known to the Department of Social Services. When the data had been compiled, the analysts found that the Department of Social Services alone was providing $5,316,824 in services to the Hamilton school and its families at an annual administrative cost of half a million dollars, a substantial sum which, used in the context of a unified plan, could go a long way toward improving the outcomes for these families.

Finally, a school migration study was performed to determine patterns of student and family mobility in and out of the Hamilton enrollment area as well as the characteristics of those families who moved around and those who stayed.

Based on all these data, New Beginnings plans to build a center located adjacent to Hamilton to house the staff and facilities for an integrated program of health services, social services, and adult education for the students and their families, in collaboration with the school.

School registration will be moved to the center so that families can become familiar with its services and to enable the staff to make an assessment of families' needs as well as those of the students. Family services advocates, drawn from the existing staff of the agencies, will be the heart of the new system. Each advocate, working with thirty to forty families, will determine eligibility, provide information about available services, and help each family develop a plan for moving toward self-sufficiency. When the plan is developed, the advocate will provide counseling and serve as the representative of the families with the agencies whose help they need. Expanded health examinations and immunizations will be offered by the center, as well as multicultural mental health services, the WIC supplemental nutrition program, and adult education, including classes in English as a second language.

But the services of the center will go far beyond its walls. New Beginnings is creating an extended team for the Hamilton Center, made up of agency professionals who, while not based at the center, will be familiar with the Hamilton families, neighborhood, and program. Their caseloads will be redefined to take into account their responsibilities to the center and its families. Police, parks and recreation, library services, children's services, probation, public housing, and many more professional personnel, including specialists from the school district and the community college, will be members of this extended team.

New Beginnings is just getting started. Its managers believe it may take ten years to put it fully in place. But it has already blazed a new trail. These hard-headed managers of some of the largest social-service and education agencies in the United States can see a plausible way to provide real help to families. They are standing on the shoulders of many of the people that Lisbeth Schorr wrote about, people who showed how smaller pieces of the system could be put together to provide far more effective services far more efficiently by organizing around the needs of families in trouble rather than around the programs of the agencies or the problems defined by the professions.

The Texas Industrial Areas Foundation

Organizing around the needs of families rather than the missions of institutions does not, however, come easily to most institutional managers. Each of the stories we have told thus far involves professionals reaching out to families to offer a new kind of help. But for every community and neighborhood that has a story like the ones we have told, there are countless others in which poor families are as powerless and their needs as unmet as they have ever been. This is a story about an organization that empowers poor families by giving them the confidence to demand what they need and the skills required to get it.

Ernie Cortes, the head of the Texas Industrial Areas Foundation (TIAF), is a legend in the state.[13] Not that he sought that status; far from it. He prefers to stay in the background. He learned the iron law of organizing from his mentor, Saul Alinsky, in the 1960s: Never do for people what they can do for themselves. The corollary, of course, is to help them learn to do everything themselves. Ernie is an unusual teacher.

He is a legend because he has taught poor Texans how to gain power—real power—and use it well. Take COPS, for example, the organization he created in 1973 in a desperately poor Mexican-American community on San Antonio's west side. The TIAF is the statewide organization that supports COPS and other local organizations.

Cortes began by talking to the leaders of the community churches. It was agreed that the organization they were to found would take no money from government agencies or from foundations. With less than one hundred thousand dollars, raised mostly from the churches themselves, Cortes got started. People make organizations; if it was their money, from their collection plates, it would be their organization. Other, less successful, organizers had started with planning, convinced that they knew what the problems were, but not Cortes. He went looking for people—not the well-known activists with their own agendas but ordinary people, natural leaders in their own neighborhoods—who led their PTAs, scout troops, or union shops. He interviewed more than a thousand people, one-on-one, taping each conversation and listening to them over and over until he was able to piece out what the community really thought the problems were. They did not talk about the things that appeared in the newspapers or the civil-rights agendas of the activists. They were concerned about skyrocketing utility bills, broken-down schools, rats coming into their homes from adjacent junk yards, the lack of swimming pools and parks, and the recurrent floods that would sweep into the West Side and into the homes of the one hundred thousand families that lived there, taking lives and destroying what little property they had.

The COPS leaders decided to concentrate on one issue: the lack of proper drainage for flood control. Cortes was teaching his growing body of members that knowledge was power. Their research showed that a bond issue had been approved by the city in 1945 for West Side drainage improvements, but the money, when raised, had been spent elsewhere. They were outraged. The city manager agreed to meet with them to discuss the problem.

Five days before the meeting, there was another destructive flood. Five hundred COPS members, fully armed with facts, figures, and a slide presentation, went to confront the city manager. Unable to counter either their facts or their arguments, and impressed by their numbers, he agreed to put the matter on the City Council agenda for the next week. At the end of that meeting, the mayor, astounded to learn that nothing had been done in three decades to solve this problem that affected forty thousand of his constituents, demanded that his staff prepare a financing plan in four hours. The $46 million bond issue they recommended was passed the following November.

COPS was to go from success to success. It has won more than $750 million worth of improvements for poor neighborhoods that formerly got nothing. The reason is simple. A major COPS effort can now generate forty thousand to fifty thousand votes. Some COPS precincts have 90 percent of the eligible voters registered. Membership drives and fundraisers produce a $150,000 annual budget. COPS is a potent force in the political life of the city.

Cortes went on to form similar organizations throughout Texas. The Texas Industrial Areas Foundation can now mobilize twenty affiliated organizations and nearly one million families from a broad range of faiths and ethnic backgrounds on behalf of its agenda. Its objective is to create "new democratic institutions to empower families and congregations to defend their integrity and to participate meaningfully in public life."[14] *Texas Business* recently named Cortes one of the most powerful people in Texas—along with Ross Perot and T. Boone Pickens.[15]

In 1986, one of the TIAF-affiliated organizations, the Allied Communities of Tarrant, developed a plan, based on James Comer's model, to turn around a predominantly black middle school where student performance was on a par with the schools Comer had taken on in New Haven. They followed much the same path that Comer had followed. The difference was that they had the skills to deeply involve the community and its institutions in the process, skills that TIAF training had given them. Just as Cortes had done years before in San Antonio's West Side, they met individually with over six hundred people, drawing out their concerns and using them to make a plan that would respond to them. They developed training programs for parents, helping them to express their views to the school authorities and to support their children's learning in the home. And they gained the parents' confidence to the point that they were willing to meet more often with their children's teachers. Community churches found ways to celebrate students' progress. The result was that hostile relations became collaborative, and, most important, student performance rose dramatically. After three years, the school, which had placed twentieth among the district's schools, placed third.

At the core of the strategy is a consistent view about the centrality of families as learning systems. Family relationships, as well as school performance, were strengthened. Cortes's belief in the power of families is best expressed in his own words:

Families teach the first lessons of relationships among persons, some of which are central not only to private life but to public life as well. Within the family one learns to act and be acted upon. It is within the family where we learn to identify ourselves with others—or fail to learn to love. It is in the family where we learn to give and take with others—or fail to learn to be reciprocal. . . . The organizations of the TIAF are mediating institutions through which families create a space to learn about power and leadership and to act on what they learn . . . they act to counter the pressures on families and to reshape other institutions in their relationships to families.[16]

No family can function effectively—as a learning system or in any other way—that is beaten down, that sees itself as powerless to affect its own destiny, that is merely the passive object of someone else's understanding of what it needs and is capable of. Cortes, like many of the other people whose work we have briefly chronicled in this chapter, starts with the assumption that effective family functioning is vital to a free society and to the development of our human resources. What he has done is find a way to give those families under the greatest stress and with the least power the skills they need to take charge of their lives and make the system do what it should do but typically will not.

Are the stories we have told in this chapter simply examples that other organizations and communities can profit from individually, or do they contain the seeds of major changes in public policy that can shape the entire system? We believe both to be true. Individual action need not await major policy changes, but only major policy changes are likely to produce widespread changes for the better in the way public institutions meet the needs of families.

The entire structure of the social-service delivery system needs to be changed from a focus on programs to a focus on results in terms of effective family functioning. Here, as elsewhere in this book, we advocate a shift to a performance-based system. To make that work in this arena will require several steps. "Performance," in terms of functioning families, rather than the narrower criteria now used by each of the fragmented pieces of the system, needs to be defined in such a way that it can be assessed. Appropriate assessment techniques need to be created that capture the spirit of that definition. New incentives, including a complete revision of the way funds flow through the system, need to be created that will induce policymakers, agency heads, and social-service professionals to reorganize the social-service delivery system to get the results that are wanted. That reorganization must stress the careful assessment of individual family needs, quick response to families in crisis, concentration of resources on those families at the time when they will do the most good, respect for the family not just as the object of the service but as the collaborator in its provision, and effective collaboration among social-service professionals in the provision of those services. The whole system must be made as easy as possible for families to use and as open as possible to the efforts of professional and community advocates to improve it.

The system, of course, extends from the federal government through the states to local governments and agencies. It must seek a whole new alignment, from top to bottom. San Diego has charted the path at the local level. Provisions in the new Kentucky legislation for public education create school-site youth centers for the provision of social services are an example of what a state can do. The U.S. Department of Health and Human Services has recently initiated an experimental and demonstration program for linking social services to the schools that may show the way to the sweeping restructuring required at the federal level. A legislative proposal for the same purpose—the Link-up for Learning Demonstration Grant Program—has also been advanced by Senators Kennedy and Bradley in the Senate Committee on Labor and Human Resources.

These are good beginnings.

CHAPTER 13

Technical and Professional Education

Rebuilding the capacity of families to care for their children, setting high standards for educational achievement, restructuring schools so that virtually all students can meet those standards, and requiring employers to invest in the continued education and training of their employees once they are on the job are essential ingredients for a renaissance in human capacity in the United States. But they are not sufficient. In addition, our non-college-bound students must be given the work and technical skills they will need in the years ahead to connect them to the labor market of which they will form what may be the most vital part.

In this country, you are nothing if you have not gone to college. As in much else, our budgetary priorities tell the story. The public spends $19,940 on average on the education of youth between ages sixteen through twenty-four if they go to college, but only $9,130 if they do not.[1] The true measure is not dollars; it is our failure to attend to any of the real needs of non-college-bound students: to help them at an early age to learn enough about what people do for a living to make intelligent career choices, to enable them to develop good work habits, to give them the opportunity to acquire strong technical and professional skills, or to connect them to jobs and people that will get them started on a strong career path when they are leave school. The extent of our failure can best be seen by comparing what we do with the systems common in other countries.

Japanese schools, for instance, are closely linked with employers and typically provide a smooth transition to the workplace for their graduates.[2] Japanese firms look at the schools as they look at any other supplier, cultivating close relations with individual schools and demanding from them the highest quality they can command. The process by which young people enter the work force takes place in stages. First, firms send literature and videotapes about themselves to schools at all levels.[3] Recruiters stay in touch with the teachers at those high schools with which they have established relationships, taking them out to lunch and inquiring about the quality of their students, urging them to encourage their best students to consider employment at their firms.[4] Such schools are known as "contract schools," because of the informal contract between the school and the firm under which the firm agrees to recruit from the school as long as the candidates put forward by the school meet the firm's requirements. The best offers go to the best schools.

In the second stage of the selection process, about eight months before graduation, seniors, advised by their homeroom teachers, choose from among the jobs that have been offered to the school and apply for their school's nomination for those jobs. Finally, a committee of teachers nominates and ranks the candidates for the available jobs.

Candidates are selected based on their academic performance, not on the basis of vocational skills. As we have already explained, Japanese firms, especially the large firms that comprise about one-third of the Japanese economy, provide at their own expense all the vocational skill training these youngsters need after they are hired. The mating game we have just described is the result of Japanese employers' conviction that what is most important to them is the candidates' capacity to continue to learn throughout their working lives.

The Japanese system provides a powerful motivation to all non-college-bound Japanese youth to do well in school, because the judgment of one's teachers is the crucial element in getting the job one wants. For the same reason, it provides teachers with far more authority than teachers of the non-college-bound in the United States have ever dreamed of having. Most important, it provides a dependable, swift, and smooth transition for Japanese youth into real careers in the labor market. Without ever actually having to enter that market, they are, by the age of nineteen, experienced workers with strong academic and technical skills, already well embarked on a real career.

The Swedish system, on the other hand, combines school and work. Work experience begins at age seven, in first grade. Each year, Swedish students spend from one to several weeks in various kinds of workplaces—often including a visit to their parents' place of employment—finding out what people do and how they do it. Representatives of employers also visit the school, describing the industries of which they are a part and the careers that are possible within them.

When Swedish students are sixteen, they choose from among twenty-seven "lines" or courses of study the one they will pursue through upper secondary school. The "lines" are grouped in six divisions, arts and social sciences, the care professions, economics and commerce, technology and science, technology and industry, and agriculture, horticulture, and forestry. All of these programs are three years in length. All include core courses in Swedish, English, and mathematics. The rest is a blend of the theoretical and the practical. For the 75 percent of Swedish students who do not plan to go to college, 10 to 20 percent of their first and second years, and as much as 60 percent of their third year, are spent in the workplace. School vocational counselors, advised by industry committees, are responsible for organizing the "worklife" experiences of these students. Through the three years of upper secondary school, the field of vision of the student narrows from familiarization with the occupational requirements of a broad industry group to the development of strong skills in a particular job classification.

The Swedes have taken great care to design a system which does not commit youth to a narrow specialization for life. One feature of this system, to which we have already alluded, is the exposure of young people to a very broad range of occupations within an equally broad industry group. This is intended to provide students with a broad enough grounding so that they can shift to some other occupation with relative ease whenever they wish, picking up only the specifics of the new occupation for which they wish to train. Another important aspect of the system is its modular approach to the training curriculum. Developed years ago by the Swedish adult training system, this approach uses common curricular building blocks or modules for many occupations. Because people who want at some point to change occupations need not take these modules again if they have once passed them, the process of change is much easier than it would otherwise be. This modular system is now being incorporated into the upper secondary-school system for initial training as well.

One of the most attractive features of the Swedish system is the youth centers. The Swedish system of grade-school education is highly structured and every-where the same. But a significant number of students fail to prosper in this system and drop out. In striking contrast to the United States, Swedish employ-ers do not want employees who have not met the national education standard and will rarely employ them, so these youth find that they are virtually unemploy-able. Despite Sweden's reputation in the United States as the prototypical welfare state, the reality is otherwise. This Calvinist country will go to almost any length to avoid having to put people on welfare. In 1980, The Swedish parliament enacted legislation holding every municipality responsible for locating disadvan-taged and disaffected out-of-school youth between the ages of sixteen and eight-een, recruiting them into the program, and finding education and work oppor-tunities for them. It is a national dropout recovery program, and it is highly successful, putting the vast majority of their dropouts back on track toward productive careers.

The youth centers are staffed by teachers, career counselors, a social worker, and a nurse. Each has access to a full range of health and social services. In contrast to the highly structured regular schools, the youth centers are more flexible and even experimental. Full of opportunities for personal attention, they feel more like family than an institution. Programs for each student are individually tailored, allowing them to mix and match from many options. Among these are on-the-job training, which permits them to earn a small salary trying out a variety of jobs four days a week and attending classes one day; vocational courses in a regular school; a day or more a week of academic courses (assuming that they would like to return to an academic program at some point); a full-time position as an assistant to the regular employees in a firm, with one day a week of academic study; a two-year apprenticeship in an apprenticeable trade; joining a craft workshop; or working in the youth center print shop. And there are other alternatives for students who have special needs. Some of the youth centers are operated by school systems, others are not. The municipalities are free to use a variety of program operators; their only obligation is to find some way of meeting the needs of these youngsters for successful integration into the work force and the society.

One of the most interesting of the European approaches to skill development is being taken by the Danes.[5] When the export market for this tiny country of five million collapsed after the Second World War, the Danes realized that their only hope for preserving their standard of living lay in developing a highly skilled work force and exporting very high-quality goods and services. In recent years, they have engaged in a major revision of their system for developing the skills of the non-college-bound.

As in Germany and Sweden, most Danish youth not going on to university participate in a three-year program of combined work and study after they complete the tenth grade. Periods of work alternate with time spent in study at a technical college. What is particularly interesting about the Danish approach is its conception of appropriate goals and courses of study.

Based on extensive consultation with their employers, the Danes have divided the qualities that they want in their workers into two broad groups: metacognitive qualities and qualifications. Among the metacognitive qualities they seek are learning to learn, knowledge transfer, information processing, management, the capacity for self-motivation, communication, and teamwork. Qualifications are divided into four categories: subject matter, personal, teamwork, and management and organization.

By teamwork, they mean flexibility, negotiation skills, the capacity to be helpful and caring, awareness, doing the right thing at the right time, and the capacity to figure out "what's in it for you." Personal qualifications involve active listening, energy, selling ideas, the ability to concentrate, creativity, quality consciousness, tidiness, willingness to run risks, responsibility, patience, and stamina. Management and organization qualifications include the capacity to pinpoint problems and tasks quickly, formulate strategies, take action, follow through, finish what has been begun, and evaluate the consequences.

The Danes have constructed a set of explicit goals for trainees that incorporate but go beyond the academic and technical skills required for success to include a specified set of work skills essential for participation in high-performance work organizations. In addition, they have devised an ingenious way to develop those skills in their young people.

In describing that approach, we will concentrate on its implementation in a large company. The program begins with three to five days of orientation and introduction, followed by six to twelve months of training in teamwork and the functioning of self-governing groups. Then there is a brief period of individual formal training. The rest of the program, lasting approximately two years, consists of project-based, self-directed learning. Groups of trainees are formed, comprising young people who intend to specialize in very different but complementary areas. They are given large, long-term, complex projects to accomplish that require the skills of everyone in the group. The teams are expected to organize themselves and to reach their goals on their own. Without any formal instruction or supervision, they are provided access to any member of the firm they wish to consult and to the information resources available to the permanent employees, but they must locate these people and information resources on their own.

Through this whole process, each team member must keep a diary recording the problems encountered, the approaches taken to address them, and the progress made in acquiring the skills needed to meet the standards set by the employers. Each trainee meets regularly with his or her teachers, and uses the diary as a basis for discussion with the teacher to evaluate progress. The students are expected to manage their own learning process and constantly to assess their learning. The teachers act like mentors and coaches, but they do not engage in direct instruction. The learning process in this scheme has become a paradigm of the work environment—and learning process—in a high-performance work organization.

Furthermore, as the Danish youth progress through the system we have just described, they can take, at their option, a set of courses, which, if passed, qualify them for admission to a university. In this way, the Danes made explicit provisions for a no-dead-end system, one in which people can always advance through their own efforts to a higher level of the education system and to the opportunities that more education affords.

In comparison with the school-to-work-transition programs of other countries, the American picture is bleak.[6]

Some 25 percent of our high-school students drop out of school before they finish. We do not know exactly how many because there is no uniform definition of a high-school dropout. About half of those who drop out eventually get a G.E.D. certificate, which certifies to their having an education at a level slightly above the seventh grade[7] on average—not much above the primary-school standard of many less developed countries. The United States has no dropout recovery system at all.

As for those who complete school, about half of our high-school students are in the general track, enrolled neither in the academic track for the college-bound nor in the vocational track. These students leave school with little more than the seventh-grade education that the G.E.D. holders have and no more than one vocational course related to any work that they will do. In short, they leave school with no worthwhile skills.

There is no school-to-work transition program for these students, the vast majority of whom will constitute our front-line work force. Census records show that they will get an unskilled, low-pay job for a while, leave it, go on unemployment, get another job like the first one, and continue in this way, alternating between dead-end jobs and unemployment until they are in their midtwenties, when they will finally get their first "real" job. Along the way, they may take a course or two in a community college, but, as we show later in this chapter, the chance that they will actually get a degree qualifying them for a decent career is very slim. Most of the jobs they get in their early twenties are in places in which their colleagues are young people just like themselves. Their supervisors are likely to be no more skilled than they are. They learn, as a consequence, almost nothing in the way of technical skills or work habits that they did not know when they graduated from high school. Their view of work is dismal indeed. There is a very great gulf—a chasm, in fact—between the qualifications of our youth at twenty-five and those of the young people in all the countries we have just described. The question is what to do about it.

Looked at from one vantage point, the German and Japanese systems represent polar opposites on the continuum of possible school-to-work transition systems for the United States. The foundation of the German system is the strong identification of the German worker with a trade or occupation through which one progresses over time from apprentice through journeyman to master. This is the pride, yet also the Achilles heel of the system. The drive to master one's trade produces exceptionally well-qualified workers, but they are also highly specialized and cannot easily move to some other occupation or to a redefinition of their own occupation when changing technology or consumer tastes require it. The system is a formula both for high quality and social and economic rigidity.

The whole drift of the German system of vocational education is to produce people with very high technical qualifications for their life's work. The Japanese, on the other hand, are mainly interested in producing highly educated people who can learn anything quickly and well, taking on an endless succession of changing jobs over a lifetime of work. In the Japanese system, the schools are responsible for producing graduates with a high level of "general intelligence." The employers take it from there, providing their new workers with whatever technical and work skills they will need. The Japanese system would appear to be much better adapted to a world in which job requirements will change rapidly with increasingly frequent introductions of new technologies and shifts in consumer taste. But the real strength of the Japanese vocational system lies in the massive efforts of the large employers to provide first-rate vocational skills to their new employees. These firms, however, employ only about one-third of

Japanese workers, leaving the others to depend on a weak backup system of state-run vocational schools. The other weakness of the Japanese system, from an American point of view, is the lack of any formal national system for recognizing vocational qualifications. In a country like Japan, where employees of large firms are expected to stay with their first employer for most of their working lives, this is no handicap. But in a highly mobile country like the United States, a system of nationally recognized vocational qualifications is essential if individuals are to invest in themselves and have the opportunity to realize that investment when they move.

Within Europe, the Swedes and the Germans would appear to be at opposite ends of another continuum. While the German system is heavily employer-based, the Swedish is heavily school-based, with the Danes in the middle. The great advantage of an employer-based system is that the trainees have direct access to the latest ideas, technology, and methods; learn from masters of their trades who can be expected to be up-to-date; and can immediately apply in real settings the book and laboratory knowledge they are acquiring. But the price of an employer-based system is that employers can be expected to train narrowly rather than educate broadly. A school-based system of vocational education, on the other hand, expands rather than narrows options for individuals, and provides a more flexible work force for national economies.

In practice, the European systems are moving toward one another rapidly. The Swedes are adding a year to their system to provide for more workplace experience and the Germans recently added a year to provide a "foundation year" of broad career exploration and exposure. Each system recognizes its shortcomings and is moving to overcome them by adding time for the missing element.[8] Nevertheless, the distinctive biases of these national systems remain and provide food for thought for those who would design a new system for the United States.

It is not clear, however, how thoughtful Americans will be as they belatedly attempt to learn from the experience of other countries. There appears to be something of a rush to judgment going on, a drive among many—particularly state government leaders—to emulate the German system without giving much thought to the attractive features of other systems. It is not at all clear that we would serve this country well by replicating a system of narrow lifelong specialization in trades and occupations. The Germans are themselves concerned about the rigidity of their system—as we should be. The strong pride in the ancient German system that motivates German employers voluntarily to invest large sums in vocational education is wholly lacking in the American experience.

In describing what other countries do to assure a successful transition from school to work, we do not mean to imply that nothing of value goes on in this country. We know of secondary vocational schools, proprietary schools, and community colleges that prepare their students very well for challenging and rewarding careers, that have strong ties to the employer community, that are very responsive to shifting industry requirements, and have the latest equipment on which their students can train. We know of good grade-school programs that enable students to become acquainted with a wide range of careers, dropout recovery programs that plainly do what they were intended to do, and curricula that are explicitly designed to help students develop many of the qualities that are important to the Danes.

But these are all isolated occurrences, running against the grain of a system that produces, overall, the dismal results we reported earlier. The country does not need more programs and projects. What it so sorely lacks and so desperately needs is a system that embraces the great majority of our students and prepares them to become productive members of what could be—but certainly is not now—the most capable front-line work force in the world.

As we see it, this country must construct a new system that builds on the best practices of the leading industrial nations for developing strong technical and professional skills in high-school students not going directly to a four-year college.

To begin with, a period of weeks must be set aside in every year of grade school experience during which students visit work sites and gain an understanding of the range of career opportunities the society affords, as in Sweden.

All students need this, not just those headed directly for the workplace right out of school. The joke about bachelor's degree holders who decide to go to law school because they do not know what else to do is only too true. The great majority of our children learn about what goes on at work from the movies and from television, a highly distorted picture of the occupational options open to them when they finish their schooling. The problem is particularly severe for poor and minority children whose access to people who perform roles in the society is very limited, but it applies in some measure to almost everyone. Watching films and tapes and reading books on careers is no substitute for visiting real workplaces and talking to the people who work in them.

Such a change in policy will be resisted by many American educators who, more than most educators in the rest of the world, reject the idea that schools exist in part to prepare people for work. This view partly accounts for the primacy of college as the only goal worth working for in school. But this has to change. The necessary change will not come about simply as a matter of policy; the teachers themselves will have to be persuaded that work not requiring a college degree can be challenging, rewarding, and the source of real status in our society. The true companion to respect for ordinary work in school is the implementation of high performance work organizations outside the school.

In addition a system of youth centers must be created, modeled on the Swedish system, through which municipalities are made responsible for dropout recovery.

This was the second recommendation of the Commission on the Skills of the American Workforce. No nation in which one-quarter of the students fail to complete secondary education can hope to have a world-class work force. We pointed out earlier that South Korea's dropout rate is 10 percent. Sweden's rate, due to its youth center program, is even less than that if youth who complete the program are counted as school completers. Every state should require its municipalities to create youth center programs on the Swedish model, with the aim of bringing all dropouts they recruit up to the standard set by the Certificate of Initial Mastery and to connect all of those students to the labor force. These youth centers, in addition to operating alternative education and work experience programs, should ally themselves closely with the health and social-services programs available to them. Whenever a student drops out of school, the school district should be required to notify the nearest youth center, which should then actively recruit that student into its program.

Many existing programs already have the capacity to perform some or all of the functions that we would assign to the youth centers—ranging from the Job Corps to other programs operated under the aegis of the Joint Training Partnership Act legislation and still others operated by churches and community-based organizations. We would have the youth centers contract with such organizations and with school districts prepared to meet their requirements in order to get the job done. The point is not to create new institutions and agencies to replace the old, but rather to make sure that some designated agency sees it as its sole responsibility to recover every dropout in the municipality.

Funding is one of the key issues that will face the states as they design statewide youth center programs. In our view, every local, state, and federal dollar to which the student is entitled while enrolled in a regular high school should follow the dropout to the youth center. While this will not be an easy requirement to meet for states and localities experiencing hard fiscal times, we owe no less to these youngsters. There is overwhelming evidence that the nation would save far more from reduced costs of welfare and prison cells than such a policy would cost. It is simply a matter of which line in the local, state or federal budget gets reduced and which goes up. The net savings are indisputable.

It is also necessary to set a very high general academic standard that all are expected to meet before they begin vocational education, as the aim is to give students the skills they will need to continue to learn all their lives, as in Japan.

We addressed this point earlier when we repeated the call of the Commission on the Skills of the American Workforce for Certificates of Initial Mastery, set at a world-class standard, to be awarded to most students around the age of sixteen, when they successfully complete an appropriate examination. By setting a single standard for everyone, we break ranks with the Europeans, who use their exams to sort students out, dividing those who will go to college from those who will not. Students who get their certificate will be able to choose whether they begin a Technical and Professional Certificate Program, enroll in a college preparatory program, or go directly into the work force. This is not a tracking program. To the contrary, it will spell the end of the American tracking system. It is the beginning of real opportunity for everyone.

Furthermore, we must provide access for all students who want it to a high-quality, structured, on-the-job learning experience leading to a universally recognized qualification, as in Germany.

The third recommendation of the Commission on the Skills of the American Workforce was to create a system of Technical and Professional Certificates covering most of the trades and occupations not requiring a four-year college degree. The certificates would be awarded when students who had their Certificates of Initial Mastery complete a three-year program of combined schooling and structured on-the-job training, and successfully pass a written and practical examination drawn to criteria set by industry groups. Programs could be offered by many different kinds of institutions—high schools, area vocational schools, employers, community colleges, and proprietary schools among them—working singly or in combination, but always teamed up with employers prepared to offer the job-site component of the program. These institutions would compete with one another for the tuition the students bring with them.

Student participation in the Technical and Professional Certificate Program would be paid for in two ways. First, students who had just received their Certificate of Initial Mastery would receive an entitlement from combined state and federal funds of the equivalent of four years of continued full-time education and training. This entitlement could be used for any combination of four-year college study or participation in programs leading to a Technical and Professional Certificate. Much of the money required to meet this commitment would come from a repackaging of the money now being spent by government on the last two years of secondary school and the first two years of college. The other source of funds would be the money spent by employers on their employees as a result of the requirement that they spend an amount equal to at least 1 percent of salaries and wages on the continued education and training of their employees.

Several key policy issues must be addressed as the nation designs the system. To what extent should the Technical and Professional Certificate Program be school-based and to what extent employer-based? What balance should be struck between specialization and breadth of training? To what extent should each industry define its own standards and requirements and to what extent should there be one integrated system? How should the balance be determined between state-devised and administered systems and the prerogative of national policy? And, finally, should industry standards be based on current industry practice and needs, or instead on the needs defined by high-performance work organizations in each industry?

In our view, this country cannot afford to have a system in which each state and each industry goes its own way. Each state and industry should have a strong voice in constructing the system and an equally strong role in administering it, but it must be a national system, with national standards, nationally recognized certificates, and a system of occupational classifications for which one can train that do not vary by jurisdiction. Anything less will lead to a system that will reduce the mobility of our work force or reduce the incentive individuals have to train or both. The country will almost surely begin to create this system industry by industry and state by state, but the aim from the start must be to make it truly national.

We must devise a structure for the school-based portion of the vocational education system that is based, as in Sweden, on a modular curriculum and broad occupational categories, rather than on narrow specialization. Schooling must educate as well as train, and provide the broadest possible foundation for worker mobility and choice.

We have a strong bias toward development of a system that educates and trains as broadly as possible. The rigidities of the German system strike us as a serious problem that this country would do well to avoid. Much of the success of the Japanese economy, we believe, is attributable to the flexible system of imparting a changing array of skills to Japanese workers, who are constantly expected to take on new jobs in a variety of occupations over their working careers. That is the ideal. As we pointed out earlier, we do not have the kind of lifetime employment system that Japan uses to realize that ideal, but we may be able to approximate the results the Japanese achieve by borrowing the modular curriculum structure and the broad training classifications of the Swedes. This will require an enormous effort to determine the common requirements of many industries across many occupations in a country far larger than Sweden. But we believe that it can be done and that it will be worth the effort.

We must create a Danish-style curriculum for the work-based portion of the program that is designed to develop the qualities needed for the high-performance work organizations of the future.

The United States faces something of a dilemma. Many people feel, as we do, the urgent necessity of developing a system of technical and professional standards as rapidly as possible, and share with us the view that these standards should be largely, though not exclusively, set by employers. But most employers, as we have shown, are using methods of work organization that are outdated and must be changed. If most employers were to set the standards today, they would be the wrong standards, designed around jobs that ask little of the people who have them. Were this country to encase the current job descriptions in the concrete of a new system of technical and professional standards, it might be even more difficult to make work organization in the United States competitive with the rest of the world. That would be a sad outcome.

The Danes may have provided a good way out of this dilemma. Perhaps the United States should rely mainly on those employers in each industry who are using advanced forms of work organization to formulate the new standards and then devise a curriculum, much like that of the Danes, explicitly designed to prepare our youth to function in the new work organizations. No doubt that will mean that many youth will be employed initially by organizations that are not prepared to give them all the responsibility they have been trained to exercise or take advantage of all the skills they bring to the job. But these new employees can, on the one hand, be powerful agents of change themselves, and, on the other, make it easier for employers who are determined to change to achieve their objectives.

We must develop a no-dead-end system, based on the Danish approach, that provides explicit pathways from any point in the system to four-year college degree programs and university for everyone who wishes to take advantage of them.

The pride of the current American system of education is that it always leaves the college option open. The nation should not and need not give that up. Once again, the Danes show us how to do that in the context of the new system we advocate.

The American system for school-to-work transition is almost universally considered to be in trouble. But the United States is generally considered to be home to one of the best higher-education systems in the world, a system that is often contrasted with our elementary and secondary system which is widely acknowledged to be one of the worst among the industrialized countries. But, as is so often the case, this general assumption is actually false.[9] In fact, higher education itself, in our view, operates one of the largest and worst-performing pieces of the elementary and secondary system. Its admissions policies are responsible in no small measure for the problem in the schools. Moreover, though higher education is in a better position to provide active assistance to the schools than most of society's basic institutions, it has thus far failed to do so.

As Albert Shanker has pointed out, more than half of those going on to college here would not have qualified for admission to any college in Europe or Japan. A recent study showed that half to two-thirds of the math classes taught in our colleges are teaching high-school, not college math. The conclusion is inescapable: More than half of our "colleges" are not colleges at all, as the rest of the world defines it. They are secondary schools, the highest-cost secondary schools in the world.

Furthermore, about half of the high-school graduates who go on to college go to community colleges. To our knowledge, there are no national data on the proportion of those who seek degrees who actually get them. But in one state that we know of that has the courage to collect and report such data, about 75 percent of those who enroll in community colleges with the aim of getting an associate's degree fail to do so within six years. In the same state, two-thirds of those who enroll in four-year institutions seeking a baccalaureate degree fail to get one within six years. That is a dropout record far worse than that of our high schools. So the postsecondary sector of our secondary education system turns out to be among the least efficient secondary education systems in the world!

Last year, moreover, the National Center on Education and the Economy conducted a year-long study of the goals of the Rochester, New York, community for high school graduates—what they should know and be able to do. As a part of that study, the center asked college professors and admissions officers to talk about what their admissions standards are. Most of those who participated in the focus groups said that they have no requirements, only preferences. They said that if they were to limit enrollments only to those graduates who, in their judgment, could do college-level work, they would have to lay off professors and close down buildings and programs, and they had no intention of doing that. So they would take the best they could get, up to the limit of their capacity. Because capacity was set in the boom years of the 1970s, and the supply of eighteen-year-old youngsters has declined sharply since then, that means taking people whom they would have rejected earlier. All over the country, colleges of various descriptions are applying for authority to waive the requirement that they limit admissions to applicants who have a high-school diploma. So even the facade of "college" is disappearing.

In the years following the Second World War, officials in both Europe and the United States decided to expand greatly enrollments in higher education. It would be an oversimplification to say that America did this by lowering the standards for college and Europe decided to do it by increasing the number of high-school graduates who could qualify for college without changing the standard, but it would not do much violence to the truth.

One result of the approach the United States took is that high-school students learned that, unless one wants to go to a selective college, all a graduating senior needs to get into college is a high-school diploma. For a long time, all one needed to get a diploma was to show up most of the time and not cause too much trouble. Now, in many states, one also needs to demonstrate mastery of seventh- or eighth-grade skills in reading, writing, and mathematics.

When the National Governors' Association was putting the national educational goals together, one of the areas it addressed was goals and measures for higher education. The message NGA officials got back from higher education was that higher education would have no problems at all if the secondary schools did a better job of sending more qualified applicants. But why should students work hard at algebra in school if they can get into college by sliding by with a passing grade in general math? The colleges have no one but themselves to blame for the quality of their freshman classes.

Many people in higher education will point out that the situation we portray is not the result of the need to protect jobs and fill seats in otherwise empty institutions, but is instead the only reasonable response of people who really care about the plight of the largely poor and minority students who have been failed by the schools and who would otherwise be consigned to the scrap heap of an uncaring society. Many dedicated people in our colleges have for years devoted themselves to the needs of such youngsters and offer them the last chance they are likely to get to succeed against the odds.

A strong case can be made that the current situation is the result of both the best and worst motivating impulses. But the fact remains that the vast majority of poor and minority youth who enroll in college with the intention of getting a degree fail to do so. A large fraction of those who fail to get a degree wind up nevertheless with a debt burden around their necks that takes years to pay off, if it is paid off. What kind of favor do we do these young people by failing to tell them what they have to learn in high school to succeed in college, and then failing to give them the help they need in college to succeed once there?

One of the central themes in this book is the fact that the United States runs one of the most pernicious tracking systems in the world. Because most poor and minority students have been assigned to groups thought to have little ability, they are rarely given challenging material. Just as bad, they are given good grades for mediocre work ("Poor things, they can't do much; the least we can do is keep their self-esteem up by giving them good grades," is the thinking). By the end of elementary school the game is often over. Another version of the same reasoning applies at the transition from school to college. But there is, of course, a reckoning in the end, when these students, who have known all along that no one thought they were really capable of good work, fail in college and face a life of diminished expectations.

Why not set a clear standard for college entrance that represents the level of achievement in high school that is required to succeed at work that is college level by international standards? Why not take the money we now spend on the high-cost, low-efficiency segment of our postsecondary high-school system and use it in the schools to do the job right the first time? Why not ask the colleges to join the rest of the country in helping the schools to educate everyone—especially our poor and minority students—to a real college entrance standard?

In another context, we earlier described the ambitious program that Wegman's Food markets devised to help potential dropouts reverse course and succeed in school. The Eastman Kodak Company, also based in Rochester, recently announced a program that will eventually involve two thousand Kodak engineers, scientists, and other technical personnel in a program to upgrade the science and mathematics curriculum in the inner-city schools and work in the schools, assisting the regular staff in teaching that curriculum.

Colleges are typically among the biggest employers in their communities. Is there a reason why they cannot do as much as a grocery store and a film company for these students? Few colleges that we know of are doing anything to head off the problem in the schools on the scale just described, before remediation in college becomes necessary.

Remediation is a poor substitute for prevention. Nonexistent standards are a part of the problem, not the solution. Colleges that take whomever they can get in order to sop up unused capacity are in no position to complain about the schools. If some part of the current capacity of higher education would be shut down if we instituted appropriate standards, then so be it, if the funds that were released could be made available to the schools to do the job right the first time. If the colleges want to keep that money to do what they should have been doing all along to help the beleaguered schools, then legislatures should be ready to listen. It is time to be honest about these issues and to do something about them.

CHAPTER 14

A Labor-Market System for America

We have made the point more than once that the problem in the United States is not that nothing works—that, in fact, there are many examples of projects, programs, schools, training efforts, and the like that are among the most imaginative and effective in the world—but rather that what we lack are entire systems that work. In much of the rest of the developed world, the phrase "labor-market system" has as much currency as "school system." The two are designed to complement one another. In this country, however, the phrase "labor-market system" is virtually unknown, because we have no such system. In this chapter, we show why one is needed, and what could be accomplished if an effective labor-market system is built. In doing so, we will pull together many separate proposals made in earlier chapters to describe a way to organize and manage their implementation at every level of government as a single unified system.

A labor-market system is basically a collection of policies and institutions that bring workers and employers together and establish the rules for employment. The labor market of primary interest to us is for what we have called "front-line" labor, or all except managerial and professional jobs. In economic theory, for any market to function effectively, buyers must have good information about what is available from suppliers, sellers must have good information about what buyers are prepared to purchase, and there must be enough competition among buyers and sellers to prevent either from controlling the market. The same holds true for markets in labor. Employers need to know what the qualifications of the whole potential pool of applicants are, as well as the qualifications of individual applicants, and those seeking jobs must know what jobs are available at what rates of pay and with what advancement opportunities. Because job-related training is the key to improvement of qualifications and to the certification of skills, keen competition among the suppliers of training and accurate information about the qualifications of trainers is important to potential trainees, and accurate information about the skills of graduates is important to potential employers. These basic characteristics of a properly functioning labor market are largely missing in the United States.

But there is more to effective labor markets than that, first with respect to the relationship between labor-market policy and macroeconomic policy, and second with respect to the institutional structure required for labor markets to function effectively. For example, basic economics tells us that neither firms nor individuals will invest what they should in employee training to get the maximum return on the training dollar. For the individual, this is because the return seems very chancy and, in any event, the cash may not be available even if the eventual return is clear. For the firm, it is because other firms can hire the people that are trained, taking advantage of the investment without incurring the expense of the training. The whole society therefore underinvests in training. The only solution is for the society as whole to subsidize the investment that firms and individuals would make if left to their own devices.

Perhaps the best way to make the point about labor-market policy is to describe its development in Europe since the 1950s.[1] During the decade of the 1960s, the Europeans set themselves a target of 50 percent growth in their economy. The object of labor-market policy in this period was to facilitate manpower adjustment, through training and retraining, and to tap new sources of labor supply. But the latter half of the decade was accompanied by slowly rising inflation, the control of which was to become more important to policymakers than economic growth and the reduction of unemployment.

This change of goals placed European policymakers in the grip of a very old dilemma: how to reduce inflation without creating widespread unemployment. The classic approach to wringing inflation out of an economy is to reduce demand by increasing interest rates and decreasing government spending. When governments do that, employers, finding it hard to borrow and facing decreased demand for their goods and services, lay people off. Wages go down because employers can select qualified people who are unemployed—or fearful of being unemployed—and willing to work for less than in good times. Prices go down because the population as a whole has less to spend and is less willing to spend what it has. Because mainstream economists who base their policies on the work of John Maynard Keynes favor measures that inevitably induce inflation, modern economies typically swing through endless cycles of inflation and deliberately induced recessions that are intended to stop the inflationary spiral. For most economists, this is a zero-sum game. Reduced inflation requires increased unemployment; full employment means rising rates of inflation.

In the 1960s, two approaches had long been in use to mitigate the worst effects of this dilemma. On the one hand, various methods of controlling prices and wages were used, ranging from direct government controls to government-induced consensus between labor and management on wages and prices. On the other hand, various means had been employed to help the unemployed in periods when the government had been controlling inflation by slowing down the economy, ranging from subsidies to firms that employed people they would not otherwise have employed to the creation of public-sector jobs as a bridge to jobs that would open up in the private sector when the economy got rolling again.

But these approaches had very disappointing results. Direct government controls could only be imposed in these democracies in times of crisis. When the crisis had passed, they could no longer be maintained, and the pent-up demands for higher wages typically unleashed yet another spiral of inflation. Getting an informal consensus among the principal parties worked a little better, but it turned out that what seemed fair to one party inevitably seemed very unfair to another, so the consensus would unravel sooner or later. Similarly, subsidies to employers to hire people they would not otherwise have employed simply led them to not hire other people they would have employed, so the unemployment problem was just shifted from one group to another. When the economy did not pick up right away after the beginning of a government-induced recession, the new public employees, laid off because their "bridge" employment had run out, were left high and dry. Orthodox economists were confirmed in their view that the inflation-unemployment dilemma was as eternal as economic cycles themselves, that the only solution to unemployment was a strong economy, and the only solution for a superheated economy was to turn off the supply of money.

But policy analysts at the Organization for Economic Cooperation and Development noted that since World War II, the Swedes had evolved an approach that enabled them to keep inflation low while at the same time keeping employment up. The key was what the Swedes called "active labor-market policy."[2]

The Swedes were among those who had been using a national system of price and wage controls. But wages proved very hard to control at the level of local enterprises, and national firms that were expanding rapidly were given exemptions from the national wage controls in order to enable them to attract workers. These exceptions to the general rule fueled resentment among workers who were subject to the controls, and that resentment erupted into rejection of the system, fueling a wage explosion in 1951. Gösta Rehn and Rudolph Meidner, two Swedish Federation of Labor economists, framed a plan that built on the famous 1944 Myrdal Report which established full employment (defined as 2 percent unemployment) as national policy. Rehn and Meidner were looking for alternatives to the orthodox policies that fight inflation with unemployment.[3] Sweden is typically thought of as a welfare state, but it is not a socialist economy. The Swedes believe in work and they believe that the market operates best with private investment, not public ownership of enterprise. Acting on this set of preferences, Rehn and Meidner advocated a package of measures that would combine a balanced macroeconomic policy with an "active" labor-market policy. The

Swedes complemented other economic policies with active labor-market measures as early as the 1950s, but beginning in the late 1960s, expenditures on these policies mushroomed, reaching 3 percent of GNP and 7 percent of government expenditures by 1983–1984. Beginning in 1973, the number of people in labor-market programs exceeded the number of people officially unemployed.[4]

By active labor-market policy, the Swedes mean a policy in which passive measures like unemployment compensation are viewed as a last resort, used only when active measures, including job placement and training, are inappropriate. Whereas most European countries spend about one-third of their labor-market budgets on active measures and two-thirds on passive measures, Sweden does the reverse, spending two-thirds on active measures and only one-third on unemployment compensation.

So how does active labor-market policy relate to inflation and unemployment? Wages are driven up in particular occupations when there is a shortage of qualified people in that occupation. If additional people can be trained for occupations in high demand, wages and wage-induced inflation will come back into line as the shortage eases. In a healthy economy, people are unemployed mainly because they are not qualified for the jobs that are available. If there is a shortage of people for jobs in demand, and a surplus of people qualified only for declining occupations, then it is possible to have high unemployment at the same time that the economy is inflating, because wages are being driven up in occupations experiencing shortages of qualified people. That is exactly the situation in many parts of the United States right now. Ideally, what one would do in a situation like this is to train the unemployed to qualify them for the jobs in high demand, and pay to relocate people with the requisite skills to regions where those skills are needed, thus lowering both unemployment and inflation at the same time. That is exactly what the Swedes did.

The Swedes understand that it is more effective to reduce inflationary pressures by increasing supply than by trying to control prices that result from shortages. They also understand that it is enormously wasteful, if not inhumane, intentionally to create unemployment to reduce inflationary pressures. They understand, further, that labor-market flexibility is important but will not be achieved very effectively by merely allowing demand, supply, and wages to allocate labor among various uses. Well-trained, highly motivated workers are likely to be the most flexible component of any system. Effective labor markets therefore require policies, institutions, and rules, not just the forces of demand, supply, and prices.

At the center of the Swedish system is the Labor Market Administration, which includes the National Labor Market Board (known as the AMS) and local labor-market boards at the county level of government. The National Labor Market Board administers the local boards and the national employment service. Similarly, the county boards administer the local employment offices and the employability assessment centers.

The employment offices handle all job placement tasks in Sweden. By law, almost all available jobs in both the public and private sectors must be registered with the employment service; private employment services are forbidden. Companies need not hire from the employment service and can recruit wherever they like, but in practice, the majority of jobs are filled through employment service placements because the service meets the needs of both employers and applicants. The requirement that virtually all jobs be listed with the service is a crucial element of the whole system, because without that feature, the service would have access only to the bad jobs and no one would use the service who had other choices. If that happened, employers with good jobs would not consider applicants from the service and the whole labor-exchange function would wither on the vine, which, as we will see, is exactly what has happened to the employment service in the United States.

Representatives of both employers and labor sit on the labor-market boards at all levels, making policy and seeing to the smooth administration of the system. It is not hard to get highly qualified people to serve on the boards, because the system is vital to the agendas of both business and the unions.

The range of measures available to the employment offices is very large. The first is job matching. The Swedish system is completely computerized. A new job opening in any part of the country will appear on the terminals in every employment office in Sweden the next day. The system has all the relevant information about all the jobs and everyone who is seeking a job. But job matching requires more than efficient exchange of information. The employment offices are staffed by trained counselors who can provide information about careers and training opportunities, conduct aptitude tests, and guide job seekers through the process of thinking about career opportunities and choosing among the various options available.

If a job for which an unemployed job seeker is qualified is not available in the area, the employment office will pay the costs for the job seeker to go to interviews elsewhere in the country and will subsidize moving expenses if a job is offered. If there is nothing available, the labor-market board will pay all the costs of training for the jobs that are available, including a living subsidy in the form of training grants for the worker's family while he or she is being trained, and all the costs of living away from home for the trainee, if the nearest training center is located beyond commuting distance. The training grants range from 240 to 400 Swedish krona per day for adults (the average Swedish daily wage in that year was about 460 krona). Teenagers received about 170 krona. In the fiscal year 1986–87, about 34,000 adult Swedes were in the training system. If the same proportion of unemployed Americans were receiving training on a full-time basis, the equivalent figure would be about 700,000. These figures, of course, do not include the youngsters involved in the Swedish upper secondary vocational system, the equivalent of our vocational schools and community colleges.

The training system in Sweden is highly developed. A Labor Market Training

Group (AMU), consisting of a central board and twenty-five regional commissions, supplies most of the training to the Labor Market Board under contract, though the board also contracts with upper secondary schools and other suppliers. The AMU, which used to be part of the government, was established as an independent for-profit training and education agency in 1986.

Most of the AMU courses are vocationally oriented, but academic courses are also taught to those who need the foundation they provide for the vocational series. As we explained earlier, the whole system is set up on a modular basis, with many modules in common across different lines of study. For example, four courses in basic electricity are prerequisites for the courses of study for electricians, beginning control engineering, household appliance repair, telecom repair, and air conditioning and refrigeration. The courses in beginning control engineering are required for the course work leading to certification for elevator technicians and automation, and the courses in automation are required prerequisites for the programs in robotics, numerically controlled machine techniques, and advanced control engineering.

These are substantial programs. The course in automation, for example, lasts twenty-three weeks, and the basic course in control engineering lasts thirty-four weeks. The whole sequence required to become a robotics technician takes a total of seventy-seven weeks of study, and for those who lack the necessary fundamental academic skills, it will take longer. The equipment available in the regional training centers is state-of-the-art. Because of the high quality of training offered, many firms contract with the AMU to deliver courses for their in-house training programs.

Most of those who enroll in these labor-market training programs complete them, and about 60 to 70 percent of those who do so find jobs within six months. For those who have various forms of handicapping conditions, the centers offer vocational rehabilitation and intensive counseling. The success rate for these people is similarly high.

The Swedish labor-market system is not limited to job matching and measures intended to increase the supply of trained workers. It also uses strategies designed to increase the demand for labor. Relief work is used to create temporary jobs intended to tide workers over when the economy is slack. Public construction and civil engineering projects, for example, have been used for this purpose for years. More recently, even in good times, the country has created public jobs for youth teams to provide work experience, or to give more time to make a career decision than they would otherwise have. These measures also contribute, of course, to the very low youth unemployment rate in Sweden—a small fraction of ours. Since 1983, Swedish workers on unemployment with less than fifty days to go before their benefit expires are automatically entitled to relief work, which carries the same rate of pay as similar work on the open market. People who have medical disabilities are entitled to permanent public employment.

Sweden also pays recruitment subsidies to private employers to increase the demand for labor. Six-month subsidies are available to employ youth, the hardcore unemployed, and people whose unemployment benefit is about to expire. Three-month subsidies are provided for the occupationally handicapped. Longer subsidies are available to employers who take on the severely handicapped, with additional subsidies available to employers to purchase special equipment for these workers. Young people are likewise given employment subsidies for work in the public sector, and the jobless are provided with grants to start their own businesses.

Beyond these measures, the Swedish government also provides grants to private industry in support of in-house training to cover four situations: shortage of skilled personnel, structural change in which many workers would have to be let go if they were not trained in a new technology, other situations in which layoffs are imminent, and training to achieve gender balance in the workplace.

Only when all these measures are exhausted does the Swedish system grant unemployment compensation to an individual. Thus, as we pointed out earlier, the system minimizes the drag on the economy and the personal anguish caused by high unemployment while keeping inflation down. It also operates to equalize the distribution of income by increasing the supply of qualified people in occupations experiencing labor shortages—thereby holding the lid on wage increases in those categories—and raising the income for people in categories in oversupply by taking the surplus labor in those categories and training those people for higher-paying occupations.

In the 1960s, the Organization for Economic Cooperation and Development, recognizing the advantages of the Swedish system, recommended that the other OECD countries adopt an active labor-market policy. Most did so, though usually in modified form. Germany, for example, developed a system financed by a 5 percent tax on employers and on the salaries and wages of employees, which is used to fund an unemployment compensation system that is fully integrated with its job matching and training systems. Like the Swedes, the Germans maintain employment service centers in neighborhoods all over the country that serve as the universal intake point for the unemployed and for people seeking training for different jobs. As in Sweden, the Germans are entitled to free training, family-support subsidies while they are being trained, additional support if their training is located beyond commuting distance from their home, and more. In the German system, if employed people want training for another occupation, the amount of support they get depends on whether they want to move from an occupation in high demand to an occupation in low demand, or the reverse.

So let us return now to the conditions required for efficiency in labor markets that we laid out when we began this chapter. The active labor-market policies and programs we have described provide for good information, universally and quickly accessible, as to the jobs available and the people who are available to fill them. Equally good information is provided about the training programs that exist to qualify people for those jobs, training that is available at little or no cost. The cost of being trained is further reduced by the provision of wage subsidies for the families whose wage earners are in full-time training. More efficiency is gained by relocating people who need jobs to the places where those jobs are available, at no cost to the applicant. Even more efficiency is gained by providing jobs and job experience to people in transition, so that they will not become discouraged and they can gain further skills while waiting for regular employment. Finally, the development of a free system of training for the unemployed and a subsidized one for the employed raises the level of training to the point at which the society as a whole is investing what it should in its people. These investments will raise the whole standard of living for everyone, which would not happen if training investment decisions were left entirely to firms and individuals.

The United States, by contrast, in spite of many fragmentary efforts over the years, still does not possess an integrated labor-market system.

The United States has a job-matching agency—the Public Employment Service—created by the Wagner-Peyser Act in 1933, with many amendments since. In its current form, however, the Employment Service is a pale shadow of its European counterpart. Largely left to the states to administer, it caters mainly to the hard-core unemployed, who must be registered in order to receive benefits. Because of this, and because with very few exceptions, there is no requirement to list jobs with the service, employers rarely recruit from the people on the list, feeling, with much justice, that they cannot find skilled or even semiskilled workers by doing so. Because good jobs are not listed, few people with skills register. Starved of resources, the Employment Service is not computerized in many of its offices, does not have adequate personnel to do a serious job of counseling, and lacks most of the features, such as steady access to public-service employment openings and funds for relocation and wage subsidies, that enable European employment offices to succeed in their mission. It is little wonder that the Employment Service has a dismal reputation, and that few with any choice use it. Because they do not use it, neither the public nor employers are willing to invest in it. Because no one will invest in it, it cannot improve its services. The vicious cycle goes on, unchanging, from year to year.

It cannot be said that the government has avoided investing in adult training. The trail of training legislation is very long, though very rambling. At the head of the trail is the National Apprenticeship Act, passed in 1937. Unlike in Europe, however, apprenticeship in the United States is not a part of our system of school-to-work transition. Most people who enter the apprenticeship system do so in their late twenties. In stark contrast to the situation in Europe, few occupations outside the construction, printing, and machinist trades are apprenticeable at all, and one need not have been an apprentice to get a job in those trades and occupations that are apprenticeable. On the whole, the quality of apprenticeships here is very high, but since only a tiny fraction of the front-line workers in the

United States have gone through a registered apprenticeship program, and there are no incentives to expand the numbers, apprenticeship has never played a part in the development of the skills of American workers comparable to the role it has played in Europe.

Apart from apprenticeship, the history of national adult training policy begins with the Manpower Development and Training Act of 1962. At the time, the country was worried that advancing automation would quickly displace large numbers of workers and was seeking some way to train them for the new jobs that would become available. When the automation scare died down, the program was changed to focus, like so many to follow, on helping the disadvantaged. Two years later, in the midst of Lyndon Johnson's War on Poverty, the Economic Opportunity Act was passed. Among its other provisions, it gave birth to two programs: the Neighborhood Youth Corps, a program to provide work experience for poor youths, and the Job Corps.

The Job Corps may be the single most effective federal program for job training ever created. Its purpose is to take in unskilled recent high-school dropouts and give them the self-confidence and skills they need to succeed in the job market. There are now 106 centers, ranging in size from 100 enrollees to 2,624, and serving a total of about 100,000 young people a year all over the country.[5]

Most are residential, providing an alternative to the values learned on the street, as well as a highly structured environment in which the recruits get counseling, basic skills instruction, vocational education, and the sense of responsibility that goes with functioning effectively in the camp. The centers also provide food, housing, clothing, and medical and dental care. The system is open-entry, open-exit, meaning that corpsmen arrive and begin their studies at any time and graduate whenever they have met the criterion standard. The operators of the centers include government agencies as well as a wide range of profit and not-for-profit organizations. All get their contracts by competing for them, and retain them based on performance. Because performance is the sole criterion for keeping these contracts, the operators have a very strong incentive to innovate—to seek constantly for new and better ways to meet the needs of their clients. They naturally gravitate to the most advanced methods available to manage their operations and to educate and train their charges, as well as meet their social needs.

Seventy percent of the Job Corps graduates were placed in jobs at an average wage of $4.07 in 1983. Evaluations of the program show that graduates have higher employment rates, greater earnings, more education, better health, and less serious involvement with the criminal justice system than the comparison groups studied.[6] The program is expensive—$10,454 per person in 1986—but that cost is greatly outweighed by the tangible economic benefits—about $1.46 for every dollar spent.[7]

But the Job Corps program is a beacon of light in an otherwise dismal landscape. In 1973, the Nixon administration merged most of the Manpower and Development Administration programs into a "special revenue-sharing" program under the Comprehensive Employment and Training Act (CETA), decentralizing and decategorizing employment and training programs right down to the city level. Eventually, in the face of the oil shocks of 1973–74, CETA became largely a public-employment program. Later, in 1978, the act was amended: new local bodies were created, with mandated employer and labor participation, to oversee the local administration of the program, and funding was targeted to focus on the disadvantaged. The Carter administration further amended the legislation in 1977, 1978, and 1979 to increase greatly the sums available for training and for public-service employment. These amendments focused the program even more tightly on the needs of the poor. In 1979, the Work Incentives Tax Credit was passed to aid employers who hired eligible welfare recipients.

By the time Ronald Reagan became president, there was mounting political opposition to the CETA program, despite objective evaluations that found it to be largely successful in helping those it was intended to help. CETA's main problem was that it was a federal program administered by local governments. It was therefore very difficult for the federal government to prevent abuse of the program. Although abuse was found to be greatly exaggerated, there was certainly too much of it, especially in the early years, and adverse publicity undermined political support for the program. Another problem for CETA was that its success, like that of the program that followed, the Job Training Partnership Act (JTPA), was judged by the numbers of trainees placed in jobs, causing the program operators to select only the most qualified of the eligible applicants, and thereby to give the most help to those who needed it the least. Efforts to target CETA on the most disadvantaged stigmatized it as a "welfare" program. Given the mood of the 1980s, moreover, few taxpayers were willing to indulge in what looked like just another form of welfare for poor, mostly minority, city-dwellers.

The Reagan administration therefore replaced CETA with the Job Training Partnership Act. The act was a compromise between Reagan, who wanted to eliminate federal employment and job-training programs altogether, and Congress, which wanted to retain them. It provided for greater control by the governors and the Private Industry Councils. (Private Industry Councils comprise representatives of companies, unions, educators, and public officials.) The act virtually eliminated public-service employment programs, and greatly restricted funds for stipends for trainees and support services. Funds for federal employment and training were cut from $18.1 billion in 1978 to $11.1 billion in 1981 and $5.3 billion in 1986. Except for the elimination of public service employment, however, the program content of JTPA is essentially the same as for CETA.[8]

The JTPA legislation also amended the authority for the Employment Service for the first time since its initial authorization in 1933. The Employment Service planning function was reorganized to coincide with the areas covered by the

Private Industry Councils, clearer guidelines were established for the collection and publication of labor-market statistics, and governors were given more authority over the service within their states.

Three congressional enactments since the birth of JTPA are notable. In 1983 the Emergency Jobs Act provided $4.6 billion for government agencies to create labor-intensive projects giving employment to the long-term unemployed. In 1988, Congress passed the Worker Adjustment and Retraining Notification Act, requiring employers of one hundred or more to give at least sixty days' notice to workers of plant closings and mass layoffs. The same year saw passage of the Economic Dislocation and Worker Assistance Act, to provide assistance to workers who needed to make a transition to another job as result of jobs lost through foreign competition.

Through much of this period, especially since the 1960s, the states had put in place a vast array of small, highly targeted programs for job training and related purposes. In 1989, the Commission on the Skills of the American Workforce found that in state after state, more than eighty such programs were being run by dozens of agencies under the aegis of many different cabinet departments.[9] Many were connected with various kinds of welfare programs. Others were intended to support the economic development activities of the states. Each had its own eligibility requirements and its own application forms and procedures. One registered for these programs in different places. Few if any provided long-term training or comprehensive services, and virtually none provided for income support for trainees. None were connected to a comprehensive employment-matching program, because no such program existed anywhere. No single agency was responsible for keeping track of all these separately enacted and separately run programs, let alone for ensuring that they added up to a coherent whole. No potential client could possibly know what was available or gain access easily to the most appropriate program.

The commission discovered the same kind of disarray and inefficiency in the postsecondary training system, and could find out nothing about the quality of training offered because there are no competency requirements in the postsecondary training system. Because little or nothing is known about the real content of course offerings, completion rates for courses of study, costs of courses of study, or the quality of graduates, the commission concluded that there is no real market in postsecondary education: neither potential students nor buyers of contract services can make informed choices as to the relative costs and benefits of investing in institutions or courses of study. Choices by government are made on political grounds. The choices individuals make are based on general reputation (which rarely applies to the particular program or course of study of interest), incomplete information, and misinformation. The only career counseling available to adults looking for postsecondary training is provided by the postsecondary institutions themselves. Because these institutions have a product—their own—

to sell, and because counseling is not a core function, the service can be expected to be haphazard and often self-serving.

In the European sense of the term, the United States has no labor-market policy and no labor-market system. At a national level, as we have seen, the Employment Service (the heart of the European system) has been allowed to become moribund. Training policy has evolved over the years into myriad programs designed almost exclusively for the poor. Because they are for the poor, their graduates are stigmatized in the labor market and they lack the broad political support they need to get the funding they deserve. There is no training policy at all for the mass of American workers. And there are no serious measures to stimulate the market for labor.

At the state level, there is no system either, only a vast welter of small state programs that do not add up to a system, and a collection of postsecondary institutions that offer whatever they care to against standards that they largely set for themselves.

There is something roughly analogous to the local employment offices and labor-market boards found all over Europe—the Private Industry Councils. Some are active in defining an ambitious local program and include some of the most respected local leaders of business and labor. But too many are composed of relatively junior people who do little more than the law requires, a law which is largely confined to the provision of minimal services to the poor. None have control over the Employment Service. They can rarely command access to any but a small portion of the great range of state and federal training programs from which their clients might benefit. They are not charged with rationalizing the delivery of postsecondary training programs in the areas they serve. Virtually everywhere, they lack the resources and the measures to do anything comparable to what their counterparts abroad do, for their mission has been defined much more narrowly. But they are an important foundation on which to build.

To repeat, none of this is to say that there are no good programs or effective institutions. In fact, many state governments and some postsecondary training institutions, increasingly aware of the achievements of the labor-market systems in Europe, have lately been taking steps to put elements of those systems in place, with interesting results. Some national organizations, in particular the National Governors' Association, the German Marshall Fund, the W. T. Grant Foundation, and the National Center on Education and the Economy, have been cheering them on and providing technical assistance. It is instructive to look at some examples.[10]

In January 1990, New York State created a Human Resource Investment Subcabinet to plan and implement the Gateway Initiative, an integrated human-resource investment system that will put together the efforts of many state agencies to address all clients' education, training, and support service needs. At the local level, each participating agency or affiliate is to act as a customer service center, giving clients information about all the programs, services, and job vacancies throughout the system. The subcabinet is made up of representatives from the Job Training Partnership Council, the New York State Departments of Education, Social Services, Labor, and Economic Development, the State and City Universities of New York, the Divisions for Youth and Human Rights, and the Higher Education Services Council.

In 1988, the Massachusetts Jobs Council (MASSJOBS) was established as the policy-making and coordinating body for all employment and training programs in the Commonwealth. Council members include representatives from economic development, employment training, education, and the private sector, as well as providers and clients. Its work is supported by a network of regional employment boards, which also serve as JTPA Private Industry Councils. A council group also serves as the state JTPA Job Coordinating Council. MASSJOBS has begun to develop consistent strategies for work force development statewide, as well as to set priorities for employment-related education and training.

New Jersey has created a State Employment and Training Commission to help develop and implement a comprehensive employment and training policy for the state. The commission is implementing a plan to restructure and streamline the administration of work force readiness programs and to impose performance measures on state occupational programs. Sixty-four programs run by six state agencies are being consolidated into fifteen program areas operated by three agencies. The state expects this consolidation to save $6 million over eighteen months. The commission is also developing a single state plan for occupational education and a labor-market assessment system. Participants report that agency officials have been sharing information about each other's programs and developing joint strategies for the first time.

Since 1982, the California Employment Training Panel has been supporting customized job training for displaced workers or workers faced with displacement. The panel was established in part to promote economic development and to reduce the long-term costs of unemployment by providing workers with skills they would need to avoid unemployment altogether or reduce its length. Though the panel initially focused on attracting firms from out of state, its managers soon realized that it would serve its goals more effectively by concentrating on firms already located in California. Among its current goals is increasing business and labor investment in training by demonstrating the bottom-line value of such investment. The ETP is supported by a special tax of 0.1 percent on employers with a positive unemployment insurance tax rate. All but a small portion of the funds must be used only to train workers eligible or potentially eligible for unemployment insurance. Applications for funds come from employers, training agencies, and consortia. Projects must result in placement and retention of the worker in a job for at least ninety days at a wage level specified under a performance-based contract. Where workers are unionized, the unions must be a party to the training agreement.

Texas has been working to improve its information system for work force analysis and planning. It has developed an interactive modular software system, the Standardized Occupational Components for Regional Analysis and Trends in Employment System (SOCRATES), to help regional work-force quality planning committees analyze local labor-market dynamics. The system helps planners link employers, jobs, and educational and training resources.

All of these developments, and others like them, are encouraging. But no state has yet developed and implemented a truly comprehensive labor-market policy and system that even approaches the coherence and effectiveness of those common in Europe. What the United States must do is develop and implement a national system of employment and training boards to make and implement comprehensive labor-market policies at the national, state, and local levels. This recommendation is closely modeled on a recommendation of the Commission on the Skills of the American Workforce, but goes beyond it.[11]

We have already discussed many of the components of a successful labor market policy in this and other chapters: (1) a strong foundation of academic skills for everyone; (2) a universal dropout recovery system; (3) a national system of standards for certifying the technical and professional skills of those not going to a four-year college, designed in modular fashion to facilitate maximum work-force mobility; (4) a modern job-matching system, employing the latest in computer-based technology, in which the vast majority of front-line job vacancies are listed; (5) a career counseling system that is independent of the institutions providing education and training; and (6) a broad range of measures for upgrading the skills of the unemployed, including paid job search and relocation, free training, and subsidized employment. We have emphasized the importance of an active labor-market policy, leaving unemployment benefits as the last resort when all other measures are exhausted. We have tried to show that the natural instinct to target government programs on the disadvantaged is a mistake, that the disadvantaged are best served by a far more comprehensive system that does not stigmatize the poor.

And we have tried, as well, to show that disparate programs and projects do not add up to a system, and that patching them up will not achieve the country's goals. The question is how to create a system of policies and a management system to implement those policies that provide national coherence while at the same time devolving as many decisions as possible as close to the client as possible, and distributing decision-making authority among entities ranging from the top levels of the federal government to the local community in such a way that the whole will function effectively and efficiently.

It is that design that we now present here.

National Employment and Training Board

At the national level, what is required is a National Employment and Training Board charged with developing broad labor-market policy; making recommendations to the president, Congress and the country as a whole on national goals for that policy; and guiding the implementation of federal labor-market policy while coordinating it with national economic policies. Among its specific tasks would be (1) advancing the broad economic goals of the nation, in particular, controlling inflation, spreading advanced forms of work organization, facilitating the adjustment of workers from noncompetitive to more competitive sectors, and promoting high wages and full employment; (2) conducting analyses of national labor-market conditions; (3) overseeing the development, continual updating, and administration of a national system of competency standards for technical and professional skills; (4) promoting the development of an integrated modular design for those standards that would facilitate mobility in the national labor market; (5) redesigning the federal job-training system to ensure that it supports the broad economic goals of the nation, is easy to gain access to and efficient in its administration, is client- and outcome-oriented, and fully integrated with the unemployment insurance system and the other principal components of the labor-market system; (6) overseeing the creation of an integrated, computer-based job-matching system; (7) overseeing the creation of a career service that provides a full range of counseling and related support services for the system's clients; and (8) submitting an annual report to the nation on the condition of the labor market and the operation of the system, and making recommendations for improvement.

We do not envision the board as an administrative agency, but rather as a policymaking, coordinating, and review agency, responsible for the shape of the system as a whole. To play that role effectively, it must reflect in its membership those bodies and constituencies whose participation is vital to the successful operation of the whole system. Among those participants should be the Secretaries of Labor, Education, and Commerce, the Director of the Office of Management and Budget, the chairs of the relevant congressional committees, and a representative group of governors, heads of local and state Employment and Training Boards, chief executive officers of private-sector firms, and leaders of education, labor, and advocacy groups.

All this is very different from the way in which the United States usually does business. Various federal agencies contend with one another in the budget-building process, marshaling their constituencies and pushing their cases with Congress and with the cabinet officers, independently of one another and behind closed doors. The administration offers its proposals to a whole clutch of congressional committees, which contend with one another for precedence. The same process takes place in the states with respect to their policies and programs. The result is what we have seen—fragmented policies and programs that fall far short of what the country needs. Our alternative is simple: Get the principal parties in one room together, backed up by strong staff support, and force them to create one coherent plan to which they will all agree, as well as a reporting system to track the results so that periodic course corrections can be made on the basis of hard facts. We would replace policy development by contention in many arenas with policy development by consensus in one arena. Not that we expect conflict to disappear, but we want to create an arena in which it can be resolved rather than simply be papered over.

State Employment and Training Boards

Similarly, we believe that the states should establish statewide employment and training boards to develop their own labor-market policies within the framework of national labor-market policy, and to oversee the implementation of both the national and state policies within their jurisdiction. The membership at the state level should mirror the membership of the national body. National policy should set very broad parameters, leaving a great deal of room for the states to develop policies and organizational plans that meet their unique state needs and conditions. At both federal and state levels, the policies should emphasize the definition of the outcomes wanted at the local level, the resource flows, and the development of accountability and incentive structures that will both leave maximum flexibility for the local level to get the job done and the strongest possible incentives to get it done efficiently and well.

It will be up to the states to design their labor-market policies and programs so that they are fully integrated with their economic development objectives. The states will have the major responsibility for developing a statewide system of postsecondary training to meet the needs of the unfolding Technical and Professional Certificate programs. It will be up to them to create mechanisms to certify students who have successfully completed those programs. They will have the key responsibility for building first-class integrated statewide job-matching systems that will link up to the national and regional systems. They will have to develop the statutory framework for their statewide dropout recovery systems and design mechanisms to fund these. Finally, they will have to create the local employment and training boards that will be responsible for administering the entire system at the local level.

The examples we provided earlier show that many states are on their way to creating the needed mechanisms for integrating many of these functions at the state level. None are all the way there, and the national framework for such efforts is missing altogether. But a good beginning has been made.

Local Employment and Training Boards

We pointed out earlier that the employment service is the heart of the European system. To overcome the faults of the existing U.S. service, we need above all a network of effective local employment service offices. These offices should come under the jurisdiction of local Employment and Training Boards, created by the states and charged with developing and administering a system at the local level that will address each of these problems.

We have in mind boards that are created for each major labor market, typically a large metropolitan area or multicounty rural area. Smaller jurisdictions will not work, because the flow of labor and the provision of training do not respect smaller governmental boundaries. The typical board would be composed of the chief executive officers of respected firms, labor leaders, heads of major education and training institutions and agencies, leaders of the advocacy community and community-based organizations, and mayors and county executives, but the CEOs would have the most significant role. As we see it, these boards should be private, not-for-profit agencies chartered by the state government, with their members appointed by the governor and confirmed by the legislature. The salary schedules for their staff should be pegged to private-sector salaries, designed to attract top-notch managers and professionals.

In some states, the Private Industry Councils provide a base from which the new local Employment and Training Boards can be built. But there are many important differences between the PICs as they are now and the new structures we have in mind. If the redesign of the PICs does not take these differences into account, the new system will fail. Peter Carlson notes that "the Private Industry Councils have mainly operated on the fringes of the labor market," and he spells out the differences between their current charge and what we have in mind:

> *Broader Responsibility.* Where current public training efforts are mainly targeted on the nation's poor and long-term unemployed and operate only on the supply side of the labor market, the new system [we envision] will operate in the mainstream of the labor market, actively working on both the supply and demand sides.
>
> *Different Goals and Standards.* Where current Private Industry Councils define success as placing clients into mainly marginal jobs, the new labor-market boards will focus on the attainment of high standards of basic and technical competency in preparation for high-wage, high-career-potential jobs.
>
> *Greater Authority.* Where current Private Industry Councils have [access to the funds for only a few narrowly defined training programs], the [clients of] the new labor-market boards will have access [to a far larger funding stream and the boards themselves will have] independent staffing, independent resources derived from [firms that prefer to pay their required training allotment to the board rather than

spend it internally], and responsibility for maintaining quality control [over the whole system].

Improved Program Coordination. Where existing programs remain fragmented by institutional barriers, the new labor-market boards, using modern technology, will break down these barriers by establishing a common base of client, program, and labor-market information.[12]

To see how this new system might work, let us look at it from the point of view of a client, Terry. She might be a sixteen-year-old youngster who has just gotten her Certificate of Initial Mastery and has come into the offices of the local Employment and Training Board looking for some information about career opportunities and training options. Remember that the youngster carries with her an entitlement to four years of additional education and training from the state, and the cashier is walking in backed up by funds provided by her employer, as a result of the requirement that the employer set aside an amount equal to 1 percent of total wages and salaries for that year. In this case, the employer chose to contribute that money to the state training fund rather than spend internally.

Terry is first introduced to Mike, a counselor, who gives her a battery of aptitude and interest tests and then engages her in a conversation about what she might want to do with her life. Then the counselor flips the switch on his computer terminal and brings up reports on the short- and long-term forecasts for the area labor market. He takes Terry through the screens, explaining what industries will be experiencing demand, what kinds of careers are available in these industries, and what technical and professional certificates are required to start out at the entry level in those occupations. Mike and Terry talk for a while about the match between her interests and the occupations that are in demand in the area she resides in.

Terry selects five occupations that seem attractive. The counselor agrees that they are right for her and represent good career prospects. Terry says she is most interested in a career line that starts with the entry-level position of flexible-manufacturing technician, and asks what institutions offer technical and professional certificate programs for that career track. The counselor punches up another screen. The programs of five institutions appear—two community colleges, an area vocational school, a secondary school, and a manufacturing firm that runs a program for its own employees but also for a few nonemployees. All of them offer combined programs of schooling and structured training at a work site. They all lead, of course, to the same certificate, recognized by employers all over the country.

But some are part-time programs and some are full-time. Mike points out that they are very different in other ways, too. Two are close, within easy commuting distance, but three are not. One of the two has a free day-care center, which would be perfect for Terry, who is a single mother. But then Terry notices that the two that are close have terrible success rates for those who have enrolled over the last ten years. No more than 5 percent of those who signed up for these programs got their certificates within four years, whereas the success rates for two that are more distant exceed 80 percent, and the cost of those programs is actually lower than for the nearby ones. One of those with high success rates and lower costs also has a free day-care center and is run by a firm that Terry would really like to work for.

But she would need help to get an apartment at the location of that training program to take advantage of it. Fortunately, the local board has a policy of providing partial support in such situations, provided that the occupation being trained for is in high demand and the institution selected has high completion rates and competitive costs. So Terry's counselor signs her up for that program.

As another example we can take Bill, an unemployed twenty-year-old who does not yet have his Certificate of Initial Mastery and wants not just to get a job but to get on a track that will lead to a rewarding career. Bill's needs are being funded by a combination of the employer training contributions required under the new law, the unemployment compensation fund, and special programs for the hard-core unemployed. Mike explains the range of youth center options for getting a Certificate of Initial Mastery at no cost. After a lengthy conversation, Bill and Mike select a nearby Job Corps camp which has a contract with the youth center run by the Employment and Training Board. Mike feels that the Job Corps camp, though more expensive than some of the alternatives, is the only option that will provide Bill with the range of services that he needs to deal with some of the really tough problems he faces in overcoming his lack of self-confidence, his drug problem, and a set of values and attitudes he developed as he grew up that must change if he is to succeed.

One of the things that attracted Bill to the Job Corps program is its connection with the job experience program run by an employers' group founded by the Employment and Training Board. The group works with its members to make sure that enough entry-level jobs are developed every year to provide summer and part-time work only to young people enrolled in high school and in youth center programs, so as to give them work skills and a good record they can present when they apply for their first job.

Both Bill and Terry maintain regular contact with Mike as they pursue their certificate programs. When Bill is close to getting his Certificate of Initial Mastery, he asks Mike to help him select a technical and professional certificate program that will move him along to the next stage. As Terry gets close to getting her professional and technical certificate, Mike uses the computer system to help her locate a job in the occupation for which she has trained. Every front-line job available in the state is listed in the computer, and Mike can also access job listings in adjoining states if necessary. None are available close by, so Mike pays for her to take a bus to interview with a couple of firms elsewhere in the state. One offers Terry a job, and the board pays most of Terry's costs to relocate.

These stories hardly exhaust the range of services that Mike can offer to people who show up at his door. But they convey a feel for what could happen if the United States developed a world-class labor-market policy and a system to implement it effectively. Few steps this country could take would make a more dramatic difference to the nation's economic prospects and the lives of our people.

PART V

Two Futures:
Which Will We Choose?

CHAPTER 15

Investing in Our People

O n the eve of the presidential primaries in New Hampshire in February 1992, the Democratic candidates were quick to agree with author David Halberstam that the cold war is over and the Japanese and the Germans have won. A clever statement, but it is not yet true. The United States still has the largest and most productive economy in the world. We still generate the most patents and have the most admired research establishment of any nation. We remain the richest country on earth.

But the threat is clear. If we do not come to consensus on the need to establish our economy on new principles—the principles of human-resource capitalism outlined in this book—then our prosperity will vanish and our democracy will be under siege. If we can reach beyond our own parochialism to borrow from the most creative and successful policies in the world, if we have the will to reexamine the relevance of deeply entrenched institutions, and if we have the courage to take on a multitude of vested interests, then we can leapfrog over the best the world has to offer and build a system for the development and productive use of our human resources that will be without peer.

That will require gifted leadership and a truly bipartisan effort, the kind of bipartisan effort that characterized the foreign policy of this country at the height of the cold war. The threat is no less serious now than it was then.

But building an economy based on the principles of human-resource capitalism will require more than consensus around a new vision for this country: it will demand high levels of investment. The best firms in the world have recognized that their own restructuring plans require new investments in their future, even while they are ruthlessly paring expenditures on operations. High-performance companies understand that these are investments in sustained future growth, not just current budget costs. The following are among the larger items of investment we have recommended in this book:

• About one-quarter of our high-school students now drop out of school. We spend only $235 per year on those who drop out as opposed to over $4,000 per year on those who stay in school.[1] Most of those who drop out do so at sixteen, when they can legally do so. The proposed youth centers will be populated mainly with youth who have not been able to get their Certificate of Initial Mastery by the age of sixteen. If it took two years on average, beyond the age of sixteen, to bring these young people up to standard, then the cost of doing so would be about $8,000 per student enrolled in youth centers. It is virtually impossible to estimate the total net cost, because while the higher standard may cause more young people to drop out than do so now, the improvements made through restructuring our schools may also result in fewer dropouts. Only experience will reveal the stable rates over time, and therefore the true net additional cost of bringing these young people up to standard.

• There is no way accurately to estimate the cost of the school restructuring measures we propose. It is clear that much of what we have suggested can be accomplished at no net increase, but some proposals—more intensive use of new instructional technologies, much greater investment in professional development of teachers, more study time for students falling behind, more teacher time for scoring exams, for example—will add to current costs. But these will not be the major cost items. If we in fact establish a single high national standard of achievement for our students, then we will have to face up to the enormous disparities of expenditure among our school districts and states. In some districts there are not enough texts for each student to have one; in others there are enough for each student to keep one in school and another at home. Some districts can afford tutors for individual students, and others must crowd forty or fifty students into a classroom. Some can make advanced technologies available for small groups conducting scientific experiments, and others cannot repair leaking ceilings. The cost of eliminating these disparities depends on whether greater equity is achieved by bringing everyone up to the highest levels of expenditure or by bringing the top down while raising the bottom. Either way, however, the cost will be very high.

• We propose that all students who get their Certificate of Initial Mastery receive an entitlement equivalent to four full years of additional full-time education. Some portion of the cost of such a policy could be funded by reprogramming what is now spent on the last two years of high school and the first two years of college—local levies, state foundation funds, categorical program funds, Pell grants, college loan funds, and so on. This is not likely to fund the full cost of this proposal, because a little less than 60 percent of all high-school students now go to college, a much smaller proportion do so full-time for the first two years out of high school, and many who do go to college take only a few courses. But not all students will want to go on to four-year colleges or immediately enter a program to prepare them to get a technical and professional certificate, especially in the first few years in which such certificate programs are offered. It cannot, therefore, be known at this time what the net additional funding requirement would be for this proposal.

• We have proposed that employers make, on average, a far higher expenditure on the continued education and training of their front-line workers—on the order of 3 to 5 percent of salaries and wages, the rate of spending of most firms using high-performance forms of work organization—than they do now (1.4 percent on average).[2] Except for public-sector employers, this would be a private expenditure, and, for the amounts above the 1 percent we propose for the training fund, entirely voluntary.

• We have not costed out the net increase in expenditure for the labor-market services we propose, partly because the cost would depend greatly on the details of program design. These include the costs of the rebuilt employment service, including the creation of a fully computerized and interconnected data base; the operation of the labor-market board system; and the subsidies for job search, relocation, family living expenses, and personal living expenses while training away from home. A significant portion of these expenses would be offset by the reduced costs of unemployment compensation, but there would undoubtedly be a net increase, though of unknown proportions.

• The costs of converting to a single-payer form of universal health insurance have been much debated in Congress recently, with little consensus. We can add nothing to that debate, except to say that while a universal system would have a higher budget cost, the combined public and private costs of health care would be reduced substantially in the long run, because as other industrialized countries have found, a universal single-payer system makes it possible to control costs.

• The cost of raising the minimum wage to a level sufficient to enable a full-time wage earner making the minimum to support his or her family at or above the poverty level would be borne by employers, not the taxpayer. Opponents of such a move argue that taking such a step would cause many firms to go out of business or to reduce employment, thus contributing to increased unemployment. The experience of other countries, however, suggests that this need not be the case in the medium to long term. A low-wage strategy subsidizes inefficiency and causes wages to be more unequal than a high-wage one. The effect of raising the minimum wage would be to shut down businesses that can only survive paying low wages and to redirect investment into other businesses that can afford to pay high wages. This is exactly the outcome we advocate, because it is the only path to a high standard of living for everyone.

• The cost of providing a universal child allowance would also be high, as would be the provision of a fully integrated system of social services to families in stress. But to some extent these costs would offset one another, since a great deal of family stress is caused by poverty. We cannot estimate the net cost of these two items, because no one knows how they will interact.

Thus although the costs to the taxpayers of our proposals are unknown, it is safe to say that they will be large: undoubtedly in the tens of billions of dollars, and possibly more than a hundred billion a year. There is also no doubt that the benefits to be gained by such expenditures will vastly outweigh the out-of-pocket costs. Across-the-board improvements in the rate of productivity growth and the increased revenues from taxes paid at current rates by taxpayers who are now dependents of the state will be more than enough in time to pay for the net increases in costs we propose. But, as with all investments, the benefits will come only after the costs have been incurred for a while. Where is the money to come from for the initial investment?

This is not a good time to ask the question. The country is in a recession that seems uncommonly stubborn. In addition, much of the spending we recommend would have to come out of state budgets. But state after state is experiencing a reduction in revenues from businesses and individuals as sales dry up and consumer confidence and income languish. At the same time, state expenditures are rising as the unemployment rolls lengthen and other costs of poverty steadily increase. Just to stay even, the states must both raise taxes and cut back on services. Increasingly angry taxpayers, who see the government taking a larger and larger share of their declining real income, are closing off the tax increase option for politicians who hope to remain in office. Unable to raise taxes, and afraid of making devastating cuts in services, states are going longer into their fiscal years without budgets than ever before. Their fiscal crisis is deepening year by year, with no end in sight.

How did the states get into this mess? The answer can be found in the federal government's economic policies of the 1980s and early 1990s. The combined effects of unprecedented budget deficits, changes in the banking laws, and the reshaping of tax policy have been devastating—arguably the most disastrous of any economic policy since the nation was founded.

The federal deficit is the reason that there is no new money to spend on health insurance, child support, education and training, or any of the nation's other pressing needs. Projected to be 20 percent larger in fiscal year 1992 than in FY 1991, the deficit is far larger than ever before. Payments on the national debt in FY 92 will be $304 billion, one-third of the federal budget, up from $75 billion in 1980. The taxpayers will get no services whatsoever for this amazing sum of money. At the beginning of the 1980s, the national debt, accumulated over the first two centuries of the nation's history, stood at less than a trillion dollars. It is now more than four times that and growing fast.[3] The result is not only the hobbling of the government's capacity to meet the needs of its citizens, but an enormous drag on private investment, caused by the government's need to service its gargantuan debt with dollars that would otherwise be invested else-where. Private investment in new plant and equipment is essential to growth in productivity, and productivity growth, as every economist knows, is the only real source of economic growth. As private investment declined, real hourly wages fell from $7.78 in 1980 to $7.54 in 1990, real weekly salaries fell from $274.65 in 1980 to $259.98 in 1990, and bankruptcies rose from 360,329 in 1981 to 880,399 in 1991.[4] Through all these years, the president and Congress announced one measure after another that they promised would steadily reduce the deficit. But this year's deficit, as we just pointed out, sets an all-time record, with no end in sight.

Changes in banking and real-estate policy compounded the problems caused by the deficits. Prior to 1982, there were very strict limitations on the kinds of investments banks could make with the funds their depositors gave them. But the Garn–St. Germain Act, passed by Congress in that year, changed all that. It abolished the restrictions on bank investments in real estate; and the 1981 tax act, to which we will return in a moment, created big new tax shelters for real-estate investors. The combination of these two moves produced a boom in the construc-tion of office buildings that no one needed. Bank loans for real-estate investment soared from $284 billion in 1981 to $844 billion in 1990.[5] When the economy soured, and there was no one to pay the rent in these new buildings, the office vacancy rate went from almost 5 percent in 1980 to more than 19 percent by 1989.[6] Loan defaults started to pile up, and the banks were suddenly in deep trouble. When Congress finally took steps to close the loopholes it had created earlier, one result was that the value of these properties declined still further, causing even more distress among the banks. Now, understandably, the banks that have money to lend are very cautious about doing so, so the money available for investment in all kinds of enterprises is hard to come by even with falling interest rates. The enormous—and rising—costs of bailing out the banks have to be added to the service on the national debt as another price our children will be paying for years for the mismanagement of the 1980s. And these costs are yet another multibillion dollar drag on the nation's capacity to make vital invest-ments in the future.

The changes in tax policy have tightened the deficit squeeze still further. This year, the richest million families in the United States will make almost $700,000 each, very close to twice what they took home twelve years ago. To "compensate" for this, the federal government agreed to reduce their taxes by 17.6 percent. Tax rates fell, too, for the lowest 20 percent of wage earners, but their income fell faster, so they are worse off than before. But the worst effects were felt by the middle class. Four out of five families now pay out a greater share of their income in taxes than they did before Ronald Reagan became president. His claim, of course, was that these tax rate reductions would power the economy to a new high, raising more in taxes than a weaker economy could with higher tax rates. As we all now know, nothing of the sort happened at all.

The combination of lower government revenues and higher spending simply produced vastly higher debt. The spending produced the illusion of a healthy, growing economy even as the props were being knocked out from under it. To give the appearance, at least, that spending was under control, the federal government started squeezing the states by pushing off onto them responsibility for a growing range of services, while at the same time reducing the share of the federal budget transferred to the states and creating a climate that made it increasingly difficult for them to solve their problems by raising taxes. In this way the states have been left holding the bag, forced to deal with a crisis essentially made by the federal government's bungling of economic policy.

It is tempting to place all the blame for this state of affairs on the Reagan and Bush administrations. These events, after all, occurred on their watch and largely as a result of their policies. But they do not carry the responsibility by themselves.

Barry Bosworth, an economist at the Brookings Institution, holds us all responsible.

To me, the politicians function almost perfectly in that they perfectly represent the views of their constituents.

Conservatives would rather have deficits than raise taxes. Liberals would rather have deficits than further cuts in major social programs. Each side agrees the deficit is terrible; it's just not as bad as each group thinks the alternative is. . . .

We are more and more looking like Great Britain in the '50s and '60s. You don't collapse. You just don't do as well as everyone else. You just steadily fall behind. You argue about it, but you don't do anything about it.[7]

Economic growth during the Bush administration has been slower than at any time since World War II. That is mainly because the country has been making massive reductions in the sums allocated to investment in the future. During the decade of the 1980s, the federal budget for defense increased 10 percent, the amount required to pay interest on the national debt increased by 83 percent, and the amount required to bail out the savings and loans (not in the budget before the crisis) came to 59 billion dollars (only part of the eventual bill). None of that money can be considered investment. On the other side of the ledger, the federal budget for justice and general government declined by 42 percent, for education and training by 40 percent, for environment and natural resources by 39 percent, and for roads and transportation by 32 percent.[8]

Though these policies were to have disastrous effects. Ronald Reagan had a point in 1980 when he said that we should be arguing less about how to divide the pie and more about how to make it grow. His prescription for doing so was misguided at best, and his belief that the rich would produce that growth if left to their own devices proved wholly unfounded, but the drive to find ways to make the economy grow, to invest in its productive capacity, was right on target. At bottom, the nation's problem is not the deficit per se, but slow economic growth, and our failure to invest the borrowed money in our future.

We have argued that the principal source of our productive capacity is our people, and that the most powerful strategy for capitalizing on that resource is developing learning systems that will cause that capacity to go on growing into the indefinite future. The trick now is to find a way to make the necessary investment in our people in an era of tough economic constraints.

The first requisite is political leaders who will tell the truth to the American people. The truth is simple. We cannot go on consuming 3 to 4 percent more of GNP than we produce. We have to consume less so we can invest more. If we do not do so, then the legacy we leave our children will be a poor country. As with any family that is up to its ears in debt, whatever we save from reduced consumption has to go into three things: absolute necessities, debt reduction, and very careful investment in our future.

For years now, the American public has been listening to politicians who have told them what they want to hear: that government waste is the problem, that the greed of the lazy poor is the problem, that foreign competition is the problem, in short, that someone else is to blame. But Americans are not stupid, and they are now disgusted with politicians. Our families have to manage their own budgets every day. They are aware of the realities and they care about their future. They are ready, we believe, for straight talk and for someone who will finally propose a plan, however tough, that will plausibly produce a brighter future.

In the short term, the requirement is to get the American economy back on its feet. We would do that in two ways. First, federal grants to state and local governments should be increased on a one-time-only basis by 10 percent across the board. Much of this money would be used on roads, bridges, and other physical infrastructure, which are badly in need of renewed investment. This measure would pump about fifteen billion dollars into the economy quickly. (This is a good illustration, by the way, of the limitations of tax cuts as a device to stimulate the economy: Only a small portion of the money injected into the economy by tax cuts goes into investments, whereas all the money released by this proposal would both stimulate the economy and constitute an investment in future productivity.) Second, we would close down most of our foreign military bases, repatriate their personnel to the United States, and require all military contractors to purchase their goods and services from American-based companies. The effect would be to increase domestic demand, thus stimulating the economy without increasing debt or reducing the funds available for savings and investment. It would cause an injection of another fifteen to twenty billion dollars into the American economy.

Meeting the longer-term challenge to create a truly healthy American economy is another matter. We speculated earlier in this chapter that it might take one hundred billion dollars of additional federal spending to carry out the programs we have recommended. That sum would come to one-third of our current debt-service requirement, or one-third of our current rate of military expenditure. One hundred billion dollars is 120 dollars a year for every inhabitant of the United States.

But a surtax on our current tax rates is not the best way to raise the money required to assure our future, nor is new spending the only important requirement for the federal budget. We have both to reduce the deficit—one of several measures required to release the private investment funds required to get the economy going on a firm basis—and at the same time to make the necessary public investment in our people. It is on this balance between public and private investment that sound policy will turn.

Assume for the moment that the objective is to reduce the deficit by $300 billion and increase spending on priority investment items by $200 billion. We propose that that $200 billion be divided between $100 billion for investments in physical infrastructure and new technologies and $100 billion for the human-resources program outlined in this book. That would require a combination of revenue increases and spending reductions in other quarters of $500 billion. We would raise about half that sum with new taxes and half by reducing current expenditures. These changes, and the others we propose, should be made over a five-year period.

The idea of raising taxes will not be welcome. Americans believe themselves to be overtaxed and resent it. The problem, of course, is raising taxes when real wages are declining, because it represents a second bite into a family's standard of living. The reality is that, against the standards of the advanced industrial nations, American taxes are relatively low. If the American people were taxed at all levels at the average rate for the OECD countries, the result would be an increase in tax revenue of about $450 billion a year, almost enough to fund our entire plan. But we are not proposing such an increase.

Instead, we would make four fundamental changes in the tax law: (1) make the income tax more progressive by raising the top bracket from 28 percent to 38 percent (the level originally proposed by the Reagan administration), while reducing the total amount raised by the income tax; (2) greatly reduce corporate income taxes; (3) create a permanent research and development tax credit; and (4) institute a modest national value-added tax. All four taken together would be designed to produce a net increase in tax revenues from these sources of $250 billion.

We pointed out earlier that the United States now has the most unequal distribution of income in the developed world. The argument that is most often made for taxing the rich lightly is that higher rates will reduce the incentive of our entrepreneurs to take risks and will dry up the source of discretionary income that they invest in new business opportunities. But there is no evidence whatsoever that the much lower relative incomes of Japanese and European executives lower their incentive to work hard and take risks. The primary issue on the investment capital side is the availability of capital to business, not individuals. The evidence is overwhelming that increased consumption during the 1980s was by the wealthy, not by middle- or low-income families. The way to solve this problem is to tax wealthy individuals at much higher rates and to tax business much more lightly.

But why reduce taxes on business when the nation's budget is already running such a big deficit? First, a strong argument can be made that the consumer actually pays business taxes in the end anyway. As Lester Thurow argues: "Efforts to tax the rich by taxing corporate shareholders is in fact a disguised sales tax." Thurow points out that "even if the corporate income tax were paid by the shareholders, it is an unfair tax. Every shareholder, rich or poor, is taxed at the same rate. . . . There are much better, fairer ways than corporate income taxes to tax the rich if this is what Americans wish to do."[9] The fairer and more efficient ways are progressive personal income taxes and value-added taxes.

We would reduce somewhat the overall amount raised by the income tax and create a new value-added tax (VAT). Value added is the difference between the cost of a firm's purchase of supplies and what it takes in from the sales of goods and services. It is a measure, in other words, of the value added by the firm to the supplies it takes in when it uses them to produce the finished goods and services it sells in the market. Taxing the value added by firms has enormous advantages to a country formulating a high-performance development strategy.

• A VAT can raise a large amount of money. In 1984, for example, a 15 percent value-added tax would have raised $447 billion.

• The VAT is a tax on consumption (which we believe needs to be curtailed), not a tax on saving, investment, or work effort (all of which this country should be seeking to promote).

• Because it is a tax on consumption, it makes it possible to tax illegal underground activities; the underworld must pay the tax when it purchases goods and services in the open market with its ill-gotten gains. But it is not just organized crime that is at issue. The IRS estimates that, between 1973 and 1981, Americans evaded about $90 billion a year in taxes.[10] Getting back even half this amount would be a very large windfall.

• A value-added tax would lower the cost of American exports to consumers abroad, thus making our export products more competitive. This is because the VAT is refundable under the rules of international trade, whereas income taxes are not.

• It is easy to make the VAT a fair tax. First, one does not have to pay the tax on the things one does not choose to buy. Second, a refundable per capita tax credit can be built into the tax legislation to eliminate the tax entirely for low-income households and make it more progressive for high-income taxpayers.

• The VAT is cheap to collect. A study done in 1984 showed that a VAT with a refundable tax credit provision that would have raised $385 billion would have cost only $700 million to collect.[11]

In other countries, the VAT also seems to be more acceptable to people than the income tax, despite theoretical arguments that the income tax is preferable on equity and efficiency grounds. Americans rely much more heavily on the income tax than other countries do (36.2 percent of GDP, compared with 24.09 percent for Japan, 29.04 percent for Germany, and 12.7 percent for France).[12] Though Americans have been somewhat hostile to the VAT in the past, it is likely that they would be much less so if its introduction were accompanied by a substantial reduction in the total revenues raised by the income tax. In a recent study, Ferlinger and Mandle conjecture that the relatively high hostility to taxes in the United States could be due to "the seemingly coercive nature of the income tax . . . and . . . the seemingly voluntary nature of other forms of taxation (such as the value-added tax) induces a more benign response."[13]

It will be argued, of course, that any new taxes will retard economic growth. There is considerable evidence, however, that there is no relationship between taxes and economic growth. As we point out elsewhere, overall tax burdens in all the other leading industrial countries exceed those in this nation.[14]

Since our only hope for future economic growth is to reduce current consumption while increasing our rate of investment, the value-added tax is by far the best way to achieve this. We would call the value-added tax the "Invest in all Americans" tax. It would be deposited in a trust fund dedicated to debt reduction and to the investment program we have laid out in this book. Such trust funds for human-resource development have been used in Germany and other countries with great success for many years. The device of a trust fund may be politically essential. Again and again in recent years, the people have shown their willingness, even in the poorest of states, to dip into their pockets to spend heavily on education and on other human investments when they are convinced that the money will be spent well. Any new taxes that are simply added to general revenues, on the other hand, are fought tooth and nail. Another crucial advantage of creating such a trust fund is that investments in human resources would no longer be subject to the vagaries of the politics of the federal budgeting process, with its large fluctuations in expenditures from year to year that frustrate effective planning by the states and countless institutions and individuals.

Whether or not the proceeds from the new value-added tax are put in a trust fund, it is essential that the federal budget distinguish, as the budgets of other countries do, between capital investments and other expenditures. The lack of a capital budgeting system creates a bias against public investments.

All federal expenditures are now treated as current expenses, and none as investments in the future. The irony is that federal tax policy has long made this distinction for firms, encouraging investment in physical capital by permitting firms to spread out the cost of these investments over the useful life of the equipment purchased. Very few businesses could survive with the government's practice of counting long-term physical and human capital investments as current expenditures. These federal practices create biases against investments that yield high returns to the society as a whole, despite growing evidence that inadequate public and private investment has created major productivity and competitiveness problems for the United States.[15]

It is high time the country used the kind of accounting principles for both physical and human capital expenditures in its own budget that it has established for firms. With capital budgeting, the federal government could separate the needed long-term investments in infrastructure and human resources from current operating expenses. This would free policymakers with political concerns about budget deficits from the unwise practice of refusing to incur debt to make long-run high-yielding investments in future economic growth.

Overall, the tax policy we propose would reduce consumption, release the sums that businesses now pay in taxes for investment in future growth opportunities, and lessen the dangerous inequalities in income in the United States, inequalities that pose an increasing threat to the social fabric of this country.

Nothing like the tax proposals we have made was the subject of national discussion at the time this book was written. Leaders of both parties were talking about cutting taxes to get the economy going. The administration was continuing to insist that the best way to encourage private investment would be to lower taxes on capital gains.

We have already explained why an investment-led strategy would be far better than tax cuts to produce the economic gains the country seeks. Not even the most ardent advocates of a capital-gains tax cut believe it would do very much to stimulate the economy. Michael Boskin, chairman of the Council of Economic Advisers in the Bush administration, told the Joint Economic Committee of the Congress in 1991 that even under the most optimistic assumptions, the administration's proposal would have about the same effect on investment as a drop in interest rates of "probably 10 basis points, or something like that, [perhaps] 15."[16] To put this in perspective, the prime rate fell 250 basis points between October 1990 and December 1991, but did very little to reduce the slide in investment or improve the economy.

The interesting question is: What do America's corporate leaders think would be the best tax policy if the objective is to get them to invest in America's future? James Poterba and Lawrence Summers recently conducted a study on that point. Specifically, what they wanted to know was what would get American executives to focus less on short-term results and more on long-term growth. The managers thought that taxes would have more influence on their time horizons than any other public policies. "A cut in the corporate tax rate from 34 percent to 25 percent, a permanent research and development tax credit and allowing half of all corporate dividend payments to be deductible from corporate taxes were the three policies with the largest effect in lengthening corporate time horizons. The next two pro-lengthening [stimuli] were a 20 percent increase in corporate earnings and a credible commitment to no change in the tax system for a decade. ... Moreover, [these] policies were viewed as more attractive than restoration of the investment tax credit for equipment, a capital gains tax cut or a tax on short-term [stock market] trading."[17]

This brings us to the spending side of the federal ledger. Where would Congress find the $250 billion in reduced annual expenditures to complete our plan? We believe most of it can be found in the military budget, the budget for the space program, the CIA budget, agricultural subsidies, and the social security trust fund. The following analysis provides a few examples of how this might be done.

Take the military budget. It is now a little less than $300 billion. It was only $203 billion in 1976, when the cold war was still running strong and the Carter administration was developing a whole new generation of technologically advanced armaments to cope with anticipated threats from the Soviet Union.[18] It does not seem unreasonable to suppose that the country now needs $50 billion less than it did then to defend itself, given that the Soviet Union no longer exists, the threat from that quarter is virtually non-existent, and no new adversary has appeared on the scene whose military capacity is even remotely comparable. By that reasoning, we could get $150 billion of the amount we need from the defense budget.

The impact on those connected with the defense industry would be devastating if this was done all at once, but it should be quite possible to accomplish a cut of this magnitude over the next five years. The approach we have in mind would increase the deficit during the recession and produce net surpluses as the economy recovers, as shown in table 15.1.

If the Congress removed the current cap on required contributions to the social security trust fund, individuals with incomes over $51,300 would pay into the fund at the same rates for all their income over that level that they do for income under it. That would produce an additional $49 billion a year for the trust fund.

That money, in addition to the current surplus in the social security trust fund, would then become available to finance the whole cost of our proposal to create an entitlement for people who have their Certificate of Initial Mastery to the equivalent of another four years of full-time education and training. The mechanism for this has been proposed by Barry Bluestone, Alan Clayton-Matthews, John Havens, and Howard Young in the form of the Equity Investment in America Program (EIA).[19] Under the plan, a new fiduciary trust would be established that would make loans for higher education. Repayment could take

TABLE 15.1

Five-Year Plan for Defense Cuts (billions of dollars)

	Military Cut	**Domestic Investment**	**Net Surplus (Deficit)**
Year 1	4	30	(26)
Year 2	15	30	(15)
Year 3	27	30	(3)
Year 4	42	30	12
Year 5	62	30	32
Total	150	150	0

up to twenty-five years, with annual repayments to vary depending on the borrower's annual earnings. Repayment rates would be set so that the funds borrowed from and returned to the social security trust fund would be sufficient to exceed by a substantial amount what had been borrowed originally from that fund, thereby assuring that the fund would be able to meet its obligations to the baby-boomers when they retire in the twenty-first century.

If $250 billion were raised in new taxes, defense expenditures were cut back by $150 billion, and $50 billion were borrowed from the social security trust fund each year to pay for postsecondary education and training, that would leave only $50 billion a year to come from the other sources we have named in the federal budget for the investment program we have proposed.

In time, as the active labor-market policy takes hold, expenditures on unemployment compensation will decline radically. As the whole plan comes into effect, expenditures on welfare, the criminal-justice system, social services, and many other items in the domestic budget will fall drastically. As the proportion of people with high skills increases and those people are put to productive work, tax collections will rise greatly without any further increases in tax rates, as happened after World War II with the "G. I. Bill." This is not speculation. The evidence from other nations on these points is overwhelming. All of this is why we think of our plan as the best investment plan the country could have.

But making the case for these changes in revenue and spending will not be easy. Success will depend on convincing the public that the nation faces an invisible emergency, one that is slowly draining our future away. It will depend, too, on a convincing plan for our collective future and on persuading everyone that the pain will be fairly distributed.

The plan and the budget we have laid out is neither conservative nor liberal. It cuts across all the usual lines. Conservatives have always fought steeply graduated income taxes, but liberals have always fought value-added taxes. Liberals will be aghast at the idea of abolishing or greatly reducing taxes on business, but conservatives will be equally upset with a requirement that businesses set aside an amount equal to 1 percent of salaries and wages for training. Conservatives think school reform with tough accountability measures is long overdue, and liberals will be relieved to hear that the way business organizes work is a major part of the problem. Conservatives will deplore the children's allowance and single-payer universal health insurance, but they will applaud the reduction we propose in unemployment compensation and our proposal that many social benefits be made contingent on the recipient being willing to work and be trained. Liberals will wonder what will happen to poor children who fail to reach the standard we propose, and conservatives will take exception to the commitment to spend what is necessary to make sure that they do reach it. No plan for real change in this country can possibly succeed unless everyone who is called on to shed established positions sees others doing the same. And everyone who does so must somehow come to see that they have more to gain than lose by doing so. The new plan will require a new politics.

Can it happen? Can old antagonists join forces to create new beginnings? It is too early to tell, but we can take much comfort from some recent developments.

In the spring of 1991, President Bush called together a bipartisan group from all over the country to a special ceremony at the White House, where he announced America 2000, his education initiative. The plan was widely criticized for the pivotal role that the president's proposal for a private voucher system played in its design and for its failure to propose a major increase in federal funding for education, criticisms with which we agree. What most commentators seemed to miss, however, was the astonishing change in the federal role in education and human development that underlay the plan's whole conception.

Ronald Reagan, campaigning for the presidency in the 1980 elections, had promised to abolish the Department of Education, and to return all control of education to the states. He did his best to make good on that promise as president, and succeeded in cutting back federal job-training expenditures by two-thirds and reducing funding for other vital components of the nation's human-resource development system by similarly large amounts. Lamar Alexander, the new secretary of education and the Bush plan's principal architect, managed to engineer a 180-degree turn away from these policies.

America 2000 asserts that the federal government has a permanent and pivotal role in education; that education is far more than schooling; that virtually every major cabinet department has a vital role to play in developing America's human resources; and that the cabinet secretaries and the president must and will give personal leadership to the effort at every step of the way. No president in the entire history of the United States before Bush has ever made such a sweeping assertion of the role of the federal government in education and human-resources development. No one challenged that assertion.

President Bush made an equally important departure from well-trodden paths when he appointed Alexander, a highly regarded former governor, as secretary of education, and David Kearns, the equally well regarded former chairman of Xerox, as deputy secretary. The appointment of a governor and a CEO to these two top positions was unprecedented, signaling that education had become so important to the nation's future, and the place of federal leadership in the structure so pivotal, that the positions had to be filled by two of America's most admired leaders from government and business. In European terms, it signaled that education was to become the business not just of education, but of all the social partners.

Taken together, the message of America 2000 and the appointment of Alexander and Kearns raise education and human-resource development far higher on the national agenda than they have ever been before, and greatly improve the prospect of involving the leadership of the whole country in fashioning that agenda and taking responsibility for assuring its implementation. No less important, Secretary Alexander has from the start reached out in a thoroughly nonpartisan manner to engage people everywhere in the discussion of America 2000 and the effort to improve the nation's education system. His inclusive style has contributed greatly to the feeling that education is everyone's problem and everyone's responsibility. Long after the specifics of the president's proposal are forgotten, these aspects of his education initiative will provide later presidents with a foundation for their own initiatives far stronger than any that have been laid before.

On October 1, 1991, a year-and-a-half after the Commission on the Skills of the American Workforce released its report, *America's Choice: high skills or low wages!,* a bipartisan group of key senators and members of the House of Representatives introduced companion bills in both houses of Congress that would provide powerful incentives and support for states, local school districts, and other education and training institutions and businesses to implement the commission's proposals.

The proposed High Skills and Competitive Workforce Act of 1991 calls for federal matching funding for Youth Opportunity Centers to recover school dropouts, and a career service to help young people find jobs. It would require that companies either invest in training or pay the equivalent of 1 percent of their payroll into a state-administered training fund. The bill would amend the nation's education research authority to provide funds for research on new forms of student performance assessment, of the sort required to implement the Certificate of Initial Mastery, and calls on the administration to coordinate the work of industry committees to set standards for the proposed system of technical and professional certificates. It authorizes technical assistance to employers to help them develop high-performance work organizations, and encourages the states to develop state and regional employment and training boards as recommended by the commission.

With sponsorship from such people as Senator Hatfield, the ranking member of the Senate Appropriations Committee, Senator Kennedy, the chairman of the Committee on Labor and Human Resources, and Representative Gephardt, the majority leader in the House of Representatives, this legislative initiative has attracted wide support from governors, major national business groups, labor, and key advocacy groups. If passed by the Congress in anything like the form in which it was introduced, it will signal a major change in national policy.

The states, too, are on the move. We have already described the sweeping reform legislation in Kentucky, embracing social services integration, new incentives for students and school staff, decentralization of decisions about instructional strategy to the schools, and much more that we have recommended in these pages. Kentucky, though ahead on creating a comprehensive legislative framework for school restructuring, is certainly not alone. Furthermore, a bill being considered by the House and Senate, as this is written, would reflect and support the states' school restructuring efforts with complementary federal legislation.

Anticipating the High Skills and Competitive Workforce Act of 1991 at the federal level, the Oregon legislature initiated a comprehensive series of enactments in 1989, culminating in House Bill 2249 in 1991. This bill, like the national legislation, is largely based on the report of the Commission on the Skills of the American Workforce. The legislature began by creating the Oregon Progress Board as the state's principal strategic planning body, responsible for identifying key goals for the state and establishing benchmarks against which the state's progress in meeting those goals can be measured. The board is intended to be the key component in moving the state to a comprehensive performance-oriented public-policy system, focusing on measurements not of inputs but of outputs, such as student achievement against performance measures, and trainees who find stable jobs in the field for which they are trained.

In 1991, the legislature created the Oregon Workforce Quality Council, representing state agencies, business, labor, education and training, and local officials, and charged it with devising a comprehensive strategy for developing in Oregon—as the law puts it—"the best educated and prepared work force in America by the year 2000, and a work force equal to any in the world by 2010." The council's purview includes primary- and secondary-school reform, including the development of a Certificate of Initial Mastery and alternative learning centers for school dropouts; professional and technical education reform, including the setting of industry standards for the program and an apprenticeship system; the development of a comprehensive, integrated system for adult training for the disadvantaged, dislocated, and long-term unemployed; business, labor, and education partnerships, including collaboratively developed training programs; and methods of coordinating and centralizing education and training programs and employment services at the state and local levels. At least a dozen states are working on parallel tracks, some following Oregon's lead, some not, but all working hard on the same issues.[20]

So there are grounds for optimism. This glass is both half empty and half full. America stands poised to decide whether it will be a nation of high skills or of low wages, whether we choose to compete with Japan and Germany or with Indonesia and Thailand, whether we choose to continue to consume or to begin to invest, whether we let the future happen to us or take our future in our hands.

The plan we have presented is a plan for a new and better America, a nation restructured to live up to its promise, equal to its hopes, capable of realizing its ambitions for its people. The plan is itself ambitious, but no less so than the occasion demands.

It is a plan for new families—families made whole by a nation that cares, a nation that understands that its families are its foundation, its basic source of strength, its fundamental learning systems.

It is a plan for new community institutions—institutions that support families, that knit people together, that invite broad participation from natural community leaders and inspire the best efforts of everyone, that nurture the young and open opportunities for adults at every turn.

It is a plan for new schools—schools that draw to the teaching profession the best of our young people, that attract people who believe in their capacity to do the job, creating an environment in which they have both the incentive and the means to bring every child up to a very high standard of achievement.

It is a plan for new workplaces—workplaces where the workers no longer "leave their heads at the factory gate," but where they are called on to think, to learn, and to use the full extent of their intelligence and capacity—where workers have the dignity that comes with work that is challenging, rewarding, and interesting and with freedom and the responsibility to act on one's own initiative.

This is not just a plan for a new education and training system or for a new economy. It is a plan for a new society—a learning society.

We have not proposed new programs to fit into the existing institutional structure, but rather a new system that builds on that structure. We have taken special care to show how that system can be designed so that its pieces fit together into one whole. At each level, local, state and national, we have shown how the pieces can be made to reinforce each other. And we have shown how responsibilities can be divided among those three levels in ways that reflect our federal system, providing for both national unity and local diversity.

It is a system designed to bring out and support individual and local initiative. It stresses work, not welfare. It asserts the primacy of prevention of damage to children over measures to pick up the pieces once that damage has occurred. It replaces mountains of rules and regulations with clear standards and incentives for reaching them. In so doing, it sweeps away bureaucracy and encourages individual creativity and imagination. It assumes that everyone is capable of much more than they have been expected to accomplish before.

Most of all, it recognizes that the only resource we have is ourselves—our energy, our intellect, our confidence, and our ability to work with one another to common purpose to make American industry and American society the world leaders that they once were, and can be again.

Notes

Introduction
The American Economy

1. Peter Peterson, "The Morning After," *Atlantic Monthly,* (October 1987), p. 47.
2. Organization for Economic Cooperation and Development, *OECD Economic Outlook: Historical Statistics, 1960–1988* (Paris: OECD, 1990), pp. 73–74. Rates shown are net national savings rates. Gross national savings rates in 1988 were 15.2 percent of GNP for the United States and 20.3 percent for the seven economic-summit nations (United States, Japan, France, Germany, United Kingdom, Italy, and Canada).
3. Commission on the Skills of the American Workforce, *America's Choice: high skills or low wages!* (Rochester, N.Y.: National Center on Education and the Economy, 1990), p. 19.
4. U.S. Bureau of Labor Statistics, *Employment and Earnings,* vol. 137, no. 1, January 1990, p. 160.
5. U.S. Bureau of the Census, *Statistical Abstract of the United States 1990* (Washington, D.C.: U.S. Government Printing Office, 1990), p. 13.
6. U.S. Bureau of Labor Statistics, *Employment and Earnings,* p. 162; Howard Fullerton, Jr., "New Labor Force Projections, Spanning 1988 to 2000," *Monthly Labor Review,* vol. 112, no. 11, November 1989, p. 4.
7. Gregory Spencer, *Projections of the Population of the United States, by Age, Sex and Race: 1988 to 2080,* U.S. Bureau of the Census, Current Population Reports, Series P-25, No. 1018 (Washington, D.C.: U.S. Government Printing Office), pp. 6–7.
8. Frank Levy, *Dollars and Dreams: The Changing American Income Distribution* (New York: Basic Books, 1987), pp. 3–4.
9. Lawrence Mishel and David Frankel, eds., *The State of Working America,* 1990–91 edition (Washington, D.C.: Economic Policy Institute, 1990) pp. 69–72, 140.
10. *America's Choice,* p. 21.
11. Mishel and Frankel, *The State of Working America,* pp. 20, 69–72.
12. *America's Choice,* p. 19.

Chapter 1. The Mass-Production Economy

1. S. Kuznets, *National Income: A Summary of Findings* (New York: National Bureau of Economic Research, 1946); U.S. Bureau of the Census, *Historical Statistics of the United States, 1789–1945* (Washington, D.C.: United States Government Printing Office, 1948); J. W. Kendrick, *Productivity Trends in the United States* (Princeton, N.J.: Princeton University Press, 1961).
2. Charles M. Hession and Hyman Sardy, *Ascent to Affluence: A History of American Economic Development* (Boston, Mass.: Allyn and Bacon, 1969), p. 518.
3. See Joseph F. Wall, *Andrew Carnegie* (New York: Oxford University Press, 1970).
4. John P. Hoerr, *And the Wolf Finally Came* (Pittsburgh: University of Pittsburgh Press, 1988), p. 88.
5. See A. Nevins and F. E. Hill, *Ford: The Times, the Man and the Company,* vol. I (New York: Scribners, 1954).
6. Kendrick, *Productivity Trends in the United States,* p. 482.
7. Quoted in Raymond E. Callahan, *Education and the Cult of Efficiency: A Study of the Social Forces that Have Shaped the Administration of the Public Schools* (Chicago: University of Chicago Press, 1962), p. 28.
8. H. U. Faulkner, *The Decline of Laissez-Faire, 1897–1917* (New York: Holt Rinehart & Winston, 1951), p. 332.
9. M. Newcomer, *The Big Business Executive* (New York: Columbia University Press, 1955), p. 90.

Chapter 2. Mass-Producing Education

1. David B. Tyack, *The One Best System: A History of American Urban Education* (Cambridge: Harvard University Press, 1974), p. 43.
2. Ibid., p. 127.
3. Ibid., p. 185.
4. Robert S. and Helen M. Lynd, *Middletown: A Study in Contemporary American Culture* (New York: Harcourt Brace, 1929), p. 210.
5. Raymond E. Callahan, *Education and the Cult of Efficiency: A Study of the Social Forces that Have Shaped the Administration of the Public Schools* (Chicago: University of Chicago Press, 1962), pp. 88, 89.
6. Tyack, *The One Best System,* p. 45.
7. Ibid., p. 61.
8. Ibid., p. 62.
9. Richard Hofstadter, *Anti-Intellectualism in American Life* (New York: Alfred A. Knopf, 1963), p. 318.
10. Ibid., p. 328.
11. Ibid., p. 331.
12. Ibid., pp. 333–35.
13. Ibid., p. 341.
14. Ibid., p. 350.
15. Lawrence A. Cremin, *The Transformation of the School: Progressivism in American Education 1876–1957* (New York: Alfred A. Knopf, 1961), p. 38.
16. Ibid., p. 50.
17. Ibid., p. 57.

18. John Dewey, *Democracy and Education,* (Chicago: University of Chicago Press, 1916); see also Robert B. Westbrook, *John Dewey and American Democracy* (Ithaca, N.Y.: Cornell University Press, 1991), pp. 150–94.
19. Tyack, *The One Best System,* p. 226.

Chapter 3. Technology, Competitiveness, and the New International Economy

1. United States Bureau of the Census, *Historical Abstract of the United States: Colonial Times to 1970* (Washington, D.C.: Superintendent of Documents, U.S. Government Printing Office, 1975).
2. U.S. Department of Commerce, Bureau of the Census, *Statistical Abstract of the United States, 1990* (Washington, D.C.: U.S. Government Printing Office, 1991), p. 582.
3. *Economic Report of the President* (Washington, D.C.: U.S. Government Printing Office, 1981), pp. 233, 344.
4. Richard Nelson and Sidney Winter, *An Evolutionary Theory of Economic Change* (Cambridge, Mass.: The Belknap Press of Harvard University Press, 1982).

Chapter 4. Our Competitors Take the Lead

1. U.S. Department of Labor, Bureau of Labor Statistics, *International Comparisons of Hourly Compensation Costs of Production Workers in Manufacturing, 1975–90,* Report 817, November 1991.
2. Our review of the experience of Germany and Japan is based in part on Commission on the Skills of the American Workforce, *America's Choice: high skills or low wages!, Supporting Works* (Rochester, N.Y.: National Center on Education and the Economy, forthcoming); Ronald Dore, *British Factory—Japanese Factory: The Origins of National Diversity in Industrial Relations* (Berkeley: University of California Press, 1973); Koji Matsumoto, *Organizing for Higher Productivity: An Analysis of Japanese Systems and Practices* (Tokyo: Asian Productivity Organization, 1982); William Northdruft, *School Works: Reinventing Public Schools to Create the Workforce of the Future* (Washington, D.C.: The Brookings Institution for the German Marshall Fund, 1989); Daniel Okimoto and Thomas Rohlen, *Inside the Japanese System: Readings on Contemporary Society and Political Economy* (Stanford, Calif.: Stanford University Press, 1988); Wolfgang Streeck, "On the Institutional Conditions of Diversified Quality Production," in E. Matzner and W. Streeck, eds., *Beyond Keynesianism: The Socio-Economics of Production and Employment* (London: Edward Elgar, 1991), pp. 21–61; Herbert E. Striner, *Regaining the Lead: Policies for Economic Growth* (New York: Praeger, 1984); Marc Tucker, "Reflections on Europe," and "Reflections on Asia," unpublished memoranda, 1990; and Merry White, *The Japanese Educational Challenge: A Commitment to Children* (New York: The Free Press, 1987).
3. Striner, *Regaining the Lead,* p. 40.
4. Lawrence Mishel and David Frankel, eds., *The State of Working America* (Armonk, N.Y.: M. E. Sharpe, 1991), p. 268.
5. Department of Labor, Bureau of Labor Statistics, November 1991 (unpublished data).
6. Mishel and Frankel, *The State of Working America,* p. 256.
7. Streeck, "On the Institutional Conditions of Diversified Quality Production."
8. Ibid., p. 25.

9. Ibid., p. 26.

10. Ibid., p. 42.

11. See Ezra Vogel, *Japan as Number One: Lessons for America* (New York: Harper and Row, 1980); Organization for Economic Cooperation and Development, *The Industrial Policies in Japan* (Paris: OECD, 1972).

Chapter 5. America on the Precipice

1. Much of the data and analysis in this chapter can be found in Commission on the Skills of the American Workforce, *America's Choice: high skills or low wages!* (Rochester, N.Y.: National Center on Education and the Economy, 1990).

2. Ibid., p. 27.

3. John Bishop, "The Productivity Consequences of What Is Learned in High School," Cornell University, Center for Advanced Human Resource Studies, Working Paper 88-18, 1988.

4. Robert Rothman, "Foreigners Outpace American Students in Science," *Education Week,* January 28, 1987, p. 1.

5. International Association for the Evaluation of Educational Achievement, *Science Achievement in Seventeen Countries: A Preliminary Report* (New York: Pergamon Press, 1988).

6. Archie LaPointe, Nancy Mead, and Cary Phillips, *A World of Differences: An International Assessment of Mathematics and Science.* (Princeton, N.J.: Educational Testing Service, 1989), p. 6.

7. See Ina Mullis and Lynn Jenkins, eds., *The Science Report Card: Trends and Achievement Based on the 1986 National Assessment* (Princeton, N.J.: National Assessment of Educational Progress, Educational Testing Service, 1988); John Dossey, Ina Mullis, Mary Lindquist, and Donald Chambers, *The Mathematics Report Card: Trends and Achievement Based on the 1986 National Assessment* (Princeton, N.J.: National Assessment of Educational Progress, Educational Testing Service, 1988); Michael Martinez and Nancy Mead, *Computer Competence: The First National Assessment* (Princeton, N.J.: National Assessment of Educational Progress, Educational Testing Service, 1988); Irwin Kirsch and Ann Jungeblut, *Literacy Profiles of America's Young Adults* (Princeton, N.J.: The National Assessment of Educational Progress, Educational Testing Service, n.d.); International Association for the Evaluation of Educational Achievement, *Science Achievement in Seventeen Countries: A Preliminary Report* (New York: Pergamon Press, 1988); International Association for Educational Achievement, *The Underachieving Curriculum: Assessing U.S. School Mathematics From an International Perspective* (Champaign-Urbana: University of Illinois Press, 1987); and Lauren Resnick, "Learning in School and Out," *Educational Researcher* 16 (3 [1987]):13–20.

8. Educational Testing Service, *The Writing Report Card, 1984–1988* (Princeton: Educational Testing Service, 1989).

9. Rothman, "Foreigners Outpace American Students," p. 1.

10. *America's Choice,* p. 47.

11. Ibid., p. 46.

12. Anthony Carnevale, "The Learning Enterprise," *Training and Development Journal* 40 (1 [January 1986]):18–26.

13. John Immerwahr, Jean Johnson, and Adam Lernan-Schloss, *Cross Talk: The Public, The Experts, and Competitiveness* (Washington, D.C. and New York, The Business–Higher Education Forum and the Public Agenda Foundation, February 1991).

14. Ibid., p. 6.

15. Ibid., p. 8.

16. Ibid., p. 11.

17. Ibid., p. 16.
18. Ibid.

Chapter 6. Facing the Challenge—At Last

1. The National Commission on Excellence in Education, *A Nation at Risk: The Imperative for Educational Reform* (Washington, D.C.: U.S. Government Printing Office, 1983).
2. The initiatives briefly described here are commonly referred to as the 'first wave' of educational reform following release of *A Nation at Risk*. Among the many critiques of this period two stand out: Arthur Wise's book, *Legislated Learning* (Berkeley: University of California Press, 1979), and an article by John Chubb, "Why the Current Wave of School Reform Will Fail," *The Public Interest* 90 (Winter 1988): 28–49.
3. *A Nation at Risk* cited "a virtually unbroken decline from 1963 to 1980. Average verbal scores fell over 50 points and average mathematics scores dropped nearly 40 points." A perfect score is 800 points (pp. 8–9).
4. See above, n. 2.
5. See Sue Berryman, "The Educational Challenge of the American Economy," Teachers College, Columbia University, 1988; Robert Reich, "Education and the Next Economy," National Education Association, 1988; Lauren Resnick, *Education and Learning to Think* (Washington, D.C.: National Academy Press, 1987).
6. Jay Matthews, *Escalante: The Best Teacher in America* (New York: Henry Holt, 1988).
7. *Educating America: State Strategies for Achieving the National Education Goals (Report of the Task Force on Education)* (Washington, D.C.: The National Governors' Association, 1990), p. 12.
8. Ibid., p. 8.

Chapter 7. The Demand for Excellence

1. David Kearns and Denis Doyle, *Winning the Brain Race* (San Francisco: ICS Press, 1988).
2. The tale is well told in Gary Jacobson and John Hillkirk, *Xerox: American Samurai* (New York: Macmillan, 1986). Our understanding of that story has been greatly amplified by conversations with three Xerox executives who played important roles in the turnaround: Ed Finein, John Foley, and Norman Deets.
3. Ibid., p. 8.
4. Ibid., p. 270.
5. Quoted in ibid., p. 274.
6. Quoted in ibid., p. 306–7.
7. An interview with one of the authors.
8. Joint Economic Committee of the U.S. Congress, Subcommittee on Education and Health, *Hearings on Competitiveness and the Quality of the American Work Force,* Part 2, October 29, November 10 and 19, and December 3, 1987 (Washington, D.C.: U.S. Government Printing Office, 1988).
9. Ibid., p. 32.
10. Wiggenhorn tells this story in "Motorola U: When Training Becomes an Education," *Harvard Business Review* 68 (4 [July–August 1990]): 71–83.
11. Ibid., p. 72.
12. Quoted in Peter M. Senge, *The Fifth Discipline: The Art and Practice of the Learning Organization* (New York: Doubleday/Currency, 1990).

13. W. Edwards Deming, *Out of the Crisis* (Cambridge, Mass.: Massachusetts Institute of Technology/Center for Advanced Engineering Study, 1986), p. 6.
14. Heard by the authors at the press conference held at the release of the report of the Commission on the Skills of the American Workforce in New York City on June 15, 1990.
15. M. C. Burritt, Director of Extension at the New York State College of Agriculture, quoted in Lincoln Kelsey and Hearne, *Cooperative Extension Work* (Ithaca, N.Y.: Cornell University Press, 1949).

Chapter 8. Restructuring the Schools for High Performance

1. Task Force on Teaching as a Profession, *A Nation Prepared: Teachers for the 21st Century* (Washington, D.C.: Carnegie Forum on Education and the Economy, 1986).
2. Accounts of the Kentucky plan can be found in: House Bill 940, obtainable in four volumes with a summary from the Kentucky Legislative Research Commission; Christopher Pipho, "Reflecting on the Kentucky State Court Decision," *Education Week,* May 2, 1990, p. 28; Edward Fiske, "Kentucky Acts to Reorganize School System," *New York Times,* March 30, 1990, p. A1; Reagan Walker, "From the Backwater to the Cutting Edge," *Teacher Magazine,* June–July 1990, pp. 12–14; and "Q.A.: Improving Kentucky Schools—A Conversation with Governor Wallace G. Wilkinson," obtainable from the Office of the Governor (n.d.).
3. The political struggle to enact the Kentucky reforms provides some insight into the nature of school governance in rural areas. Most of the political jockeying was not about local control of such education matters as textbooks and curriculums, but about the allocation and control of resources. In many rural areas, the schools are important sources of good jobs. Lobbyists for the Kentucky School Boards Association therefore concentrated their efforts (unsuccessfully) on blocking the enactment of antinepotism provisions inserted to prevent local boards from putting relatives on the board payroll. According to Edward Fiske in his book *Smart Schools, Smart Kids* (New York: Simon and Schuster, 1991), a governor's aide told him, "It's a metaphor for how the system works. People care more about controlling schools than controlling education" (p. 41).

    The Kentucky plan's incentives contain penalties as well as rewards. William Ellis III reported in the February 5, 1992, issue of the *New York Times* (p. B7) that the first test of the state's punishment mechanism occurred early in 1992 when the State Education Commission charged five Harlan County school board members and the superintendent of schools with a number of infractions, including awarding school contracts to relatives and receiving kickbacks from school contractors. After a hearing before a state education panel, three school board members were removed, one school board member was acquitted, and charges against the superintendent and the other board members were dropped after they resigned. This "takeover" naturally attracted widespread attention in Kentucky. If upheld in the courts, this action could have a profound impact on control of Kentucky schools.

Chapter 9. Incentives

1. John Chubb and Terry Moe, *Politics, Markets, and America's Schools* (Washington, D.C.: Brookings Institution, 1990); see also the same authors' "Choice Is a Panacea," *Brookings Review,* Summer 1990, pp. 2–12.
2. Chubb and Moe, *Politics, Markets, and America's Schools,* p. 5.
3. Ibid, p. 6.
4. Ibid.

5. Chubb and Moe, "Choice Is a Panacea," p. 5.
6. Ibid., p. 8.
7. James Liebman, "Voice, Not Choice," *Yale Law Journal,* 101 (1 [October 1991]): 259–314.
8. Ibid., p. 271.
9. Ibid., p. 265.
10. Ina Mullis, John Dossey, Eugene Owen, and Gary Phillips, *The State of Mathematics Achievement: NAEP's 1990 Assessment of the Nation and the Trial Assessment of the States* (Washington, D.C.: National Center for Educational Statistics, U.S. Department of Education, 1991).
11. Reported to one of the authors by Albert Shanker, president of the American Federation of Teachers.
12. Liebman, "Voice, Not Choice," p. 286.
13. Ibid., p. 286.
14. Ibid., p. 287.
15. Ibid., p. 290.
16. For more information on these and other ideas from this analyst, see the following titles by Ted Kolderie from the series of newsletters of the Public Services Redesign Project, obtainable from the Center for Policy Studies in Minneapolis, Minnesota: "The States Will Have to Withdraw the Exclusive" (1990), "Leased vs. Owned Departments (And Some Implications for Schools)" (1987), "What Kind of System Would Encourage Improvement?" (1989), and a compilation of articles under the title of "What Makes an Organization *Want* to Improve?" (1988).

Chapter 10. Building a System Driven by Standards

1. In conversation with one of the authors.
2. The first two of these proposals were made by the Commission on the Skills of the American Workforce in its report, *America's Choice: high skills or low wages!* (Rochester, N.Y.: National Center on Education and the Economy, 1990).
3. Commission on the Skills of the American Workforce, *America's Choice,* pp. 71–75.
4. For a discussion of this point, see the report of the Action Council on Minority Education, *Education that Works* (Boston: Massachusetts Institute of Technology, Quality Education for Minorities Project, 1989).
5. Phillip Schlechty and V. S. Nance, *Recruitment, Selection and Retention: The Shape of the Teaching Force* (Washington, D.C.: U.S. Department of Education, National Institute of Education, 1982).
6. See Mitchell Chester and Cynthia Jorgensen, "Best Assessment Program Implemented," *Update,* (Newsletter of the Cooperating Teacher Program, Beginning Educator Support and Training Program: Support and Assessment, (Hartford: Connecticut State Department of Education, September 1989), p. 1.

Chapter 11. The Family

1. For an extended treatment of the issues addressed in this chapter, see Ray Marshall, *Losing Direction: Families, Human Resource Development and Economic Performance* (Milwaukee, Wis.: Family Service America, 1991).
2. Greg Duncan and Saul Hoffman, "Economic Consequences of Marital Instability," in *Horizontal Equity, Uncertainty and Economic Well-Being,* ed. Martin David and Timothy Smeeding (Chicago: University of Chicago Press, 1985), 434–35.

3. Arlene Saluter, Steve Rawlings, Louisa Miller, and Jeanne Moorman, *Studies in Marriage and the Family,* U.S. Bureau of the Census, Current Population Reports, Series P-23, No. 162 (Washington, D.C.: U.S. Government Printing Office, 1989), pp. 18–19.

4. Children's Defense Fund, *U.S. Children in the World,* (Washington, D.C.: Children's Defense Fund, 1990), p. 137.

5. Marion Wright Edelman, "Investing in Kids," *Service Employees Union,* June–July 1989, p. 9.

6. Ibid.; U.S. Bureau of the Census, *Statistical Abstract of the United States—1990* (Washington, D.C.: U.S. Government Printing Office, 1990). p. 66.

7. *A Vision for America's Future, An Agenda for the 1990's: A Children's Defense Budget* (Washington, D.C.: Children's Defense Fund, 1989), p. 30.

8. Ibid., pp. xvi, xxvii.

9. *Statistical Abstract of the United States—1990,* p. 458.

10. National Commission on Children, *Beyond Rhetoric: A New American Agenda for Children and Families* (Washington, D.C.: U.S. Government Printing Office, 1991).

11. Editorial in the *Democrat and Chronicle* (Rochester, N.Y.), April 4, 1991. The editorial writer attributes the data to William R. Mattox, Jr., an analyst for the Family Research Council, based in Washington, D.C.

12. National Commission on Children, *Beyond Rhetoric,* p. 261.

13. Ibid., p. 261.

14. Ibid., p. 269.

15. R. H. McKey et al., *The Impact of Head Start on Children, Families, and Communities,* pub. no. OHDS 85-31193 (Washington, D.C.: Department of Health and Human Services, 1985), p. 8.

16. Interview with Congresswoman Patricia Schroeder.

Chapter 12. Rebuilding the Community Fabric

1. William Julius Wilson, *The Truly Disadvantaged: The Inner City, the Underclass, and Public Policy* (Chicago and London: The University of Chicago Press, 1987), p. 41. In his book, Wilson acknowledges his debt to Kenneth Clark, Lee Rainwater, and Daniel Patrick Moynihan, who as long ago as the 1960s called attention to the corrosive effects of the deteriorating inner-city economy on the structure of the black family. Moynihan in particular was pilloried for his views, but time has left him fully vindicated.

2. Lisbeth Schorr, with Daniel Schorr, *Within Our Reach: Breaking the Cycle of Disadvantage* (New York: Anchor Press/Doubleday, 1988).

3. Ibid., p. 158.

4. "Keeping Families Together: Facts on Family Preservation Services," an information kit that can be obtained from the Edna McConnell Clark Foundation, 250 Park Avenue, New York, New York, 12304, describes the Family Preservation Program in detail.

5. The story of Professor Comer's work in the New Haven schools is told in two articles by James. P. Comer, "Parent Participation in the Schools," *Phi Delta Kappan,* February 1986, pp. 442–46 and "Educating Poor and Minority Children," *Scientific American,* November 1988, pp. 44–48.

6. Comer, "Educating Poor and Minority Children," p. 42.

7. Ibid., pp. 44–48.

8. Comer, "Parent Participation in the Schools," p. 445.

9. Ibid., p. 446.

10. From a Wegman's Food Markets brochure, untitled and undated.

11. This description of New Directions is based on an interview with Jake Jacobson, director

of the San Diego County Department of Social Services, a series of overhead projection slides developed by New Directions to provide an overview of the program (dated 4/5/91), and testimony delivered to the United States Senate Committee on Labor and Human Resources by Jeanne Jehl, administrator on special assignment with the San Diego Schools, on May 8, 1991.

12. Found on the seventh (unnumbered) page of the projection slides for "New Beginnings" cited above.

13. This description of the Texas Industrial Areas Foundation is based on Mary Beth Rogers, *Cold Anger: A Story of Faith and Power Politics* (Denton, Tex.: University of North Texas Press, 1990), pp. 171–82; Ernie Cortes, "Reflections on the Catholic Tradition of Family Rights," in John Coleman, ed., *One Hundred Years of Catholic Social Thought* (Maryknoll, N.Y.: Orbis Books, 1991), pp. 155–71; and Ray Marshall, *Losing Direction: Families, Human Resource Development and Economic Performance,* (Milwaukee, Wis.: Family Service America, 1991), pp. 93–96.

14. "Reflections on the Catholic Tradition of Family Rights."

15. Ibid., p. 9.

16. Ibid., p. 10.

Chapter 13. Technical and Professional Education

1. *Training Strategies: Preparing Noncollege Youth for Employment in the U.S. and Foreign Countries* (Washington, D.C.: United States General Accounting Office, 1990), p. 24.

2. This account is based on James E. Rosenbaum and Takehiko Kariya, "Japan Offers Way to Link School, Jobs," *Forum for Applied Research and Public Policy,* 4 (4 [Winter 1989]): 63–70.

3. Even the elementary schools in Japan have libraries of brochures and videotapes from the leading firms for students to peruse. This information comes from the field notes of Betsy Brown Ruzzi, a member of the research team for the Commission on the Skills of the American Workforce.

4. Ibid.

5. This description of the Danish system is based on unpublished data gathered by Sarah Cleveland for the Commission on the Skills of the American Workforce as well as on the authors' notes of remarks made by Kirsten Gibson, president of Waves Information Technology, Copenhagen, at a meeting held in Boston and organized by Jobs for the Future, a Massachusetts-based organization, in October 1991.

6. This account of the American school-to-work transition system is based on data contained in Commission on the Skills of the American Workforce, *America's Choice: high skills or low wages!,* (Rochester, N.Y.: National Center on Education and the Economy, 1990), pp. 43–48.

7. *National Education Goals Report: Building a Nation of Learners* (Washington, D.C.: National Education Goals Panel, 1991), pp. 8–9.

8. Private communication from Sarah Cleveland to Ira Magaziner, based on Ms. Cleveland's extensive cross-national research on this subject.

9. This commentary on higher education by Marc Tucker first appeared in the "Point of View" column in the *Chronicle of Higher Education,* June 5, 1991.

Chapter 14. A Labor-Market System for America

1. For a fuller discussion of this topic, see Peter Schwanse, *Labor Market Policies in the CEECS: What Lessons Are to Be Learned from the OECD Countries,* (Paris: Organization for Economic Cooperation and Development and International Labor Office, 1991).

2. This discussion of the Swedish labor market system is based on Schwanse, *Labor Market Policies;* Ray Marshall, *Youth Employment, Education, and Training in Sweden,* (Washington, D.C.: United States General Accounting Office, 1989); The Swedish Institute, *Swedish Labor Market Policy,* (Stockholm: The Swedish Institute, 1989); an unpublished background paper prepared by Sarah Cleveland for the Commission on the Skills of the American Workforce, 1989; and Allan Larsson and Per Silenstram, *The Transformation of the Swedish Labor Market Administration,* (Stockholm: Swedish National Labor Market Board, 1987).

3. Anna Hedborg and Rudolph Meidner, "The Swedish Welfare State Model," in Gregg M. Olson, ed., *Industrial Change and Labor Adjustment in Sweden and Canada* (Toronto: Garamond Press, 1988), pp. 59–70.

4. See Robert J. Flanagan, "Efficiency and Equality in Swedish Labor Markets," in Barry Bosworth and Alice Rivlin, eds., *The Swedish Economy* (Washington, D.C.: The Brookings Institution, 1987), p. 155.

5. Sar A. Levitan and Frank Gallo, *Got to Learn to Earn: Preparing Americans for Work* (Washington, D.C.: Center for Social Policy Studies, George Washington University, 1991), p. 52.

6. See Mathematica Policy Research, Inc., *Evaluation of the Economic Impact of the Job Corps: Third Follow-Up Report* (Princeton, N.J.: Mathematica, Inc., 1982) and *Relative Effectiveness of Job Corps Vocational Training by Occupational Grouping,* (Princeton, N.J.: Mathematica, Inc., March 1983); and Robert Taggart, *A Fisherman's Guide* (Kalamazoo, Mich.: W. E. Upjohn Institute for Employment Research, 1981).

7. See General Accounting Office, *Job Corps: Its Costs, Employment Outcomes and Service to the Public* (Washington, D.C.: GAO/HRD-86-121BR, July 1986).

8. Sar Levitan and Frank Gallo, *A Second Chance* (Kalamazoo, Mich.: The W. E. Upjohn Institute for Employment Research, 1988), p. 4.

9. Commission on the Skills of the American Workforce, *America's Choice: high skills or low wages!,* (Rochester, N.Y.: National Center on Education and the Economy, 1990).

10. These descriptions are based on information contained in *States and Communities on the Move: Policy Initiatives to Build a World-Class Workforce,* published jointly by the William T. Grant Foundation and thirteen other organizations in 1991 and obtainable from the William T. Grant Foundation, Washington, D.C.; National Governors' Association, *Excellence at Work: A State Action Agenda,* (Washington, D.C., National Governor's Association, 1991); and in Evelyn Ganzglass and Maria Heidkamp, *State Strategies to Train a Competitive Workforce: The Emerging Role of State-Funded Job Training Programs* (Washington, D.C.: National Governors' Association, n.d.).

11. Commission on the Skills of the American Workforce, *America's Choice,* pp. 87–90. We also draw here on a memorandum written by Peter Carlson, then a senior analyst at the National Alliance of Business and now the staff director of the National Commission on Work-Based Learning, to Ira Magaziner, Chairman of the Commission on the Skills of the American Workforce in 1990; and on an internal paper prepared for the Commission by Joan Wills, the Commission's staff director, on the subject of a revitalized job service.

12. Carlson, memorandum cited in n. 11.

Chapter 15. Investing in Our People

1. Commission on the Skills of the American Workforce, *America's Choice: high skills or low wages!* (Rochester, N.Y.: National Center on Education and the Economy), p. 47.

2. "Giving Young Americans a Square Deal," *Business Week,* August 19, 1991, p. 128.
3. President of the United States, *Economic Report of the President, 1991* (Washington, D.C.: U.S. Government Printing Office, 1991), p. 375.
4. Ibid., p. 336. Administrative Office of the U.S. Courts, *Annual Report of the Director* (Washington, D.C.: U.S. Government Printing Office, various years).
5. Federal Deposit Insurance Corporation, *Statistics of Banking* (Washington, D.C.: U.S. Government Printing Office, various years).
6. U.S. Bureau of the Census, *Statistical Abstract of the United States, 1990* (Washington, D.C.: U.S. Government Printing Office, 1990), p. 727.
7. Quoted by Robert Rankin, in "Errors of the '80s are Crippling Economy." San Jose *Mercury News,* October 6, 1991.
8. Robert McIntyre, *Inequality and the Federal Budget Deficit: 1991 Edition* (Washington, D.C.: Citizens for Tax Justice, 1991), pp. 10, 11.
9. Lester Thurow, *The Zero-Sum Solution* (New York: Simon and Schuster, 1985), p. 224.
10. Ibid., p. 231.
11. Ibid., pp. 232–34.
12. Louis Ferlinger and Jay R. Mandle, "America's Hostility to Taxes," *Challenge,* July–August 1991, pp. 53–55.
13. Ibid., p. 55.
14. "High Taxes Are Not What's Ailing the U.S. Economy," *Business Week,* February 10, 1992, p. 20.
15. "Why U.S. Companies Are Losing Ground in Their Own Backyard, *Business Week,* February 10, 1992, p. 124.
16. Cited by Jeff Faux, "Investment-Led Stimulus," Briefing Paper (Washington, D.C.: Economic Policy Institute, December 1991), p. 3.
17. James Poterba and Lawrence Summers, "Time Horizons of American Firms: New Evidence from a Survey of CEOs," paper for the Time Horizons Project of the Harvard Business School and the Council on Competitiveness, October 1991, pp. 29, 37.
18. From "Investing the Peace Dividend: How to Break the Gramm-Rudman-Hollings Stalemate," briefing paper of the Economic Policy Institute (Washington, D.C., May 1990), p. 8.
19. Barry Bluestone, Alan Clayton-Matthews, John Havens, and Howard Young, "Financing Opportunity for Post-Secondary Education in the U.S.: The Equity Investment in America Program," briefing paper of the Economic Policy Institute (Washington, D.C., June 1990).
20. See W. T. Grant Foundation Commission on Youth and America's Future, National Center on Education and the Economy, The Business Roundtable, et al., *States and Communities on the Move: Policy Initiatives to Create a World Class Workforce* (Washington, D.C.: W. T. Grant Commission on Work, Family and Citizenship, 1991), for a wide-ranging account of these developments.

Index